D1737919

# CONTENTS

# Introduction

It is generally accepted that people that live in countries surrounding the Mediterranean Sea tend to have longer life-spans and suffer less from cardiovascular ailments or cancer than. Apart from the obvious secrets like weight control and active lifestyle, the people in these regions eat food that consists of healthy foods and low on saturated fat, sugar, and red meat.

A Mediterranean diet offers a range of health benefits like diabetes control and prevention, improved brain and heart health, preventing cancer, and weight loss. If you successfully follow a Mediterranean diet, you will reduce weight and stay clear of chronic diseases.

A Mediterranean diet does not mean you have to eat the same things as people in these regions do. For instance, Italians eat differently from Greeks, who eat differently from the Spanish and French. However, these eating habits work on the same principle as a Mediterranean diet.

## What is the Mediterranean Diet?

A Mediterranean diet is based on traditional food that people used to eat in countries like Greece and Italy back during the 1960s. According to research, it has been noted that this diet is much healthier than other types of diets and provides a lower risk of lifestyle diseases. Additionally, a Mediterranean diet also prevents premature death, diabetes, type-2 diabetes, strokes, and heart attacks and helps you lose weight.

However, there is no single way to follow a Mediterranean diet, since there are several nations along the coast of the Mediterranean Sea and people in different areas follow different diets. In this book, we will discuss a dietary pattern that is healthy. You need to consider this as a general guideline since the plan will also have to be adjusted to your individual preferences and needs.

# What to Eat and Drink and What to Avoid in the Mediterranean Diet?

What types of foods you are supposed to eat and what to avoid is controversial, especially considering the fact that the climatic conditions and food availability in each country are different. Most studies conclude that a typical Mediterranean diet consists mainly of healthy plant foods and low on animal products.

However, it is important that you eat seafood like fish, at least twice a week. Additionally, you also need to ensure that you involve regular physical workouts. Some of these healthy unprocessed Mediterranean foods include:

- **Vegetables**: Cucumbers, Brussels sprouts, carrots, cauliflower, onions, spinach, kale, broccoli, tomatoes
- **Fruits**: Peaches, figs, bananas, grapes, melons, strawberries, dates, pears, oranges, and apples
- **Seeds and nuts**: Pumpkin seeds, sunflower seeds, cashews, hazelnuts, macadamia nuts, walnuts, almonds
- **Legumes**: Chickpeas, peanuts, pulses, lentils, peas, beans
- **Tubers**: Yams, turnips, sweet potatoes, potatoes
- **Whole grains**: Pasta, whole-grain bread, whole wheat, buckwheat, corn, barney, rye, rice, brown rice, whole oats
- **Seafood and fish**: Mussels, crab, clams, oysters, shrimp, mackerel, tuna, trout, sardines, salmon
- **Poultry**: Turkey, duck, chicken
- **Eggs**: Duck eggs, quail eggs, chicken eggs
- **Dairy**: Greek yogurt, yogurt, cheese
- **Spices and herbs**: Pepper, cinnamon, nutmeg, sage, rosemary, mint, basil, garlic
- **Healthy fats**: Avocado oil, avocados, olives, extra-virgin olive oil

As for drinking, the most important liquid for a Mediterranean diet is water. Your diet can also include moderate amounts of red wine; however, this is optional and should be avoided by anyone who is battling alcoholism.

Tea and coffee are acceptable; however, you need to avoid sugar-sweetened fruit juices and other beverages that contain high sugar content.

Some of the food items that you need to avoid while following the Mediterranean diet:

- Red meat (not more than once in a few months)
- Processed meats or foods like sausage, salami, and bacon
- Sugar (artificial juices, syrup-sweetened beverages like soda, most baked goods, candy, etc.)
- Hard liquor (anything apart from red wine is a no-no)
- Refined grains (like white rice, white flour, etc.)
- Butter or animal fats
- Hydrogenated oils (palm kernel oil, palm oil, etc.)

# Health Benefits of the Mediterranean Diet

A Mediterranean diet has been praised for providing a wide range of health benefits ranging from reduced risk of cancer to improved heart health. This type of diet has been studied by medical experts and diet professionals. Here are some benefits of a Mediterranean diet that is backed by science:

### 1. Increases life span and promotes heart health

Mediterranean diet is widely known to have a positive effect on the health of your heart. According to a landmark study, 7,000 people were selected to follow a strict Mediterranean diet that consisted of nuts and olive oil. These people significantly lowered the risk of major cardiovascular events like a stroke or a heart attack. They also had fewer cardiovascular disease risk factors like central obesity.

In food items like fatty fish, olive oil, and nuts, the presence of healthy fats is the key factor that contributes to this fact. For instance, 'bad' LDL cholesterol is lowered by Omega-3 fats; additionally, it also raises the 'good' HDL cholesterol levels, improves insulin resistance, and reduces inflammation. The high levels of antioxidants and fiber from red wine, fruits, and vegetables have a cardio-protective effect as well.

Since you will improve the health of your heart, a Mediterranean diet will also increase your life span.

### 2. Promotes metabolism and healthy weight

Mediterranean diets focus on food that is whole and real – particularly those that have high fiber content. This makes the diet a great choice for anyone who is looking to improve their overall metabolic health. According to experts, a Mediterranean diet that contains high-fiber content makes you less likely to gain weight by keeping you full and improving glucose and diabetes intolerance.

In fact, a Mediterranean diet is far better than a low-fat diet when it comes to weight loss. Additionally, the diet has been linked to a reduction in the risk of chronic diseases like metabolic syndrome and type-2 diabetes.

### 3. Reducing the risk of cancer

Most ingredients used in a typical Mediterranean diet contain high levels of antioxidants, especially from colorful plant foods. Antioxidants are compounds that slow down or stop oxidative damage and reduce inflammation throughout the body. Hence, a Mediterranean diet is associated with a reduced risk of neurodegenerative diseases and cancer.

According to studies, it has been found that a Mediterranean diet provides a protective effect against different types of cancers. A particular research showed that a Mediterranean diet is particularly effective against certain types of cancers like gastric, colorectal, and breast cancers. Researchers have also concluded that a Mediterranean diet that contains whole grains, vegetables, and fruits are the best bet against cancer.

### 4. Improves mood and good for your memory

For the same reasons why a Mediterranean diet is great for preventing cancer (i.e., it has anti-inflammatory and antioxidant properties), this diet is also great for improving brain health. Research has shown that a Mediterranean diet significantly reduces and/or delays the risk of depression and Alzheimer's disease. A Mediterranean diet consists of vegetables and fruits like melons, apricots, tomatoes, sweet potatoes, kale, spinach, and carrots that have higher carotenoid antioxidants; this has been linked to improving optimized and mood.

### 5. Improves your gut health

A Mediterranean diet consists of vegetables, fruits, and whole grains; this means that this diet is full of antioxidants, minerals, vitamins, and fiber. All these nutrients benefit and improve gut health by feeding the beneficial probiotic bacteria that reside there and reduces inflammation as well. In a study done of primates that fed a plant-heavy Mediterranean diet, the animals had a higher population of good gut bacteria, than those that were given a meat-based Western diet. The health of your gut is closely related to your mental health, which is another reason why a Mediterranean diet improves mood.

# A Basic Shopping List for the Mediterranean Diet

Some very basic items that you need to have in your Mediterranean diet shopping list include:

### 1. Extra-virgin olive oil

While there are many dietary patterns that can be whipped up for a Mediterranean diet, olive oil is considered the core of each one. Extra-virgin olive oil is rich in polyphenols, carotenoids, and tocopherols, giving it anti-inflammatory and antioxidant properties. It is a kitchen staple that is versatile and can be used for light and heavy cooking.

### 2. Fresh vegetables and fruits

For Mediterranean cuisine, the vegetables and fruits need to be seasonal, locally sourced, and fresh. Opt for leafy and dark greens like mustard greens, beet greens, and kale; they are often added to lentil soup, beans, and frittatas. Wild greens like dandelions, chicory, and rocket can be eaten raw or cooked.

### 3. Fresh spices and herbs

Spices and herbs are a staple of a typical Mediterranean diet. You can use these plant-based seasoning agents so that you do not have to add excess salt. Additionally, antioxidants promote good health. Bay leaves, coriander, oregano, basil, and parsley frequently.

### 4. Canned and fresh seafood

For protein and healthy fats, shellfish and fish are the best sources. Fishes like salmon, sardines, and tuna are rich in Omega-3 fats, whether they are canned or fresh. You can use shrimp, clams, and mussels on grain and pasta dishes or simply serve with herbs, olive oil, and lemon. A Mediterranean diet is all about seafood consumption.

### 5. Whole grains

Wheat is the most common ingredient used in Mediterranean diets. Another traditional grain is farro and used for both cold and hot salads in Italy. Bulger is another classic that is made from cracked wheat berries and used in tabbouleh and pilafs. Always look for the terms 'whole grain' or 'whole' when shopping for whole grains.

# How to Easily Switch to the Mediterranean Diet

A Mediterranean diet is considered one of the world's healthiest diets today since it is abundant in olive oil, legumes, whole grains, vegetables, and fruits. It also features protein sources like lean poultry and fish over red meat. For additional taste, you can also consume red wine moderately.

Moving towards a Mediterranean diet is not difficult. If you want to transition into this diet, all you need to do is follow the steps mentioned below:

### 1. Cook with olive oil

If you love cooking with coconut oil or vegetable oil, you need to switch to extra-virgin olive oil. Olive oil is rich in monounsaturated fatty acids that improve the 'good' type of cholesterol, HDL cholesterol. The HDL cholesterol removes the 'bad' LDL cholesterol out of your bloodstream. While making vinaigrettes and salad dressings, use olive oil. Additionally, you can also drizzle it on finished dishes like chicken and fish to improve flavor. For pasta and mashed potatoes, you can swap butter for olive oil.

### 2. Eat more fish

For a Mediterranean diet, fish is the go-to protein, particularly fatty fishes like mackerel, sardines, and salmon. These fishes are rich in omega-3 fatty acids that are healthy for the brain and heart. While these fishes are leaner and have lesser fat than tilapia and cod, they taste good and are a great source of protein.

If you do not eat a lot of fish, you can easily start out by eating a fish dish once a week. One of the easiest ways to cook fish is to use foil packers or parchment paper. Additionally, you can also try incorporating fish on dishes like soup, stir-fries, and tacos.

### 3. Always eat your vegetables

Vegetables are the main ingredients used in Mediterranean diet recipes. If you do not like eating greens, this is a perfect opportunity to incorporate more vegetables into your diet. If you are new to a Mediterranean diet, you can start by eating one serving during the snack time, like blending some spinach for a glass of smoothie, crunching on bell peppers, etc. For dinner, you can try out easy and quick side dishes. Try to eat at least two servings per day.

### 4. Sip some wine

People that live along the Mediterranean areas like Greek, French, Italian, and Spanish do not shy away from wine. However, this does not mean that you pour a glass down at your leisure. According to experts and dieticians, women can drink about 3-ounces per serving and 5-ounce serving for men, per day. Additionally, when you are sipping, do it with a meal. If you are a clean person, you should not start drinking wine just for the sake of this diet.

# Breakfast & Brunch Recipes

## Cauliflower Fritters With Hummus

Servings: 4      Cooking Time: 15 Minutes

**Ingredients:**
- 2 (15 oz) cans chickpeas, divided
- 2 1/2 tbsp olive oil, divided, plus more for frying
- 1 cup onion, chopped, about 1/2 a small onion
- 2 tbsp garlic, minced
- 2 cups cauliflower, cut into small pieces, about 1/2 a large head
- 1/2 tsp salt
- black pepper
- Topping:
- Hummus, of choice
- Green onion, diced

**Directions:**
Preheat oven to 400°F     Rinse and drain 1 can of the chickpeas, place them on a paper towel to dry off well  Then place the chickpeas into a large bowl, removing the loose skins that come off, and toss with 1 tbsp of olive oil, spread the chickpeas onto a large pan (being careful not to over-crowd them) and sprinkle with salt and pepper     Bake for 20 minutes, then stir, and then bake an additional 5-10 minutes until very crispy  Once the chickpeas are roasted, transfer them to a large food processor and process until broken down and crumble - Don't over process them and turn it into flour, as you need to have some texture. Place the mixture into a small bowl, set aside     In a large pan over medium-high heat, add the remaining 1 1/2 tbsp of olive oil  Once heated, add in the onion and garlic, cook until lightly golden brown, about 2 minutes. Then add in the chopped cauliflower, cook for an additional 2 minutes, until the cauliflower is golden     Turn the heat down to low and cover the pan, cook until the cauliflower is fork tender and the onions are golden brown and caramelized, stirring often, about 3-5 minutes  Transfer the cauliflower mixture to the food processor, drain and rinse the remaining can of chickpeas and add them into the food processor, along with the salt and a pinch of pepper. Blend until smooth, and the mixture starts to ball, stop to scrape down the sides as needed  Transfer the cauliflower mixture into a large bowl and add in 1/2 cup of the roasted chickpea crumbs (you won't use all of the crumbs, but it is easier to break them down when you have a larger amount.), stir until well combined     In a large bowl over medium heat, add in enough oil to lightly cover the bottom of a large pan  Working in batches, cook the patties until golden brown, about 2-3 minutes, flip and cook again  Distribute among the container, placing parchment paper in between the fritters. Store in the fridge for 2-3 days     To Serve: Heat through in the oven at 350F for 5-8 minutes. Top with hummus, green onion and enjoy!  Recipe Notes: Don't add too much oil while frying the fritter or they will end up soggy. Use only enough to cover the pan. Use a fork while frying and resist the urge to flip them every minute to see if they are golden

**Nutrition Info:Per Serving:** Calories:333;Total Carbohydrates: 45g;Total Fat: 13g;Protein: 14g

## Italian Breakfast Sausage With Baby Potatoes And Vegetables

Servings: 4      Cooking Time: 30 Minutes

**Ingredients:**
- 1 lbs sweet Italian sausage links, sliced on the bias (diagonal)
- 2 cups baby potatoes, halved
- 2 cups broccoli florets
- 1 cup onions cut to 1-inch chunks
- 2 cups small mushrooms -half or quarter the large ones for uniform size
- 1 cup baby carrots
- 2 tbsp olive oil
- 1/2 tsp garlic powder
- 1/2 tsp Italian seasoning
- 1 tsp salt
- 1/2 tsp pepper

**Directions:**
Preheat the oven to 400 degrees F     In a large bowl, add the baby potatoes, broccoli florets, onions, small mushrooms, and baby carrots     Add in the olive oil, salt, pepper, garlic powder and Italian seasoning and toss to evenly coat     Spread the vegetables onto a sheet pan in one even layer     Arrange the sausage slices on the pan over the vegetables     Bake for 30 minutes – make sure to sake halfway through to prevent sticking  Allow to cool     Distribute the Italian sausages and vegetables among the containers and store in the fridge for 2-3 days     To Serve: Reheat in the microwave for 1-2 minutes, or until heated through and enjoy!     Recipe Notes: If you would like crispier potatoes, place them on the pan and bake for 15 minutes before adding the other ingredients to the pan.

**Nutrition Info:Per Serving:** Calories:321;Total Fat: 16g;Total Carbs: 23g;Fiber: 4g;Protein: 22g

## Greek Quinoa Breakfast Bowl

Servings: 6      Cooking Time: 20 Minutes

**Ingredients:**
- 12 eggs
- ¼ cup plain Greek yogurt
- 1 tsp onion powder
- 1 tsp granulated garlic
- ½ tsp salt
- ½ tsp pepper
- 1 tsp olive oil
- 1 (5 oz) bag baby spinach
- 1 pint cherry tomatoes, halved
- 1 cup feta cheese
- 2 cups cooked quinoa

**Directions:**
In a large bowl whisk together eggs, Greek yogurt, onion powder, granulated garlic, salt, and pepper, set aside
In a large skillet, heat olive oil and add spinach, cook the spinach until it is slightly wilted, about 3-4 minutes
Add in cherry tomatoes, cook until tomatoes are softened, 4 minutes    Stir in egg mixture and cook until the eggs are set, about 7-9 minutes, stir in the eggs as they cook to scramble    Once the eggs have set stir in the feta and quinoa, cook until heated through
Distribute evenly among the containers, store for 2-3 days    To serve: Reheat in the microwave for 30 seconds to 1 minute or heated through
**Nutrition Info:Per Serving:** Calories:357;Total Carbohydrates: ;Total Fat: 20g;Protein: 23g

## Egg, Prosciutto, And Cheese Freezer Sandwiches

Servings: 6      Cooking Time: 20 Minutes

**Ingredients:**
- Cooking spray or oil to grease the baking dish
- 7 large eggs
- ½ cup low-fat (2%) milk
- ½ teaspoon garlic powder
- ½ teaspoon onion powder
- 1 tablespoon Dijon mustard
- ½ teaspoon honey
- 6 whole-wheat English muffins
- 6 slices thinly sliced prosciutto
- 6 slices Swiss cheese

**Directions:**
Preheat the oven to 375°F. Lightly oil or spray an 8-by--inch glass or ceramic baking dish with cooking spray. In a large bowl, whisk together the eggs, milk, garlic powder, and onion powder. Pour the mixture into the baking dish and bake for    minutes, until the eggs are set and no longer jiggling. Cool.    While the eggs are baking, mix the mustard and honey in a small bowl. Lay out the English muffin halves to start assembly. When the eggs are cool, use a biscuit cutter or drinking glass about the same size as the English muffin diameter to cut 6 egg circles. Divide the leftover egg scraps evenly to be added to each sandwich.    Spread

½ teaspoon of honey mustard on each of the bottom English muffin halves. Top each with 1 slice of prosciutto, 1 egg circle and scraps, 1 slice of cheese, and the top half of the muffin.    Wrap each sandwich tightly in foil.    STORAGE: Store tightly wrapped sandwiches in the freezer for up to 1 month. To reheat, remove the foil, place the sandwich on a microwave-safe plate, and wrap with a damp paper towel. Microwave on high for 1½ minutes, flip over, and heat again for another 1½ minutes. Because cooking time can vary greatly between microwaves, you may need to experiment with a few sandwiches before you find the perfect amount of time to heat the whole item through.
**Nutrition Info:Per Serving:** Total calories: 361; Total fat: 17g; Saturated fat: 7g; Sodium: 953mg; Carbohydrates: 26g; Fiber: 3g; Protein: 24g

## Healthy Zucchini Kale Tomato Salad

Servings: 4      Cooking Time: 20 Minutes

**Ingredients:**
- 1 lb kale, chopped
- 2 tbsp fresh parsley, chopped
- 1 tbsp vinegar
- 1/2 cup can tomato, crushed
- 1 tsp paprika
- 1 cup zucchini, cut into cubes
- 1 cup grape tomatoes, halved
- 2 tbsp olive oil
- 1 onion, chopped
- 1 leek, sliced
- Pepper
- Salt

**Directions:**
Add oil into the inner pot of instant pot and set the pot on sauté mode.    Add leek and onion and sauté for 5 minutes.    Add kale and remaining ingredients and stir well.    Seal pot with lid and cook on high for 15 minutes.    Once done, allow to release pressure naturally for 10 minutes then release remaining using quick release. Remove lid.    Stir and serve.
**Nutrition Info:**Calories: 162;Fat: 3 g;Carbohydrates: 22.2 g;Sugar: 4.8 g;Protein: 5.2 g;Cholesterol: 0 mg

## Cheese And Cauliflower Frittata With Peppers

Servings: 6     Cooking Time: 30 Minutes
**Ingredients:**
- 10 eggs
- 1 seeded and chopped bell pepper
- ½ cup grated Parmigiano-Reggiano
- ½ cup milk, skim
- ½ teaspoon cayenne pepper
- 1 pound cauliflower, floret
- ½ teaspoon saffron
- 2 tablespoons chopped chives
- Salt and black pepper as desired

**Directions:**
Prepare your oven by setting the temperature to 370 degrees Fahrenheit. You should also grease a skillet suitable for the oven.     In a medium-sized bowl, add the milk and eggs. Whisk them until they are frothy. Sprinkle the grated Parmigiano-Reggiano cheese into the frothy mixture and fold the ingredients together. Pour in the salt, saffron, cayenne pepper, and black pepper and gently stir.     Add in the chopped bell pepper and gently stir until the ingredients are fully incorporated.     Pour the egg mixture into the skillet and cook on medium heat over your stovetop for 4 minutes.     Steam the cauliflower florets in a pan. To do this, add ½ inch of water and ½ teaspoon sea salt. Pour in the cauliflower and cover for 3 to 8 minutes. Drain any extra water.     Add the cauliflower into the mixture and gently stir.     Set the skillet into the preheated oven and turn your timer to 13 minutes. Once the mixture is golden brown in the middle, remove the frittata from the oven.     Set your skillet aside for a couple of minutes so it can cool.     Slice and garnish with chives before you serve.
**Nutrition Info:**calories: 207, fats: grams, carbohydrates: 8 grams, protein: 17 grams.

## Avocado Kale Omelet

Servings: 1     Cooking Time: 5 Minutes
**Ingredients:**
- 2 eggs
- 1 teaspoon milk
- 2 teaspoons olive oil
- 1 cup kale (chopped)
- 1 tablespoon lime juice
- 1 tablespoon cilantro (chopped)
- 1 teaspoon sunflower seeds
- Pinch of red pepper (crushed)
- ¼ avocado (sliced)
- sea salt or plain salt
- freshly ground black pepper

**Directions:**
Toss all the Ingredients: (except eggs and milk) to make the kale salad.     Beat the eggs and milk in a bowl. Heat oil in a pan over medium heat. Then pour in the egg mixture and cook it until the bottom settles. Cook for 2 minutes and then flip it over and further cook for 20 seconds.     Finally, put the omelet in containers. Top the omelet with the kale salad.     Serve warm.
**Nutrition Info:Per Serving:**Calories: 399, Total Fat: 28.8g, Saturated Fat: 6.2, Cholesterol: 328 mg, Sodium: 162 mg, Total Carbohydrate: 25.2g, Dietary Fiber: 6.3 g, Total Sugars: 9 g, Protein: 15.8 g, Vitamin D: 31 mcg, Calcium: 166 mg, Iron: 4 mg, Potassium: 980 mg

## Mediterranean Breakfast Burrito

Servings: 6     Cooking Time: 5 Minutes
**Ingredients:**
- 9 eggs whole
- 6 tortillas whole 10 inch, regular or sun-dried tomato
- 3 tbsp sun-dried tomatoes, chopped
- 1/2 cup feta cheese I use light/low-fat feta
- 2 cups baby spinach washed and dried
- 3 tbsp black olives, sliced
- 3/4 cup refried beans, canned
- Garnish:
- Salsa

**Directions:**
Spray a medium frying pan with non- stick spray, add the eggs and scramble and toss for about 5 minutes, or until eggs are no longer liquid     Add in the spinach, black olives, sun-dried tomatoes and continue to stir and toss until no longer wet     Add in the feta cheese and cover, cook until cheese is melted     Add 2 tbsp of refried beans to each tortilla     Top with egg mixture, dividing evenly between all burritos, and wrap Frying in a pan until lightly browned     Allow to cool completely before slicing     Wrap the slices in plastic wrap and then aluminum foil and place in the freezer for up to 2 months or fridge for 2 days     To Serve: Remove the aluminum foil and plastic wrap, and microwave for 2 minutes, then allow to rest for 30 seconds, enjoy! Enjoy hot with salsa and fruit
**Nutrition Info:Per Serving:** Calories:252;Total Carbohydrates: 21g;Total Fat: 11g;Protein: 14g |

## Shakshuka With Feta

Servings: 4-6      Cooking Time:40 Minutes
**Ingredients:**
- 6 large eggs
- 3 tbsp extra-virgin olive oil
- 1 large onion, halved and thinly sliced
- 1 large red bell pepper, seeded and thinly sliced
- 3 garlic cloves, thinly sliced
- 1 tsp ground cumin
- 1 tsp sweet paprika
- ⅛ tsp cayenne, or to taste
- 1 (28-ounce) can whole plum tomatoes with juices, coarsely chopped
- ¾ tsp salt, more as needed
- ¼ tsp black pepper, more as needed
- 5 oz feta cheese, crumbled, about 1 1/4 cups
- To Serve:
- Chopped cilantro
- Hot sauce

**Directions:**
Preheat oven to 375 degrees F      In a large skillet over medium-low heat, add the oil      Once heated, add the onion and bell pepper, cook gently until very soft, about 20 minutes      Add in the garlic and cook until tender, 1 to 2 minutes, then stir in cumin, paprika and cayenne, and cook 1 minute      Pour in tomatoes, season with 3/4 tsp salt and 1/4 tsp pepper, simmer until tomatoes have thickened, about 10 minutes      Then stir in crumbled feta      Gently crack eggs into skillet over tomatoes, season with salt and pepper      Transfer skillet to oven      Bake until eggs have just set, 7 to 10 minutes      Allow to cool and distribute among the containers, store in the fridge for 2-3 days      To Serve: Reheat in the oven at 360 degrees F for 5 minutes or until heated through
**Nutrition Info:Per Serving:** Calories:337;Carbs: 17g;Total Fat: 25g;Protein:

## Spinach, Feta And Egg Breakfast Quesadillas

Servings: 5      Cooking Time: 15 Minutes
**Ingredients:**
- 8 eggs (optional)
- 2 tsp olive oil
- 1 red bell pepper
- 1/2 red onion
- 1/4 cup milk
- 4 handfuls of spinach leaves
- 1 1/2 cup mozzarella cheese
- 5 sun-dried tomato tortillas
- 1/2 cup feta
- 1/4 tsp salt
- 1/4 tsp pepper
- Spray oil

**Directions:**
In a large non-stick pan over medium heat, add the olive oil      Once heated, add the bell pepper and onion, cook for 4-5 minutes until soft      In the meantime, whisk together the eggs, milk, salt and pepper in a bowl      Add in the egg/milk mixture into the pan with peppers and onions, stirring frequently, until eggs are almost cooked through      Add in the spinach and feta, fold into the eggs, stirring until spinach is wilted and eggs are cooked through      Remove the eggs from heat and plate      Spray a separate large non-stick pan with spray oil, and place over medium heat      Add the tortilla, on one half of the tortilla, spread about ½ cup of the egg

mixture      Top the eggs with around ⅓ cup of shredded mozzarella cheese      Fold the second half of the tortilla over, then cook for 2 minutes, or until golden brown      Flip and cook for another minute until golden brown      Allow the quesadilla to cool completely, divide among the container, store for 2 days or wrap in plastic wrap and foil, and freeze for up to 2 months      To Serve: Reheat in oven at 375 for 3-5 minutes or until heated through
**Nutrition Info:Per Serving:** (1/2 quesadilla):
Calories:213;Total Fat: 11g;Total Carbs: 15g;Protein: 15g

## Breakfast Cobbler

Servings: 4      Cooking Time: 12 Minutes
**Ingredients:**
- 2 lbs apples, cut into chunks
- 1 1/2 cups water
- 1/4 tsp nutmeg
- 1 1/2 tsp cinnamon
- 1/2 cup dry buckwheat
- 1/2 cup dates, chopped
- Pinch of ground ginger

**Directions:**
Spray instant pot from inside with cooking spray. Add all ingredients into the instant pot and stir well. Seal pot with a lid and select manual and set timer for 12 minutes.      Once done, release pressure using quick release. Remove lid.      Stir and serve.
**Nutrition Info:**Calories: 195;Fat: 0.9 g;Carbohydrates: 48.3 g;Sugar: 25.8 g;Protein: 3.3 g;Cholesterol: 0 mg

## Egg-topped Quinoa Bowl With Kale

Servings: 2      Cooking Time: 5 Minutes
**Ingredients:**
- 1-ounce pancetta, chopped
- 1 bunch kale, sliced
- ½ cup cherry tomatoes, halved
- 1 teaspoon red wine vinegar
- 1 cup cooked quinoa
- 1 teaspoon olive oil
- 2 eggs
- 1/3 cup avocado, sliced
- sea salt or plain salt
- fresh black pepper

**Directions:**
Start by heating pancetta in a skillet until golden brown. Add in kale and further cook for 2 minutes.      Then, stir in tomatoes, vinegar, and salt and remove from heat. Now, divide this mixture into 2 bowls, add avocado to both, and then set aside.      Finally, cook both the eggs and top each bowl with an egg.      Serve hot with toppings of your choice.
**Nutrition Info:Per Serving:**Calories: 547, Total Fat: 22., Saturated Fat: 5.3, Cholesterol: 179 mg, Sodium: 412 mg, Total Carbohydrate: 62.5 g, Dietary Fiber: 8.6 g, Total Sugars: 1.7 g, Protein: 24.7 g, Vitamin D: 15 mcg, Calcium: 117 mg, Iron: 6 mg, Potassium: 1009 mg

## Strawberry Greek Frozen Yogurt

Servings: 5     Cooking Time: 2-4 Hours
**Ingredients:**
- 3 cups plain Greek low-fat yogurt
- 1 cup sugar
- ¼ cup lemon juice, freshly squeezed
- 2 teaspoons vanilla
- 1/8 teaspoon salt
- 1 cup strawberries, sliced

**Directions:**
In a medium-sized bowl, add yogurt, lemon juice, sugar, vanilla, and salt.     Whisk the whole mixture well. Freeze the yogurt mix in a 2-quart ice cream maker according to the given instructions.     During the final minute, add the sliced strawberries.     Transfer the yogurt to an airtight container.     Place in the freezer for 2-4 hours.     Remove from the freezer and allow it to stand for 5-15 minutes.     Serve and enjoy!

**Nutrition Info:Per Serving:**Calories: 251, Total Fat: 0.5 g, Saturated Fat: 0.1 g, Cholesterol: 3 mg, Sodium: 130 mg, Total Carbohydrate: 48.7 g, Dietary Fiber: 0.6 g, Total Sugars: 47.3 g, Protein: 14.7 g, Vitamin D: 1 mcg, Calcium: 426 mg, Iron: 0 mg, Potassium: 62 mg

## Almond Peach Oatmeal

Servings: 2     Cooking Time: 10 Minutes
**Ingredients:**
- 1 cup unsweetened almond milk
- 2 cups of water
- 1 cup oats
- 2 peaches, diced
- Pinch of salt

**Directions:**
Spray instant pot from inside with cooking spray. Add all ingredients into the instant pot and stir well. Seal pot with a lid and select manual and set timer for 10 minutes.     Once done, allow to release pressure naturally for 10 minutes then release remaining using quick release. Remove lid.     Stir and serve.

**Nutrition Info:**Calories: 234;Fat: 4.8 g;Carbohydrates: 42.7 g;Sugar: 9 g;Protein: 7.3 g;Cholesterol: 0 mg

## Peanut Butter Banana Pudding

Servings: 1     Cooking Time: 25 Minutes
**Ingredients:**
- 2 bananas, halved
- ¼ cup smooth peanut butter
- Coconut for garnish, shredded

**Directions:**
Start by blending bananas and peanut butter in a blender and mix until smooth or desired texture obtained.     Pour into a bowl and garnish with coconut if desired.     Enjoy.

**Nutrition Info:Per Serving:**Calories: 589, Total Fat: 33.3g, Saturated Fat: 6.9, Cholesterol: 0 mg, Sodium: 13 mg, Total Carbohydrate: 66.5 g, Dietary Fiber: 10 g, Total Sugars: 38 g, Protein: 18.8 g, Vitamin D: 0 mcg, Calcium: 40 mg, Iron: 2 mg, Potassium: 1264 mg

## Coconut And Banana Mix

Servings: 4     Cooking Time: 4 Minutes
**Ingredients:**
- 1 cup coconut milk
- 1 banana
- 1 cup dried coconut
- 2 tablespoons ground flax seed
- 3 tablespoons chopped raisins
- ⅛ teaspoon nutmeg
- ⅛ teaspoon cinnamon
- Salt to taste

**Directions:**
Set a large skillet on the stove and set it to low heat. Chop up the banana.     Pour the coconut milk, nutmeg, and cinnamon into the skillet.     Pour in the ground flaxseed while stirring continuously.     Add the dried coconut and banana. Mix the ingredients until combined well.     Allow the mixture to simmer for 2 to 3 minutes while stirring occasionally.     Set four airtight containers on the counter.     Remove the pan from heat and sprinkle enough salt for your taste buds. Divide the mixture into the containers and place them into the fridge overnight. They can remain in the fridge for up to 3 days.     Before you set this tasty mixture in the microwave to heat up, you need to let it thaw on the counter for a bit.

**Nutrition Info:**calories: 279, fats: 22 grams, carbohydrates: 25 grams, protein: 6.4 grams.

## Raspberry-lemon Olive Oil Muffins

Servings: 12     Cooking Time: 20 Minutes
**Ingredients:**
- Cooking spray to grease baking liners
- 1 cup all-purpose flour
- 1 cup whole-wheat flour
- 1/2 cup tightly packed light brown sugar
- 1/2 teaspoon baking soda
- 1/2 teaspoon aluminum-free baking powder
- 1/8 teaspoon kosher salt
- 1 1/4 cups buttermilk
- 1 large egg
- 1/4 cup extra-virgin olive oil
- 1 tablespoon freshly squeezed lemon juice
- Zest of 2 lemons
- 1 1/4 cups frozen raspberries (do not thaw)

**Directions:**
Preheat the oven to 400°F and line a muffin tin with baking liners. Spray the liners lightly with cooking spray.     In a large mixing bowl, whisk together the all-purpose flour, whole-wheat flour, brown sugar, baking soda, baking powder, and salt.     In a medium bowl, whisk together the buttermilk, egg, oil, lemon juice, and lemon zest.     Pour the wet ingredients into the dry ingredients and stir just until blended. Do not overmix. Fold in the frozen raspberries.     Scoop about 1/4 cup of batter into each muffin liner and bake for 20 minutes, or until the tops look browned and a paring knife comes out clean when inserted. Remove the muffins from the tin to cool.     STORAGE: Store covered containers at room temperature for up to 4 days. To freeze muffins for up to 3 months, wrap them in foil and place in an airtight resealable bag.

**Nutrition Info:Per Serving:** Total calories: 166; Total fat: 5g; Saturated fat: 1g; Sodium: 134mg; Carbohydrates: 30g; Fiber: 3g; Protein: 4g

## Pearl Couscous Salad

Servings: 6     Cooking Time: 10 Minutes
**Ingredients:**
- lemon juice, 1 large lemon
- 1/3 cup extra-virgin olive oil
- 1 teaspoon dill weed
- 1 teaspoon garlic powder
- salt
- pepper
- 2 cups Pearl Couscous
- 2 tablespoons extra virgin olive oil
- 2 cups grape tomatoes, halved
- water as needed
- 1/3 cup red onions, finely chopped
- 1/2 English cucumber, finely chopped
- 1 15-ounce can chickpeas
- 1 14-ounce can artichoke hearts, roughly chopped
- 1/2 cup pitted Kalamata olives
- 15-20 pieces fresh basil leaves, roughly torn and chopped
- 3 ounces fresh mozzarella

**Directions:**
Start by preparing the vinaigrette by mixing all Ingredients: in a bowl. Set aside.     Heat olive oil in a medium-sized heavy pot over medium heat.     Add couscous and cook until golden brown.     Add 3 cups of boiling water and cook the couscous according to package instructions.     Once done, drain in a colander and put it to the side.     In a large mixing bowl, add the rest of the Ingredients: except the cheese and basil. Add the cooked couscous, basil, and mix everything well.     Give the vinaigrette a gentle stir and whisk it into the couscous salad. Mix well.     Adjust/add seasoning as desired.     Add mozzarella cheese. Garnish with some basil.     Enjoy!

**Nutrition Info:Per Serving:**Calories: 578, Total Fat: 25.3g, Saturated Fat: 4.6, Cholesterol: 8 mg, Sodium: 268 mg, Total Carbohydrate: 70.1g, Dietary Fiber: 17.5 g, Total Sugars: 10.8 g, Protein: 23.4 g, Vitamin D: 0 mcg, Calcium: 150 mg, Iron: 6 mg, Potassium: 1093 mg

## Mushroom Tomato Egg Cups

Servings: 4     Cooking Time: 5 Minutes
**Ingredients:**
- 4 eggs
- 1/2 cup tomatoes, chopped
- 1/2 cup mushrooms, chopped
- 2 tbsp fresh parsley, chopped
- 1/4 cup half and half
- 1/2 cup cheddar cheese, shredded
- Pepper
- Salt

**Directions:**
In a bowl, whisk the egg with half and half, pepper, and salt.     Add tomato, mushrooms, parsley, and cheese and stir well.     Pour egg mixture into the four small jars and seal jars with lid.     Pour 1 1/2 cups of water into the instant pot then place steamer rack in the pot. Place jars on top of the steamer rack.     Seal pot with lid and cook on high for 5 minutes.     Once done, release pressure using quick release. Remove lid.     Serve and enjoy.

**Nutrition Info:**Calories: 146;Fat: 10.g;Carbohydrates: 2.5 g;Sugar: 1.2 g;Protein: 10 g;Cholesterol: 184 mg

## Mediterranean Breakfast Salad

Servings: 2    Cooking Time: 10 Minutes
**Ingredients:**
- 4 eggs (optional)
- 10 cups arugula
- 1/2 seedless cucumber, chopped
- 1 cup cooked quinoa, cooled
- 1 large avocado
- 1 cup natural almonds, chopped
- 1/2 cup mixed herbs like mint and dill, chopped
- 2 cups halved cherry tomatoes and/or heirloom tomatoes cut into wedges
- Extra virgin olive oil
- 1 lemon
- Sea salt, to taste
- Freshly ground black pepper, to taste

**Directions:**
Cook the eggs by soft-boiling them - Bring a pot of water to a boil, then reduce heat to a simmer. Gently lower all the eggs into water and allow them to simmer for 6 minutes. Remove the eggs from water and run cold water on top to stop the cooking, process set aside and peel when ready to use    In a large bowl, combine the arugula, tomatoes, cucumber, and quinoa    Divide the salad among 2 containers, store in the fridge for 2 days    To Serve: Garnish with the sliced avocado and halved egg, sprinkle herbs and almonds over top. Drizzle with olive oil, season with salt and pepper, toss to combine. Season with more salt and pepper to taste, a squeeze of lemon juice, and a drizzle of olive oil
**Nutrition Info:Per Serving:** Calories:2;Carbs: 18g;Total Fat: 16g;Protein: 10g

## Breakfast Carrot Oatmeal

Servings: 2    Cooking Time: 10 Minutes
**Ingredients:**
- 1 cup steel-cut oats
- 1/2 cup raisins
- 1/2 tsp ground nutmeg
- 1/2 tsp ground cinnamon
- 2 carrots, grated
- 2 cups of water
- 2 cups unsweetened almond milk
- 1 tbsp honey

**Directions:**
Spray instant pot from inside with cooking spray. Add all ingredients into the instant pot and stir well. Seal pot with lid and cook on high for 10 minutes. Once done, release pressure using quick release. Remove lid.    Stir and serve.
**Nutrition Info:** Calories: 3;Fat: 6.6 g;Carbohydrates: 73.8 g;Sugar: 33.7 g;Protein: 8.1 g;Cholesterol: 0 mg

## Rum-raisin Arborio Pudding

Servings: 2    Cooking Time: 4 Hours
**Ingredients:**
- ¾ cup Arborio rice
- 1 can evaporated milk
- ½ cup raisins
- ¼ teaspoon nutmeg, grated
- 1½ cups water
- 1/3 cup sugar
- ¼ cup dark rum
- sea salt or plain salt

**Directions:**
Start by mixing rum and raisins in a bowl and set aside. Then, heat the evaporated milk and water in a saucepan and then simmer.    Now, add sugar and stir until dissolved.    Finally, convert this milk mixture into a slow cooker and stir in rice and salt. Cook on low heat for hours.    Now, stir in the raisin mixture and nutmeg and let sit for 10 minutes.    Serve warm.
**Nutrition Info:Per Serving:** Calories: 3, Total Fat: 10.1g, Saturated Fat: 5.9, Cholesterol: 36 mg, Sodium: 161 mg, Total Carbohydrate: 131.5 g, Dietary Fiber: 3.3 g, Total Sugars: 54.8 g, Protein: 14.4 g, Vitamin D: 0 mcg, Calcium: 372 mg, Iron: 2 mg, Potassium: 712 mg

## Mediterranean Quinoa And Feta Egg Muffins

Servings: 12    Cooking Time: 30 Minutes
**Ingredients:**
- 8 eggs
- 1 cup cooked quinoa
- 1 cup crumbled feta cheese
- 1/4 tsp salt
- 2 cups baby spinach finely chopped
- 1/2 cup finely chopped onion
- 1 cup chopped or sliced tomatoes, cherry or grape tomatoes
- 1/2 cup chopped and pitted Kalamata olives
- 1 tbsp chopped fresh oregano
- 2 tsp high oleic sunflower oil plus optional extra for greasing muffin tins

**Directions:**
Pre-heat oven to 350 degrees F    Prepare 1silicone muffin holders on a baking sheet, or grease a 12-cup muffin tin with oil, set aside    In a skillet over medium heat, add the vegetable oil and onions, sauté for 2 minutes    Add tomatoes, sauté for another minute, then add spinach and sauté until wilted, about 1 minute    Remove from heat and stir in olives and oregano, set aside    Place the eggs in a blender or mixing bowl and blend or mix until well combined    Pour the eggs in to a mixing bowl (if you used a blender) then add quinoa, feta cheese, veggie mixture, and salt, and stir until well combined    Pour mixture in to silicone cups or greased muffin tins, dividing equally, and bake for 30 minutes, or until eggs have set and muffins are a light golden brown    Allow to cool completely    Distribute among the containers, store in fridge for 2-3 days    To Serve: Heat in the microwave for 30 seconds or until slightly heated through    Recipe Notes: Muffins can also be eaten cold. For the quinoa, I recommend making a large batch {2 cups water per each cup of dry, rinsed quinoa} and saving the extra for leftovers.
**Nutrition Info:Per Serving:** Calories:1Total Carbohydrates: 5g;Total Fat: 7g;Protein: 6g

## Blueberry Greek Yogurt Pancakes

Servings: 6    Cooking Time: 15 Minutes
**Ingredients:**
- 1 1/4 cup all-purpose flour
- 2 tsp baking powder
- 1 tsp baking soda
- 1/4 tsp salt
- 1/4 cup sugar
- 3 eggs
- 3 tbsp vegan butter unsalted, melted
- 1/2 cup milk
- 1 1/2 cups Greek yogurt plain, non-fat
- 1/2 cup blueberries optional
- Toppings:
- Greek yogurt
- Mixed berries – blueberries, raspberries and blackberries

**Directions:**
In a large bowl, whisk together the flour, salt, baking powder and baking soda    In a separate bowl, whisk together butter, sugar, eggs, Greek yogurt, and milk until the mixture is smooth    Then add in the Greek yogurt mixture from step to the dry mixture in step 1, mix to combine, allow the patter to sit for 20 minutes to get a smooth texture – if using blueberries fold them into the pancake batter    Heat the pancake griddle, spray with non-stick butter spray or just brush with butter    Pour the batter, in 1/4 cupful's, onto the griddle    Cook until the bubbles on top burst and create small holes, lift up the corners of the pancake to see if they're golden browned on the bottom    With a wide spatula, flip the pancake and cook on the other side until lightly browned    Distribute the pancakes in among the storage containers, store in the fridge for 3 day or in the freezer for 2 months    To Serve: Reheat microwave for 1 minute (until 80% heated through) or on the stove top, drizzle warm syrup on top, scoop of Greek yogurt, and mixed berries (including blueberries, raspberries, blackberries)
**Nutrition Info:Per Serving:** Calories:258;Total Carbohydrates: 33g;Total Fat: 8g;Protein: 11g

## Vegetable Breakfast Bowl

Servings: 2    Cooking Time: 5 Minutes
**Ingredients:**
- Breakfast Bowl:
- 1 ½ cups cooked quinoa
- 1 lb asparagus[1], cut into bite-sized pieces, ends trimmed and discarded
- 1 tbsp avocado oil or olive oil
- 3 cups shredded kale leaves
- 1 batch lemony dressing
- 3 cups shredded, uncooked Brussels sprouts
- 1 avocado, peeled, pitted and thinly-sliced
- 4 eggs, cooked to your preference (optional)
- Garnishes:
- Toasted sesame seeds
- Crushed red pepper
- Sunflower seeds
- Sliced almonds
- Hummus
- Lemon Dressing:
- 2 tsp Dijon mustard
- 1 garlic clove, minced
- 2 tbsp avocado oil or olive oil

- 2 tbsp freshly-squeezed lemon juice
- Salt, to taste
- Freshly-cracked black pepper, to taste

**Directions:**
In a large sauté pan over medium-high heat, add the oil Once heated, add the asparagus and sauté for 4-5 minutes, stirring occasionally, until tender. Remove from heat and set side    Add the Brussels sprouts, quinoa, and cooked asparagus, and toss until combined Distribute among the container, store in fridge for 2-3 days    To serve: In a large, mixing bowl combine the kale and lemony dressing. Use your fingers to massage the dressing into the kale for 2-3 minutes, or until the leaves are dark and softened, set aside. In a small mixing bowl, combine the avocado, lemon juice, dijon mustard, garlic clove, salt, and pepper. Assemble the bowls by smearing a spoonful of hummus along the side of each bowl, then portion the kale salad evenly between the four bowls. Top with the avocado slices, egg, and your desired garnishes    Recipe Note: Feel free to sub the asparagus with your favorite vegetable(s), sautéing or roasting them until cooked
**Nutrition Info:Per Serving:** Calories:632;Carbs: 52g;Total Fat: 39g;Protein: 24g

## Egg-artichoke Breakfast Casserole

Servings: 8    Cooking Time: 30 To 35 Minutes
**Ingredients:**
- 14 ounces artichoke hearts, if using canned remember to drain them
- 16 eggs
- 1 cup shredded cheddar cheese
- 10 ounces chopped spinach, if frozen make sure it is thawed and well-drained
- 1 clove of minced garlic
- ½ cup ricotta cheese
- ½ cup parmesan cheese
- ½ teaspoon crushed red pepper
- 1 teaspoon sea salt
- ½ teaspoon dried thyme
- ¼ cup onion, shaved
- ¼ cup milk

**Directions:**
Grease a 9 x -inch baking pan or place a piece of parchment paper inside of it.    Turn the temperature on your oven to 350 degrees Fahrenheit.    Crack the eggs into a bowl and whisk them well.    Pour in the milk and whisk the two ingredients together. Squeeze any excess moisture from the spinach with a paper towel.    Toss the spinach and leafless artichoke hearts into the bowl. Stir until well combined.    Add the cheddar cheese, minced garlic, parmesan cheese, red pepper, sea salt, thyme, and onion into the bowl. Mix until all the ingredients are fully incorporated. Pour the eggs into the baking pan.    Add the ricotta cheese in even dollops before placing the casserole in the oven.    Set your timer for 30 minutes, but watch the casserole carefully after about 20 minutes. Once the eggs stop jiggling and are cooked, remove the meal from the oven. Let the casserole cool down a bit and enjoy!
**Nutrition Info:**calories: 302, fats: 18 grams, carbohydrates: grams, protein: 22 grams.

## Breakfast Cauliflower Rice Bowl

Servings: 6     Cooking Time: 12 Minutes
**Ingredients:**
- 1 cup cauliflower rice
- 1/2 tsp red pepper flakes
- 1 1/2 tsp curry powder
- 1/2 tbsp ginger, grated
- 1 cup vegetable stock
- 4 tomatoes, chopped
- 3 cups broccoli, chopped
- Pepper
- Salt

**Directions:**
Spray instant pot from inside with cooking spray. Add all ingredients into the instant pot and stir well. Seal pot with lid and cook on high for 12 minutes. Once done, allow to release pressure naturally for 10 minutes then release remaining using quick release. Remove lid.     Stir and serve.
**Nutrition Info:** Calories: 44; Fat: 0.8 g; Carbohydrates: 8.2 g; Sugar: 3.8 g; Protein: 2.8 g; Cholesterol: 0 mg

## Savory Cucumber-dill Yogurt

Servings: 4     Cooking Time: 10 Minutes
**Ingredients:**
- 2 cups low-fat (2%) plain Greek yogurt
- 4 teaspoons minced shallot
- 4 teaspoons freshly squeezed lemon juice
- ¼ cup chopped fresh dill
- 2 teaspoons olive oil
- ¼ teaspoon kosher salt
- Pinch freshly ground black pepper
- 2 cups chopped Persian cucumbers (about 4 medium cucumbers)

**Directions:**
Combine the yogurt, shallot, lemon juice, dill, oil, salt, and pepper in a large bowl. Taste the mixture and add another pinch of salt if needed.     Scoop ½ cup of yogurt into each of 4 containers. Place ½ cup of chopped cucumbers in each of 4 separate small containers or resealable sandwich bags.     STORAGE: Store covered containers in the refrigerator for up to 5 days.
**Nutrition Info:Per Serving:** Total calories: 127; Total fat: 5g; Saturated fat: 2g; Sodium: 200mg; Carbohydrates: 9g; Fiber: 2g; Protein: 11g

## Cranberry Spice Tea

Servings: 2     Cooking Time: 18 Minutes
**Ingredients:**
- 1-ounce cranberries
- ½ lemon, juice, and zest
- 1 cinnamon stick
- 2 teabags
- ½ inch ginger, peeled and grated
- raw honey to taste
- 3 cups water

**Directions:**
Start by adding all the Ingredients: except honey into a pot or saucepan.     Bring to a boil and then simmer for about 115 minutes.     Strain and serve the tea.     Add honey or any other sweetener of your preference. Enjoy.

**Nutrition Info:Per Serving:** Calories: 38, Total Fat: 0.3g, Saturated Fat: 0.1, Cholesterol: 0 mg, Sodium: 2 mg, Total Carbohydrate: 10 g, Dietary Fiber: 4.9 g, Total Sugars: 1.1 g, Protein: 0.7 g, Vitamin D: 0 mcg, Calcium: 77 mg, Iron: 1 mg, Potassium: 110 mg

## Zucchini Pudding

Servings: 4     Cooking Time: 10 Minutes
**Ingredients:**
- 2 cups zucchini, grated
- 1/2 tsp ground cardamom
- 1/4 cup swerve
- 5 oz half and half
- 5 oz unsweetened almond milk
- Pinch of salt

**Directions:**
Spray instant pot from inside with cooking spray. Add all ingredients into the instant pot and stir well. Seal pot with lid and cook on high for 10 minutes. Once done, allow to release pressure naturally for 10 minutes then release remaining using quick release. Remove lid.     Stir well and serve.
**Nutrition Info:** Calories: ; Fat: 4.7 g; Carbohydrates: 18.9 g; Sugar: 16 g; Protein: 1.9 g; Cholesterol: 13 mg

## Breakfast Burrito Mediterranean Style

Servings: 6     Cooking Time: 20 Minutes
**Ingredients:**
- 9 eggs
- 3 tablespoons chopped sun-dried tomatoes
- 6 tortillas that are 10 inches
- 2 cups baby spinach
- ½ cup feta cheese
- ¾ cups of canned refried beans
- 3 tablespoons sliced black olives
- Salsa, sour cream, or any other toppings you desire

**Directions:**
Wash and dry your spinach.     Grease a medium frying pan with oil or nonstick cooking spray.     Add the eggs into the pan and cook for about 5 minutes. Make sure you stir the eggs well, so they become scrambled. Combine the black olives, spinach, and sun-dried tomatoes with the eggs. Stir until the ingredients are fully incorporated.     Add the feta cheese and then set the lid on the pan so the cheese will melt quickly. Spoon a bit of egg mixture into the tortilla.     Wrap the tortillas tightly.     Wash your pan or get a new skillet. Remember to grease the pan.     Set each tortilla into the pan and cook each side for a couple of minutes. Once they are lightly brown, remove them from the pan and allow the burritos to cool on a serving plate. Top with your favorite condiments and enjoy!     To store the burritos, wrap them in aluminum foil and place them in the fridge. They can be stored for up to two days.
**Nutrition Info:** calories: 252, fats: grams, carbohydrates: 21 grams, protein: 14 grams.

## Healthy Dry Fruit Porridge

Servings: 6     Cooking Time: 8 Hours
**Ingredients:**
- 2 cups steel-cut oats
- 1/8 tsp ground nutmeg
- 1 tsp vanilla
- 1 1/2 tsp cinnamon
- 1/2 cup dry apricots, chopped
- 1/2 cup dry cranberries, chopped
- 1/2 cup dates, chopped
- 1/2 cup raisins
- 8 cups of water
- Pinch of salt

**Directions:**
Spray instant pot from inside with cooking spray. Add all ingredients into the instant pot and stir well. Seal the pot with a lid and select slow cook mode and cook on low for 8 hours.     Stir well and serve.
**Nutrition Info:**Calories: 196;Fat: 2 g;Carbohydrates: 42 g;Sugar: 18.4 g;Protein: 4.g;Cholesterol: 0 mg

## Pesto Scrambled Eggs

Servings: 2     Cooking Time: 10 Minutes
**Ingredients:**
- 5 eggs
- 2 tablespoons butter
- 2 tablespoons pesto
- 4 tablespoons milk
- salt to taste
- pepper to taste

**Directions:**
Beat the eggs into a bowl and add salt and pepper as per your taste.     Then, heat a pan and add the butter, then the eggs, stirring continuously.     While stirring continuously, add the pesto.     Switch off the heat and quickly add the creamed milk and mix it well with eggs. Serve hot.
**Nutrition Info:Per Serving:**Calories: 342, Total Fat: 29.8g, Saturated Fat: 12.3, Cholesterol: 44mg, Sodium: 345 mg, Total Carbohydrate: 3.4g, Dietary Fiber: 0.3 g, Total Sugars: 3.2 g, Protein: 16.8 g, Vitamin D: 47 mcg, Calcium: 148 mg, Iron: 2 mg, Potassium: 168 mg

## Breakfast Sweet Potatoes With Spiced Maple Yogurt And Walnuts

Servings: 4     Cooking Time: 45 Minutes
**Ingredients:**
- 4 red garnet sweet potatoes, about 6 inches long and 2 inches in diameter
- 2 cups low-fat (2%) plain Greek yogurt
- ¼ teaspoon pumpkin pie spice
- 1 tablespoon pure maple syrup
- ½ cup walnut pieces

**Directions:**

Preheat the oven to 425°F. Line a sheet pan with a silicone baking mat or parchment paper.     Prick the sweet potatoes in multiple places with a fork and place on the sheet pan. Bake until tender when pricked with a paring knife, 40 to 45 minutes.     While the potatoes are baking, mix the yogurt, pumpkin pie spice, and maple syrup until well combined in a medium bowl. When the potatoes are cool, slice the skin down the middle vertically to open up each potato. If you'd like to eat the sweet potatoes warm, place 1 potato in each of containers and ½ cup of spiced yogurt plus 2 tablespoons of walnut pieces in each of 4 other containers. If you want to eat the potatoes cold, place ½ cup of yogurt and 2 tablespoons of walnuts directly on top of each of the 4 potatoes in the 4 containers. STORAGE: Store covered containers in the refrigerator for up to days.
**Nutrition Info:Per Serving:** Total calories: 350; Total fat: 13g; Saturated fat: 3g; Sodium: 72mg; Carbohydrates: 4; Fiber: 5g; Protein: 16g

## Peach Blueberry Oatmeal

Servings: 4     Cooking Time: 4 Hours
**Ingredients:**
- 1 cup steel-cut oats
- 1/2 cup blueberries
- 3 1/2 cups unsweetened almond milk
- 7 oz can peach
- Pinch of salt

**Directions:**
Spray instant pot from inside with cooking spray. Add all ingredients into the instant pot and stir well. Seal the pot with a lid and select slow cook mode and cook on low for 4 hours.     Stir well and serve.
**Nutrition Info:**Calories: 1;Fat: 4.5 g;Carbohydrates: 25.4 g;Sugar: 8.6 g;Protein: 3.9 g;Cholesterol: 0 mg

## Veggie Mediterranean Quiche

Servings: 8     Cooking Time: 55 Minutes
**Ingredients:**
- 1/2 cup sundried tomatoes - dry or in olive oil*
- Boiling water
- 1 prepared pie crust
- 2 tbsp vegan butter
- 1 onion, diced
- 2 cloves garlic, minced
- 1 red pepper, diced
- 1/4 cup sliced Kalamata olives
- 1 tsp dried oregano
- 1 tsp dried parsley
- 1/3 cup crumbled feta cheese
- 4 large eggs
- 1 1/4 cup milk
- 2 cups fresh spinach or 1/2 cup frozen spinach, thawed and squeezed dry
- Salt, to taste
- Pepper, to taste
- 1 cup shredded cheddar cheese, divided

**Directions:**
If you're using dry sundried tomatoes - In a measure cup, add the sundried tomatoes and pour the boiling water over until just covered, allow to sit for 5 minutes or until the tomatoes are soft. The drain and chop tomatoes, set aside     Preheat oven to 375 degrees F Fit a 9-inch pie plate with the prepared pie crust, then flute edges, and set aside     In a skillet over medium high heat, melt the butter     Add in the onion and garlic, and cook until fragrant and tender, about 3 minutes     Add in the red pepper, cook for an additional 3 minutes, or until the peppers are just tender     Add in the spinach, olives, oregano, and parsley, cook until the spinach is wilted (if you're using fresh) or heated through (if you're using frozen), about 5 minutes     Remove the pan from heat, stir in the feta cheese and tomatoes, spoon the mixture into the prepared pie crust, spreading out evenly, set aside     In a medium-sized mixing bowl, whisk together the eggs, 1/2 cup of the cheddar cheese, milk, salt, and pepper Pour this egg and cheese mixture evenly over the spinach mixture in the pie crust     Sprinkle top with the remaining cheddar cheese     Bake for 50-55 minutes, or until the crust is golden brown and the egg is set Allow to cool completely before slicing     Wrap the slices in plastic wrap and then aluminum foil and place in the freezer.     To Serve: Remove the aluminum foil and plastic wrap, and microwave for 2 minutes, then allow to rest for 30 seconds, enjoy!     Recipe Notes: You'll find two types of sundried tomatoes available in your local grocery store—dry ones and ones packed in olive oil. Both will work for this recipe.     If you decide to use dry ones, follow the directions in the recipe to reconstitute them. If you're using oil-packed sundried tomatoes, skip the first step and just remove them from the oil, chop them, and continue with the recipe. Season carefully! Between the feta, cheddar, and olives, this recipe is naturally salty.

**Nutrition Info:Per Serving:**
Calories:239;Carbs: ;Total Fat: 15g;Protein: 7g

## Mediterranean Scrambled Eggs

Servings: 2     Cooking Time: 10 Minutes
**Ingredients:**
- 1 tbsp oil
- 1 yellow pepper, diced
- 2 spring onions, sliced
- 8 cherry tomatoes, quartered
- 2 tbsp sliced black olives
- 1 tbsp capers
- 4 eggs
- 1/4 tsp dried oregano
- Black pepper
- Topping:
- Fresh parsley, to serve

**Directions:**
In a frying pan over medium heat, add the oil     Once heated, add the diced pepper and chopped spring onions, cook for a few minutes, until slightly soft     Add in the quartered tomatoes, olives and capers, and cook for 1 more minute     Crack the eggs into the pan, immediately scramble with a spoon or spatula Sprinkle with oregano and plenty of black pepper, and stir until the eggs are fully cooked     Distribute the eggs evenly into the containers, store in the fridge for 2-3 days     To Serve: Reheat in the microwave for 30 seconds or in a toaster oven until warmed through **Nutrition Info:Per Serving:** Calories:249;Carbs: 13g;Total Fat: 17g;Protein: 14g

## Chia Pudding

Servings: 2     Cooking Time: 15 Minutes
**Ingredients:**
- ½ cup chia seeds
- 2 cups milk
- 1 tablespoon honey

**Directions:**
Combine and mix the chia seeds, milk, and honey in a bowl.     Put the mixture in the freezer and let it set. Take the pudding out of the freezer only when you see that the pudding has thickened.     Serve chilled.
**Nutrition Info:Per Serving:**Calories: 429, Total Fat: 22.4g, Saturated Fat: 4.9, Cholesterol: 20 mg, Sodium: 124 mg, Total Carbohydrate: 44.g, Dietary Fiber: 19.5 g, Total Sugars: 19.6 g, Protein: 17.4 g, Vitamin D: 1 mcg, Calcium: 648 mg, Iron: 4 mg, Potassium: 376 mg

## Breakfast Rice Bowls

Servings: 4     Cooking Time: 8 Minutes
**Ingredients:**
- 1 cup of brown rice
- 1 tsp ground cinnamon
- 1/4 cup almonds, sliced
- 2 tbsp sunflower seeds
- 1/4 cup pecans, chopped
- 1/4 cup walnuts, chopped
- 2 cup unsweetened almond milk
- Pinch of salt

**Directions:**
Spray instant pot from inside with cooking spray. Add all ingredients into the instant pot and stir well. Seal pot with lid and cook on high for 8 minutes. Once done, allow to release pressure naturally for 5 minutes then release remaining using quick release. Remove lid.     Stir well and serve.
**Nutrition Info:**Calories: 291;Fat: 12 g;Carbohydrates: 40.1 g;Sugar: 0.4 g;Protein: 7.g;Cholesterol: 0 mg

## Tahini Egg Salad With Pita

Servings: 4     Cooking Time: 12 Minutes
**Ingredients:**
- 4 large eggs
- ¼ cup freshly chopped dill
- 1 tablespoon plus 1 teaspoon unsalted tahini
- 2 teaspoons freshly squeezed lemon juice
- ⅛ teaspoon kosher salt
- 4 whole-wheat pitas, quartered

**Directions:**
Place the eggs in a saucepan and cover with water. Bring the water to a boil. As soon as the water starts to boil, place a lid on the pan and turn the heat off. Set a timer for     minutes.     When the timer goes off, drain the hot water and run cold water over the eggs to cool. When the eggs are cool, peel them, place the yolks in a medium bowl, and mash them with a fork. Then chop the egg whites.     Add the chopped egg whites, dill, tahini, lemon juice (to taste), and salt to the bowl, and mix to combine.     Place a heaping ⅓ cup of egg salad in each of 4 containers. Place the pita in 4 separate containers or resealable bags so that the bread does not get soggy.     STORAGE: Store covered containers in the refrigerator for up to 5 days.
**Nutrition Info:Per Serving:** Total calories: 242; Total fat: 10g; Saturated fat: 2g; Sodium: 300mg; Carbohydrates: 29g; Fiber: 5g; Protein: 13g

## Strawberry-mango Green Smoothie

Servings: 2     Cooking Time: 10 Minutes
**Ingredients:**
- 1½ cups low-fat (2%) milk
- 2 cups packed baby spinach leaves
- ½ cup sliced Persian or English cucumber, skin on
- ⅔ cup frozen strawberries
- ⅔ cup frozen mango chunks
- 1 medium very ripe banana, sliced (about ⅔ cup)
- ½ small avocado
- 1 teaspoon honey

**Directions:**
Place the milk, spinach, cucumber, strawberries, mango, banana, and avocado in a blender.     Blend until smooth and taste. If the smoothie isn't sweet enough, add the honey.     Distribute the smoothie between 2 to-go cups.     STORAGE: Store smoothie cups in the refrigerator for up to 3 days.
**Nutrition Info:Per Serving:** Total calories: 261; Total fat: 8g; Saturated fat: 2g; Sodium: 146mg; Carbohydrates: 40g; Fiber: ; Protein: 11g

## Breakfast Taco Scramble

Servings: 4     Cooking Time: 1 Hour 25 Minutes
**Ingredients:**
- 8 large eggs, beaten
- 1/4 tsp seasoning salt
- 1 lb 99% lean ground turkey
- 2 tbsp Greek seasoning
- 1/2 small onion, minced
- 2 tbsp bell pepper, minced
- 4 oz. can tomato sauce
- 1/4 cup water
- 1/4 cup chopped scallions or cilantro, for topping
- For the potatoes:
- 12 (1 lb) baby gold or red potatoes, quartered
- 4 tsp olive oil
- 3/4 tsp salt
- 1/2 tsp garlic powder
- fresh black pepper, to taste

**Directions:**
In a large bowl, beat the eggs, season with seasoning salt     Preheat the oven to 4 degrees F     Spray a 9x12 or large oval casserole dish with cooking oil     Add the potatoes 1 tbsp oil, 3/teaspoon salt, garlic powder and black pepper and toss to coat     Bake for 4minutes to 1 hour, tossing every 15 minutes     In the meantime, brown the turkey in a large skillet over medium heat, breaking it up while it cooks     Once no longer pink, add in the Greek seasoning     Add in the bell pepper, onion, tomato sauce and water, stir and cover, simmer on low for about 20 minutes     Spray a different skillet with nonstick spray over medium heat     Once heated, add in the eggs seasoned with 1/4 tsp of salt and scramble for 2–3 minutes, or cook until it sets     Distribute 3/4 cup turkey and 2/3 cup eggs and divide the potatoes in each storage container, store for 3-4 days     To Serve: Reheat in the microwave for 1-minute (until 90% heated through) top with shredded cheese if desired, and chopped scallions
**Nutrition Info:Per Serving:** (¼ of a the scramble): Calories:450;Total Fat: 19g;Total Carbs: 24.5g;Fiber: 4g;Protein: 46g

## Whole-wheat Pancakes With Spiced Peach And Orange Compote

Servings: 6     Cooking Time: 15 Minutes
**Ingredients:**
- 1½ cups whole-wheat flour
- 1 teaspoon baking powder
- ½ teaspoon baking soda
- ½ teaspoon ground cinnamon
- ⅛ teaspoon kosher salt
- 1 large egg
- 1 cup low-fat (2%) plain Greek yogurt
- 1 tablespoon honey
- 1 cup low-fat (2%) milk
- 2 teaspoons olive oil, divided
- 1 (10-ounce) package frozen sliced peaches
- ½ cup orange juice
- ¼ teaspoon pumpkin pie spice

**Directions:**
TO MAKE THE PANCAKES     Combine the flour, baking powder, baking soda, cinnamon, and salt in a large mixing bowl and whisk to make sure everything is distributed evenly. In a separate bowl, whisk together the egg, yogurt, honey, and milk. Pour the liquid ingredients into the dry ingredients and stir until just combined. Do not overmix.     Heat ½ teaspoon of oil in a 12-inch skillet or griddle over medium heat. Once the pan is hot, spoon ¼ cup of pancake batter into the pan. You should be able to fit pancakes in a 12-inch skillet. Cook each side for about 1 minute and 30 seconds, watching carefully and checking the underside for a golden but not burnt color before flipping. Repeat until all the batter has been used.     Place 2 pancakes in each of 6 containers.     TO MAKE THE COMPOTE Thaw the peaches in the microwave just to the point that they can be cut, about 30 seconds on high. Cut the peaches into 1-inch pieces.     Bring the peaches, orange juice, and pumpkin pie spice to a boil in a saucepan. As soon as bubbles appear, lower the heat to medium-low and cook for 12 minutes, until the juice has thickened and the peaches are very soft. Allow to cool, then mash with a potato masher.     Place 2 tablespoons of compote in each of 6 sauce containers.     STORAGE: Store covered pancake containers in the refrigerator for up to 5 days or in the freezer for up to 2 months. Peach compote will last up to 2 weeks in the refrigerator and up to 2 months in the freezer.
**Nutrition Info:Per Serving:** Total calories: 209; Total fat: 5g; Saturated fat: 2g; Sodium: 289mg; Carbohydrates: 34g; Fiber: 4g; Protein: 11g

## Peanut Butter Banana Greek Yogurt

Servings: 4     Cooking Time: 5 Minutes
**Ingredients:**
- 3 cups vanilla Greek yogurt
- 2 medium bananas sliced
- 1/4 cup creamy natural peanut butter
- 1/4 cup flaxseed meal
- 1 tsp nutmeg

**Directions:**
Divide yogurt between four jars with lids     Top with banana slices     In a bowl, melt the peanut butter in a microwave safe bowl for -40 seconds and drizzle one tbsp on each bowl on top of the bananas     Store in the fridge for up to 3 days     When ready to serve, sprinkle with flaxseed meal and ground nutmeg     Enjoy!
**Nutrition Info:Per Serving:** Calories:3;Carbs: 47g;Total Fat: 10g;Protein: 22g

## Green Shakshuka

Servings: 2     Cooking Time: 15 Minutes
**Ingredients:**
- 1 tbsp olive oil
- 1 onion, peeled and diced
- 1 clove garlic, peeled and finely minced
- 3 cups broccoli rabe, chopped
- 3 cups baby spinach leaves
- 2 tbsp whole milk or cream
- 1 tsp ground cumin
- 1/4 tsp black pepper
- 1/4 tsp salt (or to taste)
- 4 Eggs
- Garnish:
- 1 pinch sea salt
- 1 pinch red pepper flakes

**Directions:**
Pre-heat the oven to 350 degrees F     Add the broccoli rabe to a large pot of boiling water, cook for minutes, drain and set aside     In a large oven-proof skillet or cast-iron pan over medium heat, add in the tablespoon of olive oil along with the diced onions, cook for about 10 minutes or until the onions become translucent     Add the minced garlic and continue cooking for about another minute     Cut the par-cooked broccoli rabe into small pieces, stir into the onion and garlic mixture     Cook for a couple of minutes, then stir in the baby spinach leaves, continue to cook for a couple more minutes, stirring often, until the spinach begins to wilt     Stir in the ground cumin, salt, ground black pepper, and milk     Make four wells in the mixture, crack an egg into each well – be careful not to break the yolks. Also, note that it's easier to crack each egg into a small bowl and then transfer them to the pan     Place the pan with the eggs into the pre-heated oven, cook for 10 to 15 minutes until the eggs are set to preference     Sprinkle the cooked eggs with a dash of sea salt and a pinch of red pepper flakes     Allow to cool, distribute among the containers, store for 2-3 days     To Serve: Microwave for 1-minute or until heated through, serve with crusty whole-wheat bread or warmed slices of pita or naan
**Nutrition Info:Per Serving:** Calories:278;Carbs: 18g;Total Fat: 16g;Protein: 16g

## Clean Breakfast Cookies

Servings: 4     Cooking Time: 20 Minutes
**Ingredients:**
- 2 cups oats (rolled)
- 1 cup whole wheat flour
- ¼ cup flax seed
- 2½ teaspoons cinnamon (ground)
- 1 cup honey
- ½ teaspoon baking soda
- 2 egg whites
- ½ teaspoon vanilla extract
- 4 tablespoons almond butter
- pinch of salt

**Directions:**
Preheat oven to 325 degrees F.     Whisk oats, flour, flaxseed, cinnamon, salt, and baking soda together in a bowl.     Then, stir honey, egg whites, almond butter, and vanilla extract into the oats mixture until dough is blended.     Now, prepare the baking sheets and scoop the dough in them.     Finally, bake for about 20 minutes.     Serve warm or room temperature.
**Nutrition Info:Per Serving:**Calories: 686, Total Fat: 14.3g, Saturated Fat: 1.3, Cholesterol: 0 mg, Sodium: 185 mg, Total Carbohydrate: 131.4 g, Dietary Fiber: 11.9 g, Total Sugars: .2 g, Protein: 15.6 g, Vitamin D: 0 mcg, Calcium: 100 mg, Iron: 9 mg, Potassium: 456 mg

## Omelet With Cheese And Broccoli

Servings: 4     Cooking Time: 30 Minutes
**Ingredients:**
- 6 eggs
- 2 ½ cups of broccoli florets
- ¼ cup of milk
- 1 tablespoon olive oil
- ⅓ cup Romano cheese, grated
- ¼ teaspoon pepper
- ⅕ teaspoon salt

- ⅓ cup Greek olives, sliced
- Parsley and more Romano cheese for garnish

**Directions:**
Turn your oven to broil.     Set a steamer basket in a large pan and add 1 inch of water.     Add the broccoli to the steamer basket and turn the range to medium. Once the water starts to boil, reduce the temperature to low. Steam the broccoli for 4 to 5 minutes. You will know the vegetable is done when it is soft and tender.     In a large bowl, whisk the eggs.     Pour in the milk, pepper, and salt.     Once the broccoli is done, toss into the large bowl and add the olives and grated cheese.     Grease an oven-proof 10-inch skillet and turn the heat on the burner to medium.     Add in the egg mixture, then cook for 4 to 5 minutes.     Set the skillet into the oven but make sure it's at least 4 inches from the heating source. Broil the eggs for 3 minutes. If the eggs are not completely set, continue cooking for another minute or two.     Remove the eggs from the oven and set on the stove so they can cool for a few minutes.     Garnish the omelet with cheese and parsley. Then, cut into wedges and enjoy!
**Nutrition Info:**calories: 229, fats: 17 grams, carbohydrates: 5 grams, protein: 15 grams.

## Greek Yogurt Breakfast Bowl

Servings: 1     Cooking Time: 5 Minutes
**Ingredients:**
- 1 cup Greek Yogurt plain
- 13 cup Pomegranate Seeds (or fresh fruit of your choice)
- 1 tsp honey

**Directions:**
In a jar with a lid, add the Greek yogurt in a bowl top with fruit and drizzle honey over the top     Close the lid and refrigerate for 3 days
**Nutrition Info:Per Serving:** Calories116;Carbs 24g;Total Fat 1.2g;Protein 4g

## Cucumber Celery Lime Smoothie

Servings: 2     Cooking Time: 15 Minutes
**Ingredients:**
- 8 stalks of celery, chopped
- 1 lemon, juiced
- 2 cucumbers, peeled and chopped
- ½ cup ice
- sweetener of your choice
- 1 cup water

**Directions:**
Place all the Ingredients: in a blender.     Blend well until smooth and frothy or desired texture.     Serve chilled.     Enjoy.
**Nutrition Info:Per Serving:**Calories: 64, Total Fat: 0., Saturated Fat: 0.2, Cholesterol: 0 mg, Sodium: 63 mg, Total Carbohydrate: 15.7 g, Dietary Fiber: 3.4 g, Total Sugars: 6.7 g, Protein: 2.8 g, Vitamin D: 0 mcg, Calcium: 85 mg, Iron: 1 mg, Potassium: 660 mg

## Chocolate-almond Banana Bread

Servings: 4    Cooking Time: 25 Minutes
**Ingredients:**
- Cooking spray or oil to grease the pan
- 1 cup almond meal
- 2 large eggs
- 2 very ripe bananas, mashed
- 1 tablespoon plus 2 teaspoons maple syrup
- ½ teaspoon vanilla extract
- ½ teaspoon baking powder
- ¼ teaspoon ground cardamom
- ⅓ cup dark chocolate chips, very roughly chopped

**Directions:**
Preheat the oven to 350°F and spray an 8-inch cake pan or baking dish with cooking spray or rub with oil. Combine all the ingredients in a large mixing bowl. Then pour the mixture into the prepared pan.    Place the pan in the oven and bake for 25 minutes. The edges should be browned, and a paring knife should come out clean when the banana bread is pierced.    When cool, slice into wedges and place 1 wedge in each of 4 containers.    STORAGE: Store covered containers at room temperature for up to 2 days, refrigerate for up to 7 days, or freeze for up to 3 months.
**Nutrition Info:Per Serving:** Total calories: 3; Total fat: 23g; Saturated fat: 6g; Sodium: 105mg; Carbohydrates: 37g; Fiber: 6g; Protein: 10g

## Mediterranean Breakfast Egg White Sandwich

Servings: 1    Cooking Time: 30 Minutes
**Ingredients:**
- 1 tsp vegan butter
- ¼ cup egg whites
- 1 tsp chopped fresh herbs such as parsley, basil, rosemary
- 1 whole grain seeded ciabatta roll
- 1 tbsp pesto
- 1-2 slices muenster cheese (or other cheese such as provolone, Monterey Jack, etc.)
- About ½ cup roasted tomatoes
- Salt, to taste
- Pepper, to taste
- Roasted Tomatoes:
- 10 oz grape tomatoes
- 1 tbsp extra virgin olive oil
- Kosher salt, to taste
- Coarse black pepper, to taste

**Directions:**
In a small nonstick skillet over medium heat, melt the vegan butter    Pour in egg whites, season with salt and pepper, sprinkle with fresh herbs, cook for 3-4 minutes or until egg is done, flip once    In the meantime, toast the ciabatta bread in toaster    Once done, spread both halves with pesto    Place the egg on the bottom half of sandwich roll, folding if necessary, top with cheese, add the roasted tomatoes and top half of roll sandwich    To make the roasted tomatoes: Preheat oven to 400 degrees F. Slice tomatoes in half lengthwise. Then place them onto a baking sheet and drizzle with the olive oil, toss to coat. Season with salt and pepper and roast in oven for about 20 minutes, until the skin appears wrinkled
**Nutrition Info:Per Serving:** Calories:458;Total Carbohydrates: 51g;Total Fat: 0g;Protein: 21g

## Strawberry-apricot Smoothie

Servings: 2    Cooking Time: 15 Minutes
**Ingredients:**
- 1 cup strawberries, frozen
- ¾ cup almond milk, unsweetened
- 2 apricots, pitted and sliced

**Directions:**
Put all the Ingredients: into the blender.    Blend them for a minute or until you reach desired foamy texture. Serve the smoothie.    Enjoy.
**Nutrition Info:Per Serving:**Calories: 247, Total Fat: 21.9 g, Saturated Fat: 19 g, Cholesterol: 0 mg, Sodium: 1mg, Total Carbohydrate: 14.4 g, Dietary Fiber: 4.1 g, Total Sugars: 9.7 g, Protein: 3 g, Vitamin D: 0 mcg, Calcium: 30 mg, Iron: 2 mg, Potassium: 438 mg

## Apple Quinoa Breakfast Bars

Servings: 12    Cooking Time: 40 Minutes
**Ingredients:**
- 2 eggs
- 1 apple peeled and chopped into ½ inch chunks
- 1 cup unsweetened apple sauce
- 1 ½ cups cooked & cooled quinoa
- 1 ½ cups rolled oats
- 1/4 cup peanut butter
- 1 tsp vanilla
- 1/2 tsp cinnamon
- 1/4 cup coconut oil
- ½ tsp baking powder

**Directions:**
Heat oven to 350 degrees F    Spray an 8x8 inch baking dish with oil, set aside    In a large bowl, stir together the apple sauce, cinnamon, coconut oil, peanut butter, vanilla and eggs    Add in the cooked quinoa, rolled oats and baking powder, mix until completely incorporated    Fold in the apple chunks    Spread the mixture into the prepared baking dish, spreading it to each corner    Bake for 40 minutes, or until a toothpick comes out clean    Allow to cool before slicing    Wrap the bars individually in plastic wrap. Store in an airtight container or baggie in the freezer for up to a month.
To serve: Warm up in the oven at 350 F for 5 minutes or microwave for up to 30 seconds
**Nutrition Info:Per Serving:** (1 bar):
Calories:230;Total Fat: 10g;Total Carbs: 31g;Protein: 7g

## Pepper, Kale, And Chickpea Shakshuka

Servings: 5    Cooking Time: 35 Minutes
**Ingredients:**
- 1 tablespoon olive oil
- 1 small red onion, thinly sliced
- 1 red bell pepper, thinly sliced
- 1 green bell pepper, thinly sliced
- 1 bunch kale, stemmed and roughly chopped
- ½ cup packed cilantro leaves, chopped
- ½ teaspoon kosher salt
- 1 teaspoon smoked paprika
- 1 (14.5-ounce) can diced tomatoes
- 1 (14-ounce) can low-sodium chickpeas, drained and rinsed
- ⅔ cup water
- 5 eggs
- 2½ whole-wheat pitas (optional)

**Directions:**
Preheat the oven to 375°F.    Heat the oil in an oven-safe 1inch skillet over medium-high heat. Once the oil is shimmering, add the onions and red and green bell peppers. Sauté for 5 minutes, then cover, leaving the lid slightly ajar. Cook for 5 more minutes, then add the kale and cover, leaving the lid slightly ajar. Cook for 10 more minutes, stirring occasionally.    Add the cilantro, salt, paprika, tomatoes, chickpeas, and water, and stir to combine.    Make 5 wells in the mixture. Break an egg into a small bowl and pour it into a well. Repeat with the remaining eggs.    Place the pan in the oven and bake until the egg whites are opaque and the eggs still jiggle a little when the pan is shaken, about 12 to 1minutes, but start checking at 8 minutes.    When the shakshuka is cool, scoop about 1¼ cups of veggies into each of 5 containers, along with 1 egg each. If using, place ½ pita in each of 5 resealable bags.    STORAGE: Store covered containers in the refrigerator for up to 5 days.
**Nutrition Info:Per Serving:** Total calories: 244; Total fat: 9g; Saturated fat: 2g; Sodium: 529mg; Carbohydrates: 29g; Fiber: ; Protein: 14g

## Rosemary Broccoli Cauliflower Mash

Servings: 3    Cooking Time: 12 Minutes
**Ingredients:**
- 2 cups broccoli, chopped
- 1 lb cauliflower, cut into florets
- 1 tsp dried rosemary
- 1/4 cup olive oil
- 1 tsp garlic, minced
- Salt

**Directions:**
Add broccoli and cauliflower into the instant pot. Pour enough water into the pot to cover broccoli and cauliflower.    Seal pot with lid and cook on high for 1minutes.    Once done, allow to release pressure naturally. Remove lid.    Drain broccoli and cauliflower well and clean the instant pot.    Add oil into the pot and set the pot on sauté mode.    Add broccoli, cauliflower, rosemary, garlic, and salt and cook for 10

minutes.    Mash the broccoli and cauliflower mixture using a potato masher until smooth.    Serve and enjoy.
**Nutrition Info:**Calories: 205;Fat: 17.2 g;Carbohydrates: 12.6 g;Sugar: 4.7 g;Protein: 4.8 g;Cholesterol: 0 mg

## Pumpkin, Apple, And Greek Yogurt Muffins

Servings: 12    Cooking Time: 20 Minutes
**Ingredients:**
- Cooking spray to grease baking liners
- 2 cups whole-wheat flour
- 1 teaspoon aluminum-free baking powder (see tip)
- 1 teaspoon baking soda
- ⅛ teaspoon kosher salt
- 2 teaspoons ground cinnamon
- ½ teaspoon ground ginger
- ½ teaspoon ground allspice
- ⅔ cup pure maple syrup
- 1 cup low-fat (2%) plain Greek yogurt
- 1 cup 100% canned pumpkin
- 1 large egg
- ¼ cup extra-virgin olive oil
- 1½ cups chopped green apple (leave peel on)
- ½ cup walnut pieces

**Directions:**
Preheat the oven to 400°F and line a muffin tin with baking liners. Spray the liners lightly with cooking spray.    In a large bowl, whisk together the flour, baking powder, baking soda, salt, cinnamon, ginger, and allspice.    In a medium bowl, combine the maple syrup, yogurt, pumpkin, egg, olive oil, chopped apple, and walnuts.    Pour the wet ingredients into the dry ingredients and combine just until blended. Do not overmix.    Scoop about ¼ cup of batter into each muffin liner and bake for 20 minutes, or until the tops look browned and a paring knife comes out clean when inserted. Remove the muffins from the tin to cool. STORAGE: Store covered containers at room temperature for up to 4 days. To freeze the muffins for up to 3 months, wrap them in foil and place in an airtight resealable bag.
**Nutrition Info:Per Serving:** Total calories: 221; Total fat: 9g; Saturated fat: 1g; Sodium: 18g; Carbohydrates: 32g; Fiber: 4g; Protein: 6g

## Cocoa And Raspberry Overnight Oats

Servings: 5      Cooking Time: 10 Minutes
**Ingredients:**
- 1⅔ cups rolled oats
- 3⅓ cups unsweetened vanilla almond milk
- 2 teaspoons vanilla extract
- 1 tablespoon plus 2 teaspoons pure maple syrup
- 3 tablespoons chia seeds
- 3 tablespoons unsweetened cocoa powder
- 1⅔ cups frozen raspberries
- 5 teaspoons cocoa nibs (optional)

**Directions:**
In a large bowl, mix the oats, almond milk, vanilla, maple syrup, chia seeds, and cocoa powder until well combined.      Spoon ¾ cup of the oat mixture into each of 5 containers.      Top each serving with ⅓ cup of raspberries and 1 teaspoon of cocoa nibs, if using. STORAGE: Store covered containers in the refrigerator for up to 5 days.
**Nutrition Info:Per Serving:** Total calories: 21 Total fat: 6g; Saturated fat: <1g; Sodium: 121mg; Carbohydrates: 34g; Fiber: 10g; Protein: 7g

## Bacon Brie Omelet With Radish Salad

Servings: 6      Cooking Time: 10 Minutes
**Ingredients:**
- 200 g smoked lardons
- 3 teaspoons olive oil, divided
- 7 ounces smoked bacon
- 6 lightly beaten eggs
- small bunch chives, snipped up
- 3½ ounces sliced brie
- 1 teaspoon red wine vinegar
- 1 teaspoon Dijon mustard
- 1 cucumber, deseeded, halved, and sliced up diagonally
- 7 ounces radish, quartered

**Directions:**
Heat up the grill.      Add 1 teaspoon of oil to a small pan and heat on the grill.      Add lardons and fry them until nice and crisp.      Drain the lardon on kitchen paper. Heat the remaining 2 teaspoons of oil in a non-sticking pan on the grill.      Add lardons, eggs, chives, and ground pepper, and cook over low heat until semi-set. Carefully lay the Brie on top, and grill until it has set and is golden in color.      Remove from pan and cut into wedges.      Make the salad by mixing olive oil, mustard, vinegar, and seasoning in a bowl.      Add cucumber and radish and mix well.      Serve the salad alongside the omelet wedges in containers.      Enjoy!
**Nutrition Info:Per Serving:**Calories: 620, Total Fat: 49.3g, Saturated Fat: 22.1, Cholesterol: 295 mg, Sodium: 1632 mg, Total Carbohydrate: 4.3g, Dietary Fiber: 0.9 g, Total Sugars: 2.5 g, Protein: 39.2 g, Vitamin D: 41 mcg, Calcium: 185 mg, Iron: 2 mg, Potassium: 527 mg

## Cranberry Oatmeal

Servings: 2      Cooking Time: 6 Minutes
**Ingredients:**
- 1/2 cup steel-cut oats
- 1 cup unsweetened almond milk
- 1 1/2 tbsp maple syrup
- 1/4 tsp cinnamon
- 1/4 tsp vanilla
- 1/4 cup dried cranberries
- 1 cup of water
- 1 tsp lemon zest, grated
- 1/4 cup orange juice

**Directions:**
Add all ingredients into the heat-safe dish and stir well. Pour 1 cup of water into the instant pot then place the trivet in the pot.      Place dish on top of the trivet. Seal pot with lid and cook on high for 6 minutes. Once done, allow to release pressure naturally for 10 minutes then release remaining using quick release. Remove lid.      Serve and enjoy.
**Nutrition Info:**Calories: 161;Fat: 3.2 g;Carbohydrates: 29.9 g;Sugar: 12.4 g;Protein: 3.4 g;Cholesterol: 0 mg

## Ricotta Fig Toast

Servings: 1      Cooking Time: 15 Minutes
**Ingredients:**
- 2 slices whole-wheat toast
- 1 teaspoon honey
- ¼ cup ricotta (partly skimmed)
- 1 dash cinnamon
- 2 figs (sliced)
- 1 teaspoon sesame seeds

**Directions:**
Start by mixing ricotta with honey and dash of cinnamon.      Then, spread this mixture on the toast. Now, top with fig and sesame seeds.      Serve.
**Nutrition Info:Per Serving:**Calories: 372, Total Fat: 8.8g, Saturated Fat: 3.8, Cholesterol: 19 mg, Sodium: 373 mg, Total Carbohydrate: .7 g, Dietary Fiber: 8.8 g, Total Sugars: 27.1 g, Protein: 17 g, Vitamin D: 0 mcg, Calcium: 328 mg, Iron: 3 mg, Potassium: 518 mg

## Mushroom Goat Cheese Frittata

Servings: 4    Cooking Time: 35 Minutes
**Ingredients:**
- 1 tbsp olive oil
- 1 small onion, diced
- 10 oz crimini or your favorite mushrooms, sliced
- 1 garlic clove, minced
- 10 eggs
- 2/3 cup half and half
- 1/4 cup fresh chives, minced
- 2 tsp fresh thyme, minced
- 1/2 tsp kosher salt
- 1/2 tsp black pepper
- 4 oz goat cheese

**Directions:**
Preheat the oven to 375 degrees F    In an over safe skillet or cast-iron pan over medium heat, olive oil    Add in the onion and sauté for 5 mins until golden    Add in the sliced mushrooms and garlic, continue to sauté until mushrooms are golden brown, about 10-12 minutes    In a large bowl, whisk together the eggs, half and half, chives, thyme, salt and pepper    Place the goat cheese over the mushroom mixture and pour the egg mixture over the top    Stir the mixture in the pan and cook over medium heat until the edges are set but the center is still loose, about 8-10 minutes    Put the pan in the oven and finish cooking for an additional 10 minutes or until set    Allow to cool completely before slicing    Wrap the slices in plastic wrap and then aluminum foil and place in the freezer.    To Serve: Remove the aluminum foil and plastic wrap, and microwave for 2 minutes, then allow to rest for 30 seconds, enjoy!
**Nutrition Info:Per Serving:** Calories:243;Total Carbohydrates: 5g;Total Fat: 17g;Protein: 15g

## Honey, Dried Apricot, And Pistachio Yogurt Parfait

Servings: 3    Cooking Time: 10 Minutes
**Ingredients:**
- 1 (16-ounce) container low-fat (2%) plain Greek yogurt
- 1 tablespoon honey
- ½ teaspoon rose water (optional)
- ½ cup unsalted shelled pistachios, roughly chopped
- 12 dried apricot halves, quartered

**Directions:**
Mix the yogurt, honey, and rose water (if using) in a medium bowl.    Place ⅔ cup of yogurt in each of 3 containers. Top each mound of yogurt with equal portions of the pistachios and apricots.    STORAGE: Store covered containers in the refrigerator for up to 7 days.
**Nutrition Info:Per Serving:** Total calories: 275; Total fat: 12g; Saturated fat: 3g; Sodium: 72mg; Carbohydrates: 26g; Fiber: 3g; Protein: 19g

## Mediterranean Stuffed Sweet Potatoes With Chickpeas And Avocado Tahini

Servings: 4    Cooking Time: 40 Minutes
**Ingredients:**
- 8 medium sized sweet potatoes, rinsed well
- Marinated Chickpeas:
- 1 (15 oz) can chickpeas, drained and rinsed
- 1/2 red pepper, diced
- 3 tbsp extra virgin olive oil
- 1 tbsp fresh lemon juice
- 1 tbsp lemon zest
- 1 clove;about 1/2 teaspoon garlic, crushed
- 1 tbsp freshly chopped parsley
- 1 tbsp fresh oregano
- 1/4 tsp sea salt
- Avocado Tahini Sauce:
- 1 medium sized ripe avocado
- 1/4 cup tahini
- 1/4 cup water
- 1 clove garlic, crushed
- 1 tbsp fresh parsley
- 1 tbsp fresh lemon juice
- Toppings:
- 1/4 cup pepitas, hulled pumpkin seeds
- Crumbled vegan feta or regular feta

**Directions:**
Preheat the oven to 400 degrees F    With a fork to pierce a few holes in the sweet potatoes    Place them on a baking sheet and bake for 45 minutes to an hour, or until the potatoes are tender to the touch. (Note that larger sweet potato will take longer to bake)    In the meantime, prepare the chickpeas by placing them in a medium sized bowl, combine the chickpeas with the extra virgin olive oil, lemon juice, lemon zest, red bell peppers, garlic, parsley, oregano, and sea salt. Toss the chickpeas until they're all coated in the marinade, set aside    Avocado Tahini Sauce:    Create the sauce by adding the ripe avocado, tahini, water, garlic, parsley, and lemon juice into a blender and process until smooth - If you would like a thinned consistency add another 1-2 tbsp of water    Once smooth transfer the sauce to a small bowl, set aside    To Assembly: Once the sweet potatoes are tender, remove them from the oven and set aside until they are cool enough to handle    Then cut a slit down the middle of each potato and carefully spoon the chickpeas inside    Place the potato and chickpeas bake into container, store for 2-3 days    To Serve: Heat through in the oven at 374 degrees F for 5-8 minutes or until heated through. Top with the avocado tahini and sprinkle the pepitas and crumbled feta. Enjoy    Recipe Notes: There will be leftover chickpeas & avocado tahini - save the extras to make more sweet potatoes or create a big salad for a different lunch
**Nutrition Info:Per Serving:** Calories:308;Carbs: 38g;Total Fat: 15g;Protein: 7g

## Walnut Banana Oatmeal

Servings: 2     Cooking Time: 3 Minutes
**Ingredients:**
- 1/2 cup steel-cut oats
- 1 cup of water
- 1 cup unsweetened almond milk
- 1 tsp honey
- 2 tbsp walnuts, chopped
- 1/2 banana, chopped

**Directions:**
Spray instant pot from inside with cooking spray. Add oats, water, and almond milk into the instant pot and stir well.     Seal pot with lid and cook on high for minutes.     Once done, release pressure using quick release. Remove lid.     Stir in honey, walnut, and banana and serve.
**Nutrition Info:**Calories: 183;Fat: 7.8 g;Carbohydrates: 25.2 g;Sugar: 8 g;Protein: 5.4 g;Cholesterol: 0 mg

## Super-seed Granola

Servings: 8     Cooking Time: 40 Minutes
**Ingredients:**
- 1½ cups rolled oats
- ⅓ cup raw quinoa
- ⅓ cup green pumpkin seeds (pepitas)
- ⅓ cup raw, unsalted sunflower seeds
- 2 tablespoons chia seeds
- 1 teaspoon ground cinnamon
- ⅓ cup pure maple syrup
- ⅓ cup unsweetened, unsalted sunflower seed butter

**Directions:**
Preheat the oven to 325°F. Line a baking sheet with a silicone mat or parchment paper.     In a large mixing bowl, combine the oats, quinoa, pumpkin seeds, sunflower seeds, chia seeds, and cinnamon.     Place the maple syrup and sunflower seed butter in a small microwaveable bowl and microwave for 20 to     seconds to melt the seed butter. Pour it over the oat mixture and stir to coat.     Spread the granola evenly across the lined pan, bake for 15 minutes, stir, bake for 15 more minutes, stir, and bake for 10 more minutes. Remove the granola from the oven; it will get crunchier as it cools.     Place ½ cup of granola in each of 8 containers and store at room temperature.     STORAGE: Store covered containers at room temperature for 2 weeks.
**Nutrition Info:Per Serving:** Total calories: 258; Total fat: 13g; Saturated fat: 1g; Sodium: 19mg; Carbohydrates: 30g; Fiber: 4g; Protein: 9g

## Ham And Egg Muffins

Servings: 6     Cooking Time: 25 Minutes
**Ingredients:**
- ¼ cup crumbled feta cheese
- ⅛ teaspoon salt
- 1 ½ tablespoons of pesto sauce
- 9 slices of deli ham
- ⅓ cup chopped spinach
- 5 eggs
- ⅛ teaspoon of pepper
- ½ cup roasted red pepper plus a little for garnish
- Basil for garnish

**Directions:**
Turn the temperature on your oven to 400 degrees Fahrenheit.     Grease the cups of the muffin tin. Line each muffin tin cup with a slice of ham. The trick is to ensure there are no holes within the ham so none of the egg mixture seeps out.     Add some roasted peppers into the muffin cup.     Add 1 tablespoon of chopped spinach on top of the roasted pepper.     Sprinkle ½ tablespoon of feta cheese on top of the spinach. Combine the eggs in a bowl with the salt and pepper. Whisk well.     Divide the egg mixture evenly between the 6 muffin tins.     Set in your oven and turn the timer for 15 minutes. If the eggs are not set and puffy after 15 minutes, keep them in the oven for another minute or two.     Carefully remove the muffins from the muffin tin cups and let them cool completely.     Garnish and enjoy your breakfast muffins, or you can store them in the fridge for up to three days. To warm them up, microwave them for 30 seconds.
**Nutrition Info:**calories: 109, fats: 6 grams, carbohydrates: 2 grams, protein: 9 grams.

## Almond Pancakes

Servings: 6     Cooking Time: 30 Minutes
**Ingredients:**
- ½ cup melted coconut oil, plus a little on the side for grease
- 2 cups unsweetened, room temperature almond milk
- 2 teaspoons raw honey
- 1 ½ cups whole wheat flour
- 2 eggs, room temperature
- ¼ teaspoon ground cinnamon
- ½ cup almond flour
- ¼ teaspoon sea salt
- ½ teaspoon baking soda
- 1 ½ teaspoons baking powder

**Directions:**
In a large bowl, whisk your eggs.     Add in the coconut oil, honey, and almond milk. Whisk thoroughly.     In a separate bowl, sift together your baking soda, baking powder, sea salt, almond flour, cinnamon, and whole wheat flour. Ensure the ingredients are well incorporated.     Combine the two mixtures by slowly adding your powdered ingredients into your wet ingredients. Stir as you combine as it will be easier to fully mix the ingredients.     Grease a large skillet with oil and set it on medium-high heat.     Using ½ cup measurements, pour the batter into the skillet. Make sure the pancakes are not touching each other when they cook.     Let your pancakes cook for about 3 to 5 minutes on each side. Once bubbles start to break the surface and the edges become firm, flip the pancake over to cook the other side.     Once they are cooked thoroughly, place them on a plate and continue the process until all your batter is used up. You might need to grease your skillet again between batches.     To give your pancakes more of a Mediterranean flavor, add some fresh fruit on top.
**Nutrition Info:**calories: 286, fats: 17 grams, carbohydrates: 26 grams, protein: 7 grams.

## Mediterranean Egg Muffins With Ham

Servings: 6     Cooking Time: 15 Minutes
**Ingredients:**
- 9 Slices of thin cut deli ham
- 1/2 cup canned roasted red pepper, sliced + additional for garnish
- 1/3 cup fresh spinach, minced
- 1/4 cup feta cheese, crumbled
- 5 large eggs
- Pinch of salt
- Pinch of pepper
- 1 1/2 tbsp Pesto sauce
- Fresh basil for garnish

**Directions:**
Preheat oven to 400 degrees F      Spray a muffin tin with cooking spray, generously      Line each of the muffin tin with 1 ½ pieces of ham - making sure there aren't any holes for the egg mixture come out of      Place some of the roasted red pepper in the bottom of each muffin tin      Place 1 tbsp of minced spinach on top of each red pepper      Top the pepper and spinach off with a large 1/2 tbsp of crumbled feta cheese      In a medium bowl, whisk together the eggs salt and pepper, divide the egg mixture evenly among the 6 muffin tins      Bake for 15 to 17 minutes until the eggs are puffy and set      Remove each cup from the muffin tin      Allow to cool completely      Distribute the muffins among the containers, store in the fridge for 2 - 3days or in the freezer for 3 months      To Serve: Heat in the microwave for 30 seconds or until heated through. Garnish with 1/4 tsp pesto sauce, additional roasted red pepper slices and fresh basil.
**Nutrition Info:Per Serving:** Calories:109;Carbs: 2g;Total Fat: 6g;Protein: 9g

## Overnight Berry Chia Oats

Servings: 1     Cooking Time: 5 Minutes
**Ingredients:**
- 1/2 cup Quaker Oats rolled oats
- 1/4 cup chia seeds
- 1 cup milk or water
- pinch of salt and cinnamon
- maple syrup, or a different sweetener, to taste
- 1 cup frozen berries of choice or smoothie leftovers
- Toppings:
- Yogurt
- Berries

**Directions:**
In a jar with a lid, add the oats, seeds, milk, salt, and cinnamon, refrigerate overnight      On serving day, puree the berries in a blender      Stir the oats, add in the berry puree and top with yogurt and more berries, nuts, honey, or garnish of your choice      Enjoy!      Recipe Notes: Make 3 jars at a time in individual jars for easy grab and go breakfasts for the next few days.
**Nutrition Info:Per Serving:** Calories:405;Carbs: g;Total Fat: 11g;Protein: 17g

## Quinoa

Servings: 4     Cooking Time: 8 Hours

**Ingredients:**
- 1 cup quinoa (uncooked)
- 2 cups water
- 1 tablespoon raw honey
- 1 cup coconut milk
- Topping(s) of your preference (nuts, cinnamon, etc.)
- sea salt or plain salt

**Directions:**
Start by rinsing the quinoa under running water. Then, add all the Ingredients: in a slow cooker and cover with a lid. Cook the mixture for 8 hours on low. Serve hot with toppings of your choice.
**Nutrition Info:Per Serving:**Calories: 310, Total Fat: 16.8g, Saturated Fat: 13, Cholesterol: 0 mg, Sodium: 11 mg, Total Carbohydrate: 39 g, Dietary Fiber: 4.3 g, Total Sugars: 6.3 g, Protein: 7.4 g, Vitamin D: 0 mcg, Calcium: 30 mg, Iron: 3 mg, Potassium: 400 mg

## Egg, Feta, Spinach, And Artichoke Freezer Breakfast Burritos

Servings: 6     Cooking Time: 5 Minutes
**Ingredients:**
- 8 large eggs
- ½ teaspoon dried Italian herbs
- ½ teaspoon garlic powder
- ½ teaspoon onion powder
- 3 teaspoons olive oil, divided
- 10 ounces baby spinach leaves
- ½ cup crumbled feta cheese
- 1 (14-ounce) can quartered artichoke hearts, super-tough leaves removed
- 6 (8- or 9-inch) whole-wheat tortillas
- 6 tablespoons prepared hummus or homemade hummus

**Directions:**
Beat the eggs and whisk in the Italian herbs, garlic powder, and onion powder.      Heat 1 teaspoon of oil in a 1inch skillet. When the oil is shimmering, add the spinach and sauté for 2 to 3 minutes, until the spinach is wilted. Remove the spinach from the pan.      In the same pan, heat the remaining 2 teaspoons of oil. When the oil is hot, add the eggs. When the eggs start to set, stir to scramble. Cook for about minutes, then add the cooked spinach, feta, and artichoke hearts. Cool the mixture and pour off any liquid if it accumulates. Place 1 tortilla on a cutting board. Spread 1 tablespoon of hummus down the middle of the tortilla. Place ¾ cup of the egg filling on top of the hummus. Fold the bottom end and sides over the filling and tightly roll up. Repeat for the remaining 5 tortillas.      Wrap each burrito in foil and place in a resealable plastic bag.      STORAGE: Store sealed bags in the freezer for up to 3 months. To reheat burritos, unwrap and remove the foil. Cover the burrito with a damp paper towel, place on a microwaveable plate, and microwave on high until the center of the burrito is hot, about 2 minutes.
**Nutrition Info:Per Serving:** Total calories: 359; Total fat: 18g; Saturated fat: 6g; Sodium: 800mg; Carbohydrates: 32g; Fiber: 6g; Protein: 18g

## Breakfast Jalapeno Egg Cups

Servings: 6      Cooking Time: 8 Minutes
**Ingredients:**
- 12 eggs, lightly beaten
- 1/4 tsp garlic powder
- 1/2 tsp lemon pepper seasoning
- 3 jalapeno peppers, chopped
- 1 cup cheddar cheese, shredded
- Pepper
- Salt

**Directions:**
Pour 1/2 cups of water into the instant pot then place steamer rack in the pot.      In a bowl, whisk eggs with lemon pepper seasoning, garlic powder, pepper, and salt.      Stir in jalapenos and cheese.      Pour mixture between six jars and seal jar with a lid.      Place jars on top of the rack in the instant pot.      Seal pot with a lid and select manual and set timer for 8 minutes.      Once done, allow to release pressure naturally for 10 minutes then release remaining using quick release. Remove lid. Serve and enjoy.
**Nutrition Info:**Calories: 212;Fat: 15.2 g;Carbohydrates: 3.2 g;Sugar: 2.1 g;Protein: 16.1 g;Cholesterol: 347 mg

## Low Carb Waffles

Servings: 2      Cooking Time: 10 Minutes
**Ingredients:**
- 4 egg whites
- 2 whole eggs
- ½ teaspoon baking powder
- 4 tablespoons milk
- 4 tablespoons coconut flour
- sugar or sweetener to taste

**Directions:**
Whip the egg whites to a stiff peak.      When the stiff peaks are attained, add the coconut flour, milk, baking powder, and the whole egg; mix.      Start heating your waffle iron to the required temperature. Grease it and pour in the batter. Cook until brown.      Serve warm and top with your choice of fruit or other toppings.
**Nutrition Info:Per Serving:**Calories: 234, Total Fat: 9.1g, Saturated Fat: 7, Cholesterol: 166 mg, Sodium: 204 mg, Total Carbohydrate: 18.9 g, Dietary Fiber: 10 g, Total Sugars: 4.2 g, Protein: 17.7 g, Vitamin D: 16 mcg, Calcium: 118 mg, Iron: 1 mg, Potassium: 310 mg

## Potato Breakfast Hash

Servings: 2      Cooking Time: 10 Minutes
**Ingredients:**
- 1 sweet potato, diced
- 1 cup bell pepper, chopped
- 1 tsp cumin
- 1 tbsp olive oil
- 1 potato, diced

- 1/2 tsp pepper
- 1 tsp paprika
- 1/2 tsp garlic, minced
- 1/4 cup vegetable stock
- 1/2 tsp salt

**Directions:**
Add all ingredients into the instant pot and stir well. Seal pot with lid and cook on high for 10 minutes. Once done, release pressure using quick release. Remove lid.      Stir and serve.
**Nutrition Info:**Calories: 206;Fat: 7.7 g;Carbohydrates: 32.9 g;Sugar: 7.6 g;Protein: 4 g;Cholesterol: 0 mg

## Farro Porridge With Blackberry Compote

Servings: 4      Cooking Time: 30 Minutes
**Ingredients:**
- 1¼ cups uncooked semi-pearled farro
- 5 cups unsweetened vanilla almond milk
- 1 tablespoon pure maple syrup
- 1 (10-ounce) package frozen blackberries (2 cups)
- 2 teaspoons pure maple syrup
- 2 teaspoons balsamic vinegar

**Directions:**
TO MAKE THE FARRO      Place the farro, almond milk, and maple syrup in a saucepan. Bring the liquid to a boil, then turn the heat down to low and simmer until the farro is tender and has absorbed much of the liquid, about 30 minutes. It should still look somewhat liquidy and will continue to absorb liquid as it cools.      Scoop ¾ cup of farro into each of 4 containers.      TO MAKE THE BLACKBERRY COMPOTE      While the farro is cooking, place the frozen blackberries, maple syrup, and balsamic vinegar in a separate saucepan on medium-low heat. Cook for 12 to 1minutes, until the blackberry juices have thickened. Cool.      Spoon ¼ cup of the blackberry compote into each of the 4 farro containers. STORAGE: Store covered containers in the refrigerator for up to 5 days.
**Nutrition Info:Per Serving:** Total calories: 334; Total fat: 5g; Saturated fat: 0g; Sodium: 227mg; Carbohydrates: 64g; Fiber: 11g; Protein: 11g

## Bulgur Fruit Breakfast Bowl

Servings: 6    Cooking Time: 15 Minutes
**Ingredients:**
- 2 cups 2% milk
- ½ teaspoon ground cinnamon
- 1 ½ cups bulgur
- ½ cup almonds, chopped
- ½ cup mint, chopped (fresh is preferred)
- 8 dried and chopped figs
- 1 cup water
- 2 cups frozen sweet cherries - you can also substitute in blueberries or blackberries

**Directions:**
Turn your stovetop to medium heat and combine the bulger, water, milk, and cinnamon. Lightly stir as the ingredients come to a boil.    Cover your mixture and turn the stove range temperature down to medium-low heat. Let the mixture simmer for 8 to 11 minutes. It is done simmering when about half of the liquid has been absorbed    Without removing the pan, turn off the rangetop heat and add the frozen cherries, almonds, and figs. Lightly stir and then cover for one minute so the cherries can thaw, and the mixture can combine. Remove the cover and add in the mint before scooping your breakfast into a bowl.

**Nutrition Info:** calories: 301, fats: 6 grams, carbohydrates:   grams, protein: 9 grams.

## Acorn Squash Eggs

Servings: 5    Cooking Time: 30 Minutes
**Ingredients:**
- 2 acorn squash
- 4 eggs
- 2 tablespoons extra virgin olive oil
- salt
- pepper
- 5-6 dates, pitted
- 8 walnut halves
- bunch fresh parsley

**Directions:**
Preheat oven to 375 degrees F.    Cut the squashes crosswise into ¾-inch thick slices; remove seeds. Prepare slices with holes.    Line a baking sheet with parchment paper and place the slices on it.    Season with salt and pepper and bake for 20 minutes.    Chop up walnuts and dates.    Remove the baking dish from the oven and drizzle the slices with olive oil.    Crack an egg into the center of the slices (into the hole you made) and season with salt and pepper.    Sprinkle walnuts on top and put back in the oven for 10 minutes.    Add maple syrup.    Enjoy!

**Nutrition Info:Per Serving:** Calories: 198, Total Fat: 9.5g, Saturated Fat: 2, Cholesterol: 131 mg, Sodium: 97 mg, Total Carbohydrate: 25.7 g, Dietary Fiber: 3.9 g, Total Sugars: 5.7 g, Protein: 6.6 g, Vitamin D: mcg, Calcium: 107 mg, Iron: 3 mg, Potassium: 811 mg

## Green Smoothie

Servings: 2    Cooking Time: 12 Minutes
**Ingredients:**
- 4 cups spinach
- 20 almonds, raw
- 2 cups milk
- 2 scoops whey protein
- sweetener of your choice and to taste

**Directions:**
Start by blending spinach, almond, and milk in a blender.    Blend until the puree is formed.    Add the rest of the Ingredients: and blend well.    Pour into glasses and serve.    Enjoy.

**Nutrition Info:Per Serving:** Calories: 325, Total Fat: 13.1 g, Saturated Fat: 4.4 g, Cholesterol: 85 mg, Sodium: 218 mg, Total Carbohydrate: 20.4 g, Dietary Fiber: 2.8 g, Total Sugars: 12.7 g, Protein: 34.4 g, Vitamin D: 1 mcg, Calcium: 482 mg, Iron: 3 mg, Potassium: 738 mg

## Thick Pomegranate Cherry Smoothie

Servings: 4    Cooking Time: 5 Minutes
**Ingredients:**
- 16 ounces frozen dark cherries
- ¾ cup pomegranate juice
- 1 teaspoon vanilla extract
- 6 ice cubes
- ½ cup pomegranate seeds
- 1 ½ cups Greek yogurt, plain
- ⅓ cup milk
- ¾ teaspoon ground cinnamon
- ½ cup pistachios, chopped

**Directions:**
Add the ice cubes, cherries, pomegranate juice, yogurt, vanilla, milk, and cinnamon into a blender. Mix until the ingredients are smooth. It is thicker than your average smoothie.    Instead of a cup, divide the smoothie into four bowls.    Sprinkle chopped pistachios and pomegranate seeds on top of the smoothie.    Serve and enjoy!

**Nutrition Info:** calories: 212, fats: 7 grams, carbohydrates: 3grams, protein: 4 grams.

## Honey Nut Granola

Servings: 6    Cooking Time: 30 Minutes
**Ingredients:**
- ¼ cup honey
- 2 ½ cups rolled oats
- ¼ teaspoon sea salt
- 2 tablespoons ground flaxseed
- 2 teaspoons vanilla extract
- ⅓ cup chopped almonds
- ½ teaspoon ground cinnamon
- ¼ cup olive oil
- ½ cup dried apricots, chopped

**Directions:**
Set the temperature of your oven to 325 degrees Fahrenheit and line a baking pan with a piece of parchment paper. While you can grease the pan, it is easier to use parchment paper when you're cutting the granola.    Turn a burner on your stovetop to medium heat and add the salt, chopped almonds, cinnamon, and oats. Cook the mixture for 5 to 6 minutes while stirring occasionally.    Using a microwavable-safe dish, mix the flaxseed, apricots, oil, and honey. Set the mixture in your microwave and the timer for 1 minute. If the mixture does not bubble within the minute, continue for another minute or until the mixture bubbles.    Mix the vanilla into the flaxseed mixture and then pour this mixture over the almond and oats mixture. Combine the ingredients thoroughly.    Remove the skillet from heat and pour onto the parchment paper. Spread the mixture as evenly as possible with a spatula or another sheet of parchment paper and your hand.    Set the pan into the oven and turn your timer to 15 minutes. However, you want to watch the granola closely as once it starts to brown, you'll need to remove it from heat. Set the granola aside to cool thoroughly. If you used parchment paper, you can take the granola out of the pan by holding the paper and setting it on your counter. It will cool faster so you can eat it faster! Once this waiting is done, cut or break apart the granola into small pieces and enjoy!
**Nutrition Info:**calories: 337, fats: 17 grams, carbohydrates: 42 grams, protein: 7 grams.

## Quinoa Granola

Servings: 2    Cooking Time: 25 Minutes
**Ingredients:**
- 1 cup Old-Fashioned rolled oats, or gluten-free
- 1/2 cup uncooked white quinoa
- 2 cups raw almonds, roughly chopped
- 1 Tbsp coconut sugar or sub organic brown sugar, muscovado, or organic cane sugar
- 1 pinch sea salt
- 3 1/2 tbsp coconut oil
- 1/4 cup maple syrup or agave nectar

**Directions:**
Preheat oven to 340 degrees F    In a large mixing bowl, add the quinoa, almonds, oats, coconut sugar, and salt, stir to combine    To a small saucepan, add the maple syrup and coconut oil, warm over medium heat for 2-minutes, whisking frequently until completely mixed and combined    Immediately pour over the dry ingredients, stir to combine and thoroughly all oats and nuts    Arrange on a large baking sheet, spread into an even layer    Bake for 20 minutes    Then remove from oven, stir and toss the granola - make sure to turn the pan around so the other end goes into the oven first and bakes    evenly    Bake for 5-10 minutes more - watch carefully so it doesn't burn and it's golden brown and very fragrant    Allow to cool completely, then store in a container for up to 7 days
**Nutrition Info:Per Serving:** Calories:332;Total Carbohydrates: 30g;Total Fat: 20g;Protein: 9g

## Greek Yogurt With Fresh Berries, Honey And Nuts

Servings: 1    Cooking Time: 5 Minutes
**Ingredients:**
- 6 oz. nonfat plain Greek yogurt
- 1/2 cup fresh berries of your choice
- 1 tbsp .25 oz crushed walnuts
- 1 tbsp honey

**Directions:**
In a jar with a lid, add the yogurt    Top with berries and a drizzle of honey    Top with the lid and store in the fridge for 2-days    To Serve: Add the granola or nuts, enjoy
**Nutrition Info:Per Serving:** Calories:2;Carbs: 35g;Total Fat: 4g;Protein: 19g

## Quinoa Bake With Banana

Servings: 8    Cooking Time: 1 Hour 20 Minutes
**Ingredients:**
- 3 cups medium over-ripe Bananas, mashed
- 1/4 cup molasses
- 1/4 cup pure maple syrup
- 1 tbsp cinnamon
- 2 tsp raw vanilla extract
- 1 tsp ground ginger
- 1 tsp ground cloves
- 1/2 tsp ground allspice
- 1/2 tsp salt
- 1 cup quinoa, uncooked
- 2 1/2 cups unsweetened vanilla almond milk
- 1/4 cup slivered almonds

**Directions:**
In the bottom of a 2 2-3-quart casserole dish, mix together the mashed banana, maple syrup, cinnamon, vanilla extract, ginger, cloves, allspice, molasses, and salt until well mixed    Add in the quinoa, stir until the quinoa is evenly in the banana mixture.    Whisk in the almond milk, mix until well combined, cover and refrigerate overnight or bake immediately    Heat oven to 350 degrees F    Whisk the quinoa mixture making sure it doesn't settle to the bottom    Cover the pan with tinfoil and bake until the liquid is absorbed, and the top of the quinoa is set, about 1 hour to 1 hour and 15 mins    Turn the oven to high broil, uncover the pan, sprinkle with sliced almonds, and lightly press them into the quinoa    Broil until the almonds just turn golden brown, about 2-4 minutes, watching closely, as they burn quickly    Allow to cool for 10 minutes then slice the quinoa bake    Distribute the quinoa bake among the containers, store in the fridge for 3-4 days
**Nutrition Info:Per Serving:** Calories:213;Carbs: 41g;Total Fat: 4g;Protein: 5g

## Pear And Mango Smoothie

Servings: 1    Cooking Time: 10 Minutes
**Ingredients:**
- ½ peeled, pitted, and chopped mango
- 2 cubes of ice
- 1 ripe, cored, and chopped pear
- ½ cup of plain Greek yogurt
- 1 cup chopped kale

**Directions:**
In a blender, combine the mango, ice cubes, pear, yogurt, and kale.    Blend until the mixture is smooth and thick.    Serve and enjoy!
**Nutrition Info:**calories: 293, fats: 8 grams, carbohydrates: 53 grams, protein: 8 grams.

## Cappuccino Muffins

Servings: 2    Cooking Time: 20 Minutes
**Ingredients:**
- 2 1/3 cups all-purpose flour
- 2 tsp baking powder
- 1 tsp salt
- 1 tsp ground cinnamon
- ¾ cup hot water
- 2 tbsp espresso powder or instant coffee
- 2 eggs
- 1 cup sugar
- ¾ cup vegetable oil
- 1/3 cup mini chocolate chips
- ¼ cup milk

**Directions:**
Preheat oven to 425 degree F    In a medium bowl, whisk together the flour, baking powder, salt and cinnamon, set aside    In a small bowl, combine the hot water and espresso powder, stir to dissolve, add milk, stir to combine and set aside    In a large bowl, whisk together eggs, sugar and oil, slowly add the coffee mixture, and stir to combine Then add in the dry ingredients in thirds, whisking gently until smooth Add in the chocolate chips, stir to combine    Place the muffin papers in a 12-cup muffin tin    Fill each cup half way    Bake for 17-20 minutes, until risen and set Allow to cool completely before slicing    Wrap the slices in plastic wrap and then aluminum foil and store in fridge for up to 4-5 days    To Serve: Remove the aluminum foil and plastic wrap, and microwave for 2 minutes, then allow to rest for 30 seconds, enjoy!
**Nutrition Info:Per Serving:**(1 muffin): Calories:201;Carbs: 29g;Total Fat: 8g;Protein: 2g

## Feta Spinach Egg Cups

Servings: 4    Cooking Time: 8 Minutes
**Ingredients:**
- 6 eggs
- 1/4 tsp garlic powder
- 1 tomato, chopped
- 1/4 cup feta cheese, crumbled
- 1 cup spinach, chopped
- 1/2 cup mozzarella cheese, shredded
- Pepper
- salt

**Directions:**
Pour 1/2 cups of water into the instant pot then place steamer rack in the pot.    In a bowl, whisk eggs with garlic powder, pepper, and salt.    Add remaining ingredients and stir well.    Spray four ramekins with cooking spray.    Pour egg mixture into the ramekins and place ramekins on top of the rack.    Seal pot with lid and cook on high for 8 minutes.    Once done, release pressure using quick release. Remove lid. Serve and enjoy.
**Nutrition Info:**Calories: 134;Fat: 3 g;Carbohydrates: 2 g;Sugar: 1.4 g;Protein: 11 g;Cholesterol: 256 mg

## Chocolate Almond Butter Dip

Servings: 5    Cooking Time: 10 Minutes
**Ingredients:**
- 1 cup of Plain Greek Yogurt
- ½ cup almond butter
- 1/3 cup chocolate hazelnut spread
- 1 tablespoon honey
- 1 teaspoon vanilla
- sliced up fruits as you desire, such as pears, apples, apricots, bananas, etc.

**Directions:**
Take a medium-sized bowl and add all Ingredients: except the fruit.    Take an immersion blender and blend everything well until a smooth dip forms. Alternatively, you can Directions:the Ingredients: in a food processor as well.    Serve with your favorite fruit slices!
**Nutrition Info:Per Serving:**Calories: 148, Total Fat: 7.3 g, Saturated Fat: 1.8 g, Cholesterol: 1 mg, Sodium: 26 mg, Total Carbohydrate: 17 g, Dietary Fiber: 0.7 g, Total Sugars: 15 g, Protein: 5.9 g, Vitamin D: 0 mcg, Calcium: 37 mg, Iron: 0 mg, Potassium: 15 mg

## Sun Dried Tomatoes, Dill And Feta Omelette Casserole

Servings: 6     Cooking Time: 40

**Ingredients:**
- 12 large eggs
- 2 cups whole milk
- 8 oz fresh spinach
- 2 cloves garlic, minced
- 12 oz artichoke salad with olives and peppers, drained and chopped
- 5 oz sun dried tomato feta cheese, crumbled
- 1 tbsp fresh chopped dill or 1 tsp dried dill
- 1 tsp dried oregano
- 1 tsp lemon pepper
- 1 tsp salt
- 4 tsp olive oil, divided

**Directions:**
Preheat oven to 375 degrees F    Chop the fresh herbs and artichoke salad    In a skillet over medium heat, add 1 tbsp olive oil    Sauté the spinach and garlic until wilted, about 3 minutes    Oil a 9x13 inch baking dish, layer the spinach and artichoke salad evenly in the dish    In a medium bowl, whisk together the eggs, milk, herbs, salt and lemon pepper    Pour the egg mixture over vegetables, sprinkle with feta cheese    Bake in the center of the oven for 35-40 minutes until firm in the center    Allow to cool, slice a and distribute among the storage containers. Store for 2-3 days or freeze for 3 months    To Serve: Reheat in the microwave for 30 seconds or until heated through or in the toaster oven for 5 minutes or until heated through

**Nutrition Info:Per Serving:** Calories:196;Total Carbohydrates: 5g;Total Fat: 12g;Protein: 10g

# Lunch and Dinner Recipes

## Marinated Tuna Steak

Servings: 4     Cooking Time: 15-20 Minutes
**Ingredients:**
- Olive oil (2 tbsp.)
- Orange juice (.25 cup)
- Soy sauce (.25 cup)
- Lemon juice (1 tbsp.)
- Fresh parsley (2 tbsp.)
- Garlic clove (1)
- Ground black pepper (.5 tsp.)
- Fresh oregano (.5 tsp.)
- Tuna steaks (4 - 4 oz. Steaks)

**Directions:**
Mince the garlic and chop the oregano and parsley. In a glass container, mix the pepper, oregano, garlic, parsley, lemon juice, soy sauce, olive oil, and orange juice.     Warm the grill using the high heat setting. Grease the grate with oil.     Add to tuna steaks and cook for five to six minutes. Turn and baste with the marinated sauce.     Cook another five minutes or until it's the way you like it. Discard the remaining marinade.
**Nutrition Info:**Calories: 200;Protein: 27.4 grams;Fat: 7.9 grams

## Garlic And Shrimp Pasta

Servings: 4     Cooking Time: 15 Minutes
**Ingredients:**
- 6 ounces whole wheat spaghetti
- 12 ounces raw shrimp, peeled and deveined, cut into 1-inch pieces
- 1 bunch asparagus, trimmed
- 1 large bell pepper, thinly sliced
- 1 cup fresh peas
- 3 garlic cloves, chopped
- 1 and ¼ teaspoons kosher salt
- ½ and ½ cups non-fat plain yogurt
- 3 tablespoon lemon juice
- 1 tablespoon extra-virgin olive oil
- ½ teaspoon fresh ground black pepper
- ¼ cup pine nuts, toasted

**Directions:**
Take a large sized pot and bring water to a boil     Add your spaghetti and cook them for about minutes less than the directed package instruction     Add shrimp, bell pepper, asparagus and cook for about 2- 4 minutes until the shrimp are tender     Drain the pasta and the contents well     Take a large bowl and mash garlic until a paste form     Whisk in yogurt, parsley, oil, pepper and lemon juice into the garlic paste     Add pasta mix and toss well     Serve by sprinkling some pine nuts! Enjoy!     Meal Prep/Storage Options: Store in airtight containers in your fridge for 1-3 days.
**Nutrition Info:**Calories: 406;Fat: 22g;Carbohydrates: 28g;Protein: 26g

## Paprika Butter Shrimps

Servings: 2     Cooking Time: 30 Minutes
**Ingredients:**
- ¼ tablespoon smoked paprika
- 1/8 cup sour cream

- ½ pound tiger shrimps
- 1/8 cup butter
- Salt and black pepper, to taste

**Directions:**
Preheat the oven to 390 degrees F and grease a baking dish.     Mix together all the ingredients in a large bowl and transfer into the baking dish.     Place in the oven and bake for about 15 minutes.     Place paprika shrimp in a dish and set aside to cool for meal prepping. Divide it in 2 containers and cover the lid. Refrigerate for 1-2 days and reheat in microwave before serving.
**Nutrition Info:**Calories: 330 ;Carbohydrates: 1.;Protein: 32.6g;Fat: 21.5g;Sugar: 0.2g;Sodium: 458mg

## Mediterranean Avocado Salmon Salad

Servings: 4     Cooking Time: 10 Minutes
**Ingredients:**
- 1 lb skinless salmon fillets
- Marinade/Dressing:
- 3 tbsp olive oil
- 2 tbsp lemon juice fresh, squeezed
- 1 tbsp red wine vinegar, optional
- 1 tbsp fresh chopped parsley
- 2 tsp garlic minced
- 1 tsp dried oregano
- 1 tsp salt
- Cracked pepper, to taste
- Salad:
- 4 cups Romaine (or Cos) lettuce leaves, washed and dried
- 1 large cucumber, diced
- 2 Roma tomatoes, diced
- 1 red onion, sliced
- 1 avocado, sliced
- 1/2 cup feta cheese crumbled
- 1/3 cup pitted Kalamata olives or black olives, sliced
- Lemon wedges to serve

**Directions:**
In a jug, whisk together the olive oil, lemon juice, red wine vinegar, chopped parsley, garlic minced, oregano, salt and pepper     Pour out half of the marinade into a large, shallow dish, refrigerate the remaining marinade to use as the dressing     Coat the salmon in the rest of the marinade     Place a skillet pan or grill over medium-high, add 1 tbsp oil and sear salmon on both sides until crispy and cooked through     Allow the salmon to cool     Distribute the salmon among the containers, store in the fridge for 2-3 days     To Serve: Prepare the salad by placing the romaine lettuce, cucumber, roma tomatoes, red onion, avocado, feta cheese, and olives in a large salad bowl. Reheat the salmon in the microwave for 30seconds to 1 minute or until heated through.     Slice the salmon and arrange over salad. Drizzle the salad with the remaining untouched dressing, serve with lemon wedges.
**Nutrition Info:Per Serving:** Calories:411;Carbs: 12g;Total Fat: 27g;Protein: 28g

## Beet Kale Salad

Servings: 6    Cooking Time: 50 Minutes
**Ingredients:**
- 1 bunch of kale, washed and dried, ribs removed, chopped
- 6 pieces washed beets, peeled and dried and cut into ½ inches
- ½ teaspoon dried rosemary
- ½ teaspoon garlic powder
- salt
- pepper
- olive oil
- ¼ medium red onion, thinly sliced
- 1-2 tablespoons slivered almonds, toasted
- ¼ cup olive oil
- Juice of 1½ lemon
- ¼ cup honey
- ¼ teaspoon garlic powder
- 1 teaspoon dried rosemary
- salt
- pepper

**Directions:**
Preheat oven to 400 degrees F.    Take a bowl and toss the kale with some salt, pepper, and olive oil.    Lightly oil a baking sheet and add the kale.    Roast in the oven for 5 minutes, and then remove and place to the side. Place beets in a bowl and sprinkle with a bit of rosemary, garlic powder, pepper, and salt; ensure beets are coated well.    Spread the beets on the oiled baking sheet, place on the middle rack of your oven, and roast for 45 minutes, turning twice.    Make the lemon vinaigrette by whisking all of the listed Ingredients: in a bowl.    Once the beets are ready, remove from the oven and allow it to cool.    Take a medium-sized salad bowl and add kale, onions, and beets.    Dress with lemon honey vinaigrette and toss well.    Garnish with toasted almonds.    Enjoy!

**Nutrition Info:Per Serving:**Calories: 245, Total Fat: 17.6 g, Saturated Fat: 2.6 g, Cholesterol: 0 mg, Sodium: 77 mg, Total Carbohydrate: 22.9 g, Dietary Fiber: 3 g, Total Sugars: 17.7 g, Protein: 2.4 g, Vitamin D: 0 mcg, Calcium: 50 mg, Iron: 1 mg, Potassium: 416 mg

## Moroccan Fish

Servings: 12    Cooking Time: 1 Hour 25 Minutes
**Ingredients:**
- Garbanzo beans (15 oz. Can)
- Red bell peppers (2)
- Large carrot (1)
- Vegetable oil (1 tbsp.)
- Onion (1)
- Garlic (1 clove)
- Tomatoes (3 chopped/14.5 oz can)
- Olives (4 chopped)
- Chopped fresh parsley (.25 cup)
- Ground cumin (.25 cup)
- Paprika (3 tbsp.)
- Chicken bouillon granules (2 tbsp. )

- Cayenne pepper (1 tsp.)
- Salt (to your liking)
- Tilapia fillets (5 lb.)

**Directions:**
Drain and rinse the beans. Thinly slice the carrot and onion. Mince the garlic and chop the olives. Discard the seeds from the peppers and slice them into strips. Warm the oil in a frying pan using the medium temperature setting. Toss in the onion and garlic. Simmer them for approximately five minutes.    Fold in the bell peppers, beans, tomatoes, carrots, and olives. Continue sautéing them for about five additional minutes.    Sprinkle the veggies with the cumin, parsley, salt, chicken bouillon, paprika, and cayenne. Stir thoroughly and place the fish on top of the veggies. Pour in water to cover the veggies.    Lower the heat setting and cover the pan to slowly cook until the fish is flaky (about 40 min..

**Nutrition Info:**Calories: 268;Protein: 42 grams;Fat: 5 grams

## Niçoise-inspired Salad With Sardines

Servings: 4    Cooking Time: 15 Minutes
**Ingredients:**
- 4 eggs
- 12 ounces baby red potatoes (about 12 potatoes)
- 6 ounces green beans, halved
- 4 cups baby spinach leaves or mixed greens
- 1 bunch radishes, quartered (about 1⅓ cups)
- 1 cup cherry tomatoes
- 20 kalamata or niçoise olives (about ⅓ cup)
- 3 (3.75-ounce) cans skinless, boneless sardines packed in olive oil, drained
- 8 tablespoons Dijon Red Wine Vinaigrette

**Directions:**
Place the eggs in a saucepan and cover with water. Bring the water to a boil. As soon as the water starts to boil, place a lid on the pan and turn the heat off. Set a timer for    minutes.    When the timer goes off, drain the hot water and run cold water over the eggs to cool. Peel the eggs when cool and cut in half.    Prick each potato a few times with a fork. Place them on a microwave-safe plate and microwave on high for 4 to 5 minutes, until the potatoes are tender. Let cool and cut in half.    Place green beans on a microwave-safe plate and microwave on high for 1½ to 2 minutes, until the beans are crisp-tender. Cool.    Place 1 egg, ½ cup of green beans, 6 potato halves, 1 cup of spinach, ⅓ cup of radishes, ¼ cup of tomatoes, olives, and 3 sardines in each of 4 containers. Pour 2 tablespoons of vinaigrette into each of 4 sauce containers.    STORAGE: Store covered containers in the refrigerator for up to 4 days.

**Nutrition Info:Per Serving:** Total calories: 450; Total fat: 32g; Saturated fat: 5g; Sodium: 6mg; Carbohydrates: 22g; Fiber: 5g; Protein: 21g

## Lettuce Tomato Salad

Servings: 6     Cooking Time: 15 Minutes
**Ingredients:**
- 1 heart of Romaine lettuce, chopped
- 3 Roma tomatoes, diced
- 1 English cucumber, diced
- 1 small red onion, finely chopped
- ½ cup curly parsley, finely chopped
- 2 tablespoons virgin olive oil
- lemon juice, ½ large lemon
- 1 teaspoon garlic powder
- salt
- pepper

**Directions:**
Add all Ingredients: to a large bowl.     Toss well and transfer them to containers.     Enjoy!
**Nutrition Info:Per Serving:**Calories: 68, Total Fat: 9 g, Saturated Fat: 0.8 g, Cholesterol: 0 mg, Sodium: 7 mg, Total Carbohydrate: 6 g, Dietary Fiber: 1.5 g, Total Sugars: 3.3 g, Protein: 1.3 g, Vitamin D: 0 mcg, Calcium: 18 mg, Iron: 1 mg, Potassium: 309 mg

## Mediterranean Chicken Pasta Bake

Servings: 4     Cooking Time: 30 Minutes
**Ingredients:**
- Marinade:
- 1½ lbs. boneless, skinless chicken thighs, cut into bite-sized pieces*
- 2 garlic cloves, thinly sliced
- 2-3 tbsp. marinade from artichoke hearts
- 4 sprigs of fresh oregano, leaves stripped
- Olive oil
- Red wine vinegar
- Pasta:
- 1 lb whole wheat fusilli pasta
- 1 red onion, thinly sliced
- 1 pint grape or cherry tomatoes, whole
- ½ cup marinated artichoke hearts, roughly chopped
- ½ cup white beans, rinsed + drained (I use northern white beans)
- ½ cup Kalamata olives, roughly chopped
- ⅓ cup parsley and basil leaves, roughly chopped
- 2-3 handfuls of part-skim shredded mozzarella cheese
- Salt, to taste
- Pepper, to taste
- Garnish:
- Parsley
- Basil leaves

**Directions:**
Create the chicken marinade by drain the artichoke hearts reserving the juice     In a large bowl, add the artichoke juice, garlic, chicken, and oregano leaves, drizzle with olive oil, a splash of red wine vinegar, and mix well to coat     Marinate for at least 1 hour, maximum hours     Cook the pasta in boiling salted water, drain and set aside     Preheat your oven to

42degrees F     In a casserole dish, add the sliced onions and tomatoes, toss with olive oil, salt and pepper. Then cook, stirring occasionally, until the onions are soft and the tomatoes start to burst, about 15-20 minutes     In the meantime, in a large skillet over medium heat, add 1 tsp of olive oil     Remove the chicken from the marinade, pat dry, and season with salt and pepper     Working in batches, brown the chicken on both sides, leaving slightly undercooked     Remove the casserole dish from the oven, add in the cooked pasta, browned chicken, artichoke hearts, beans, olives, and chopped herbs, stir to combine     Top with grated cheese     Bake for an additional 5-7 minutes, until the cheese is brown and bubbling     Remove from the oven and allow the dish to cool completely     Distribute among the containers, store for 2-3 days     To Serve: Reheat in the microwave for 1-2 minutes or until heated through. Garnish with fresh herbs and serve
**Nutrition Info:Per Serving:** Calories:487;Carbs: 95g;Total Fat: 5g;Protein: 22g

## Roasted Vegetable Flatbread

Servings: 12     Cooking Time: 25 Minutes
**Ingredients:**
- 16 oz pizza dough, homemade or frozen
- 6 oz soft goat cheese, divided
- ¾ cup grated Parmesan cheese divided
- 3 tbsp chopped fresh dill, divided
- 1 small red onion, sliced thinly
- 1 small zucchini, sliced thinly
- 2 small tomatoes, thinly sliced
- 1 small red pepper, thinly sliced into rings
- Olive oil
- Salt, to taste
- Pepper, to taste

**Directions:**
Preheat the oven to 400 degrees F     Roll the dough into a large rectangle, and then place it on a piece of parchment paper sprayed with non-stick spray     Take a knife and spread half the goat cheese onto one half of the dough, then sprinkle with half the dill and half the Parmesan cheese     Carefully fold the other half of the dough on top of the cheese, spread and sprinkle the remaining parmesan and goat cheese     Layer the thinly sliced vegetables over the top     Brush the olive oil over the top of the veggies and sprinkle with salt, pepper, and the remaining dill     Bake for 22-25 minutes, until the edges are medium brown, cut in half, lengthwise     Then slice the flatbread in long 2-inch slices and allow to cool     Distribute among the containers, store for 2 days     To Serve: Reheat in the oven at 375 degrees for 5 minutes or until hot. Enjoy with a fresh salad.
**Nutrition Info:Per Serving:** Calories:170;Carbs: 21g;Total Fat: 6g;Protein: 8g

## Steak Cobb Salad

Servings: 4    Cooking Time: 15 Minutes

**Ingredients:**
- 6 large eggs
- 2 tbsp unsalted butter
- 1 lb steak
- 2 tbsp olive oil
- 6 cups baby spinach
- 1 cup cherry tomatoes, halved
- 1 cup pecan halves
- 1/2 cup crumbled feta cheese
- Kosher salt, to taste
- Freshly ground black pepper, to taste

**Directions:**
In a large skillet over medium high heat, melt butter Using paper towels, pat the steak dry, then drizzle with olive oil and season with salt and pepper, to taste Once heated, add the steak to the skillet and cook, flipping once, until cooked through to desired doneness, - cook for 4 minutes per side for a medium-rare steak Transfer the steak to a plate and allow it to cool before dicing    Place the eggs in a large saucepan and cover with cold water by 1 inch    Bring to a boil and cook for 1 minute, cover the eggs with a tight-fitting lid and remove from heat, set aside for 8-10 minutes, then drain well and allow to cool before peeling and dicing Assemble the salad in the container by placing the spinach at the bottom of the container, top with arranged rows of steak, eggs, feta, tomatoes, and pecans To Serve: Top with the balsamic vinaigrette, or desired dressing    Recipe Note: You can also use New York, rib-eye or filet mignon for this recipe

**Nutrition Info:Per Serving:** Calories:640;Total Fat: 51g;Total Carbs: 9.8g;Fiber: 5g;Protein: 38.8g

## Grilled Lamb Chops

Servings: 4    Cooking Time: 10 Minutes

**Ingredients:**
- 4 8-ounce lamb shoulder chops
- 2 tablespoons Dijon mustard
- 2 tablespoons balsamic vinegar
- 1 tablespoon chopped garlic
- 1/4 teaspoon ground black pepper
- 1/2 cup olive oil
- 2 tablespoons fresh basil, shredded

**Directions:**
Pat the lamb chops dry and arrange them in a shallow glass-baking dish.    Take a bowl and whisk in Dijon mustard, garlic, balsamic vinegar, and pepper.    Mix well to make the marinade.    Whisk oil slowly into the marinade until it is smooth.    Stir in basil.    Pour the marinade over the lamb chops, making sure to coat both sides.    Cover, refrigerate and allow the chops to marinate for anywhere from 1-4 hours.    Remove the chops from the refrigerator and leave out for 30 minutes or until room temperature.    Preheat grill to medium heat and oil grate.    Grill the lamb chops until the center reads 145 degrees F and they are nicely browned, about 5-minutes per side.    Enjoy!

**Nutrition Info:Per Serving:** Calories: 1587, Total Fat: 97.5 g, Saturated Fat: 27.6 g, Cholesterol: 600 mg, Sodium: 729 mg, Total Carbohydrate: 1.3 g, Dietary Fiber: 0.4 g, Total Sugars: 0.1 g, Protein: 176.5 g, Vitamin D: 0 mcg, Calcium: 172 mg, Iron: 15 mg, Potassium: 30 mg

## Broiled Chili Calamari

Servings: 4    Cooking Time: 8 Minutes

**Ingredients:**
- 2 tablespoons extra virgin olive oil
- 1 teaspoon chili powder
- 1/2 teaspoon ground cumin
- Zest of 1 lime
- Juice of 1 lime
- Dash of sea salt
- 1 and 1/2 pounds squid, cleaned and split open, with tentacles cut into 1/2 inch rounds
- 2 tablespoons cilantro, chopped
- 2 tablespoons red bell pepper, minced

**Directions:**
Take a medium bowl and stir in olive oil, chili powder, cumin, lime zest, sea salt, lime juice and pepper    Add squid and let it marinade and stir to coat, coat and let it refrigerate for 1 hour    Pre-heat your oven to broil Arrange squid on a baking sheet, broil for 8 minutes turn once until tender    Garnish the broiled calamari with cilantro and red bell pepper    Serve and enjoy! Meal Prep/Storage Options: Store in airtight containers in your fridge for 1-2 days.

**Nutrition Info:** Calories:159;Fat: 13g;Carbohydrates: 12g;Protein: 3g

## Salmon With Corn Pepper Salsa

Servings: 2    Cooking Time: 12 Minutes

**Ingredients:**
- 1 garlic clove, grated
- 1/2 teaspoon mild chili powder
- 1/2 teaspoon ground coriander
- 1/4 teaspoon ground cumin
- 2 limes – 1, zest and juice; 1 cut into wedges
- 2 teaspoons rapeseed oil
- 2 wild salmon fillets
- 1 ear of corn on the cob, husk removed
- 1 red onion, finely chopped
- 1 avocado, cored, peeled, and finely chopped
- 1 red pepper, deseeded and finely chopped
- 1 red chili, halved and deseeded
- 1/2 a pack of finely chopped coriander

**Directions:**
Boil the corn in water for about 6-8 minutes until tender.    Drain and cut off the kernels.    In a bowl, combine garlic, spices, 1 tablespoon of limejuice, and oil; mix well to prepare spice rub.    Coat the salmon with the rub.    Add the zest to the corn and give it a gentle stir.    Heat a frying pan over medium heat. Add salmon and cook for about 2 minutes per side. Serve the cooked salmon with salsa and lime wedges. Enjoy!

**Nutrition Info:Per Serving:** Calories: 949, Total Fat: 57.4 g, Saturated Fat: 9.7 g, Cholesterol: 2mg, Sodium: 180 mg, Total Carbohydrate: 33.5 g, Dietary Fiber: 11.8 g, Total Sugars: 8.3 g, Protein: 76.8 g, Vitamin D: 0 mcg, Calcium: 100 mg, Iron: 3 mg, Potassium: 856 mg

## Italian-inspired Rotisserie Chicken And Broccoli Slaw

Servings: 4 :    Cooking Time: 15 Minutes
**Ingredients:**
- 4 cups packaged broccoli slaw
- 1 cooked rotisserie chicken, meat removed (about 10 to 12 ounces)
- 1 bunch red radishes, stemmed, halved, and thickly sliced (about 1¼ cups)
- 1 cup sliced red onion
- ½ cup pitted kalamata or niçoise olives, roughly chopped
- ½ cup sliced pepperoncini
- 8 tablespoons Dijon Red Wine Vinaigrette, divided

**Directions:**
Place the broccoli slaw, chicken, radishes, onion, olives, and pepperoncini in a large mixing bowl. Toss to combine.    Place   cups of salad in each of 4 containers. Pour 2 tablespoons of vinaigrette into each of 4 sauce containers.    STORAGE: Store covered containers in the refrigerator for up to 5 days.
**Nutrition Info:Per Serving:** Total calories: 329; Total fat: 2; Saturated fat: 4g; Sodium: 849mg; Carbohydrates: 10g; Fiber: 3g; Protein: 20g

## Flatbread With Roasted Vegetables

Servings: 12    Cooking Time: 45 Minutes
**Ingredients:**
- 5 ounces goat cheese
- 1 thinly sliced onion
- 2 thinly sliced tomatoes
- Olive oil
- ¼ teaspoon pepper
- ⅛ teaspoon salt
- 16 ounces homemade or frozen pizza dough
- ¾ tablespoon chopped dill, fresh is better
- 1 thinly sliced zucchini
- 1 red pepper, cup into rings

**Directions:**
Set your oven to 400 degrees Fahrenheit.    Set the dough on a large piece of parchment paper. Use a rolling pin to roll the dough into a large rectangle. Spread half of the goat cheese on ½ of the pizza dough. Sprinkle half of the dill on the other half of the dough. Fold the dough so the half with the dill is on top of the cheese.    Spread the remaining goat cheese on the pizza dough and then sprinkle the rest of the dill over the cheese.    Layer the vegetables on top in any arrangement you like.    Drizzle olive oil on top of the vegetables.    Sprinkle salt and pepper over the olive oil.    Set the piece of parchment paper on a pizza pan or baking pan and place it in the oven.    Set the timer for 22 minutes. If the edges are not a medium brown, leave the flatbread in the oven for another couple of minutes.    Remove the pizza from the oven when it is done and cut the flatbread in half lengthwise.    Slice the flatbread into 2-inch long pieces and enjoy!

**Nutrition Info:**calories: 170, fats: 5 grams, carbohydrates: 20 grams, protein: 8 grams.

## Seafood Paella

Servings: 4-5    Cooking Time: 40 Minutes
**Ingredients:**
- 4 small lobster tails (6-12 oz each)
- Water
- 3 tbsp Extra Virgin Olive Oil
- 1 large yellow onion, chopped
- 2 cups Spanish rice or short grain rice, soaked in water for 15 minutes and then drained
- 4 garlic cloves, chopped
- 2 large pinches of Spanish saffron threads soaked in 1/2 cup water
- 1 tsp Sweet Spanish paprika
- 1 tsp cayenne pepper
- 1/2 tsp aleppo pepper flakes
- Salt, to taste
- 2 large Roma tomatoes, finely chopped
- 6 oz French green beans, trimmed
- 1 lb prawns or large shrimp or your choice, peeled and deveined
- 1/4 cup chopped fresh parsley

**Directions:**
In a large pot, add 3 cups of water and bring it to a rolling boil    Add in the lobster tails and allow boil briefly, about 1-minutes or until pink, remove from heat Using tongs transfer the lobster tails to a plate and Do not discard the lobster cooking water    Allow the lobster is cool, then remove the shell and cut into large chunks.    In a large deep pan or skillet over medium-high heat, add 3 tbsp olive oil    Add the chopped onions, sauté the onions for 2 minutes and then add the rice, and cook for 3 more minutes, stirring regularly Then add in the lobster cooking water and the chopped garlic and, stir in the saffron and its soaking liquid, cayenne pepper, aleppo pepper, paprika, and salt Gently stir in the chopped tomatoes and green beans, bring to a boil and allow the liquid slightly reduce, then cover (with lid or tightly wrapped foil) and cook over low heat for 20 minutes    Once done, uncover and spread the shrimp over the rice, push it into the rice slightly, add in a little water, if needed    Cover and cook for another 15 minutes until the shrimp turn pink Then add in the cooked lobster chunks    Once the lobster is warmed through, remove from heat allow the dish to cool completely    Distribute among the containers, store for 2 days    To Serve: Reheat in the microwave for 1-2 minutes or until heated through. Garnish with parsley and enjoy!    Recipe Notes: Remember to soak your rice if needed to help with the cooking process
**Nutrition Info:Per Serving:** Calories:536;Carbs: 56g;Total Fat: 26g;Protein: 50g

## Mediterranean Pearl Couscous

Servings: 6    Cooking Time: 10 Minutes
**Ingredients:**
- For the Lemon Dill Vinaigrette:
- 1 large lemon, juice of
- 1/3 cup Extra virgin olive oil
- 1 tsp dill weed
- 1 tsp garlic powder
- Salt and pepper
- For the Israeli Couscous:
- 2 cups Pearl Couscous, Israeli Couscous
- Extra virgin olive oil
- 2 cups grape tomatoes, halved
- 1/3 cup finely chopped red onions
- 1/2 English cucumber, finely chopped
- 15 oz can chickpeas
- 14 oz can good quality artichoke hearts, roughly chopped if needed
- 1/2 cup good pitted kalamata olives
- 15–20 fresh basil leaves, roughly chopped or torn; more for garnish
- 3 oz fresh baby mozzarella or feta cheese, optional
- Water

**Directions:**
Make the lemon-dill vinaigrette, place the lemon juice, olive oil, dill weed, garlic powder, salt and pepper in a bowl, whisk together to combine and set aside    In a medium-sized heavy pot, heat two tbsp of olive oil Sauté the couscous in the olive oil briefly until golden brown, then add cups of boiling water (or follow the instructed on the package), and cook according to package.    Once done, drain in a colander, set aside in a bowl and allow to cool    In a large mixing bowl, combine the extra virgin olive oil, grape tomatoes, red onions, cucumber, chickpeas, artichoke hearts, and kalamata olives    Then add in the couscous and the basil, mix together gently    Now, give the lemon-dill vinaigrette a quick whisk and add to the couscous salad, mix to combine    Taste and adjust salt, if needed Distribute among the containers, store for 2-3 days To Serve: Add in the mozzarella cheese, garnish with more fresh basil and enjoy!
**Nutrition Info:Per Serving:** Calories:393;Carbs: 57g;Total Fat: 13g;Protein: 13g

## Potato And Tuna Salad

Servings: 4    Cooking Time: Nil
**Ingredients:**
- 1-pound baby potatoes, scrubbed, boiled
- 1 cup tuna chunks, drained
- 1 cup cherry tomatoes, halved
- 1 cup medium onion, thinly sliced
- 8 pitted black olives
- 2 medium hard-boiled eggs, sliced
- 1 head Romaine lettuce
- Honey lemon mustard dressing
- ¼ cup olive oil
- 2 tablespoons lemon juice
- 1 tablespoon Dijon mustard
- 1 teaspoon dill weed, chopped
- Salt as needed
- Pepper as needed

**Directions:**
Take a small glass bowl and mix in your olive oil, honey, lemon juice, Dijon mustard and dill    Season the mix with pepper and salt    Add in the tuna, baby potatoes, cherry tomatoes, red onion, green beans, black olives

and toss everything nicely    Arrange your lettuce leaves on a beautiful serving dish to make the base of your salad    Top them up with your salad mixture and place the egg slices    Drizzle it with the previously prepared Salad Dressing    Serve hot    Meal Prep/Storage Options: Store in airtight containers in your fridge for 1-2 days. Keep the fish and salad ingredients separated, mix together before serving!
**Nutrition Info:**Calories: 406;Fat: 22g;Carbohydrates: 28g;Protein: 26g

## Mediterranean Pasta Salad

Servings: 8    Cooking Time: 25 Minutes
**Ingredients:**
- Salad:
- 8 oz pasta, I used farfalle, any smallish pasta works great!
- 1 cup rotisserie chicken, chopped
- 1/2 cup sun-dried tomatoes packed in oil, drained and coarsely chopped
- 1/2 cup jarred marinated artichoke hearts, drained and coarsely chopped
- 1/2 of 1 full English cucumber, chopped
- 1/3 cup kalamata olives, coarsely chopped
- 2 cups lightly packed fresh arugula
- 1/4 cup fresh flat leaf Italian parsley, coarsely chopped
- 1 small avocado, pit removed and coarsely chopped
- 1/3 cup feta cheese
- Dressing:
- 4 tbsp red wine vinegar
- 1 ½  tbsp
- dijon mustard, do not use regular mustard
- 1/2 tsp dried oregano
- 1 tsp dried basil
- 1 clove garlic, minced
- 1-2 tsp honey
- 1/2 cup olive oil
- 3 tbsp freshly squeezed lemon juice
- Fine sea salt, to taste
- Freshly cracked pepper, to taste

**Directions:**
Prepare the pasta according to package directions until al dente, drain the pasta and allow it to completely cool to room temperature, then add it to a large bowl    Add in the chopped rotisserie chicken, chopped cucumber, coarsely chopped kalamata olives, coarsely chopped sun-dried tomatoes, coarsely chopped artichoke hearts, arugula, and parsley, toss    Distribute the salad among the containers, store for 2-days    Prepare the dressing - In a mason jar with a lid, combine the red wine vinegar, Dijon mustard, garlic, 1/2 teaspoon salt (or to taste), dried oregano, dried basil and 1/teaspoon pepper (or to taste, honey (add to sweetness preference), olive oil, and freshly squeezed lemon juice, place the lid on the mason jar and shake to combine, store in fridge To Serve: Add in the avocado and feta cheese to the salad, drizzle with the dressing, adjust any seasonings salt and pepper to taste, serve
**Nutrition Info:Per Serving:** Calories:32Carbs: 24g;Total Fat: 21g;Protein: 8g

## Lemon Herb Avocado Chicken Salad

Servings: 4     Cooking Time: 15 Minutes
**Ingredients:**
- Marinade/ Dressing:
- 2 tbsp olive oil
- 1/4 cup fresh lemon juice
- 2 tbsp water
- 2 tbsp fresh chopped parsley
- 2 tsp garlic, minced
- 1 tsp each dried thyme and dried rosemary
- 1 tsp salt
- 1/4 tsp cracked pepper, or to taste
- 1 pound skinless & boneless chicken thigh fillets or chicken breasts
- Salad:
- 4 cups Romaine lettuce leaves, washed and dried
- 1 large avocado, pitted, peeled and sliced
- 8 oz feta cheese
- 1 cup grape tomatoes, halved
- 1/4 of a red onion, sliced, optional
- 1/4 cup diced bacon, trimmed of rind and fat (optional)
- Lemon wedges, to serve

**Directions:**
In a large jug, whisk together the olive oil, lemon juice, water, chopped parsley, garlic, thyme, rosemary, salt, and pepper     Pour half of the marinade into a large, shallow dish and refrigerate the remaining marinade to use as the dressing     Add the chicken to the marinade in the bowl, allow the chicken to marinade for 15-minutes (or up to two hours in the refrigerator if you can)     In the meantime,     Once the chicken is ready, place a skillet or grill over medium-high heat add 1 tbsp of oil in, sear the chicken on both sides until browned and cooked through about 7 minutes per side, depending on thickness, and discard of the marinade Allow the chicken to rest for 5 minutes, slice and then allow the chicken to cool     Distribute among the containers, and keep in the refrigerator     To Serve: Reheat the chicken in the microwave for 30 seconds to 1 minutes. In a bowl, add the romaine lettuce, avocado, feta cheese, grape tomatoes, red onion and bacon, mix to combine. Arrange the chicken over salad. Drizzle the salad with the Untouched dressing. Serve with lemon wedges and enjoy!
**Nutrition Info:Per Serving:** Calories:378;Carbs: 6g;Total Fat: 22g;Protein: 31g

## Greek-style Braised Pork With Leeks, Greens, And Potatoes

Servings: 4     Cooking Time: 1 Hour 40 Minutes
**Ingredients:**
- 1 tablespoon olive oil, plus 2 teaspoons
- 1¼ pounds boneless pork loin chops, fat cap removed and cut into 1-inch pieces
- 2 leeks, white and light green parts quartered vertically and thinly sliced
- 1 bulb fennel, quartered and thinly sliced
- 1 cup chopped onion
- 1 teaspoon chopped garlic
- 2 cups reduced-sodium chicken broth
- 1 teaspoon fennel seed
- 1 teaspoon dried oregano
- ½ teaspoon kosher salt
- 1 pound baby red potatoes, halved
- 1 bunch chard, including stems, chopped
- 2 tablespoons freshly squeezed lemon juice

**Directions:**
Heat tablespoon of oil in a soup pot or Dutch oven over medium-high heat. When the oil is shimmering, add the pork cubes and brown for about 6 minutes, turning the cubes over after 3 minutes. Remove the pork to a plate.     Add the remaining teaspoons of oil to the same pot and add the leeks, fennel, onion, and garlic. Cook for 3 minutes.     Pour the broth into the pan, scraping up any browned bits on the bottom. Add the fennel seed, oregano, and salt, and add the pork, plus any juices that may have accumulated on the plate. Make sure the pork is submerged in the liquid. Place the potatoes on top, then place the chard on top of the potatoes.     Cover, turn down the heat to low, and simmer for 1½ hours, until the pork is tender. When the pork is done cooking, add the lemon juice. Taste and add more salt if needed. Cool.     Scoop 2 cups of the mixture into each of 4 containers.     STORAGE: Store covered containers in the refrigerator for up to 5 days.
**Nutrition Info:Per Serving:** Total calories: 3; Total fat: 13g; Saturated fat: 3g; Sodium: 1,607mg; Carbohydrates: 33g; Fiber: 8g; Protein: 34g

## Delicious Broccoli Tortellini Salad

Servings: 12     Cooking Time: 20 To 25 Minutes
**Ingredients:**
- 1 cup sunflower seeds, or any of your favorite seeds
- 3 heads of broccoli, fresh is best!
- ½ cup sugar
- 20 ounces cheese-filled tortellini
- 1 onion
- 2 teaspoons cider vinegar
- ½ cup mayonnaise
- 1 cup raisins-optional

**Directions:**
Cut your broccoli into florets and chop the onion. Follow the directions to make the cheese-filled tortellini. Once they are cooked, drain and rinse them with cold water.     In a bowl, combine your mayonnaise, sugar, and vinegar. Whisk well to give the ingredients a dressing consistency.     In a separate large bowl, toss in your seeds, onion, tortellini, raisins, and broccoli. Pour the salad dressing into the large bowl and toss the ingredients together. You will want to ensure everything is thoroughly mixed as you'll want a taste of the salad dressing with every bite!
**Nutrition Info:**calories: 272, fats: 8.1 grams, carbohydrates: 38.grams, protein: 5 grams.

## Arugula Avocado Salad

Servings: 4     Cooking Time: 15 Minutes
**Ingredients:**
- 4 cups packed baby arugula
- 4 green onions, tops trimmed, chopped
- 1½ cups shelled fava beans
- 3 Persian cucumbers, chopped
- 2 cups grape tomatoes, halved
- 1 jalapeno pepper, sliced
- 1 avocado, cored, peeled, and roughly chopped
- lemon juice, 1½ lemons
- ½ cup extra virgin olive oil
- salt
- pepper
- 1 garlic clove, finely chopped
- 2 tablespoons fresh cilantro, finely chopped
- 2 tablespoons fresh mint, finely chopped

**Directions:**
Place the lemon-honey vinaigrette Ingredients: in a small bowl and whisk them well.     In a large mixing bowl, add baby arugula, fava beans, green onions, tomatoes, cucumbers, and jalapeno.     Divide the whole salad among four containers.     Before serving, dress the salad with the vinaigrette and toss.     Add the avocado to the salad.     Enjoy!

**Nutrition Info:Per Serving:**Calories: 229, Total Fat: 11.1 g, Saturated Fat: 2.5 g, Cholesterol: 0 mg, Sodium: 24 mg, Total Carbohydrate: 32.1 g, Dietary Fiber: 12 g, Total Sugars: 10.1 g, Protein: 3 g, Vitamin D: 0 mcg, Calcium: 163 mg, Iron: 3 mg, Potassium: 1166 mg

## Quinoa Stuffed Eggplant With Tahini Sauce

Servings: 2     Cooking Time: 30 Minutes
**Ingredients:**
- 1 eggplant
- 2 tbsp olive oil, divided
- 1 medium shallot, diced, about 1/2 cup
- 1 cup chopped button mushrooms, about 2 cups whole
- 5-6 Tuttorosso whole plum tomatoes, chopped
- 1 tbsp tomato juice from the can
- 1 tbsp chopped fresh parsley, plus more to garnish
- 2 garlic cloves, minced
- 1/2 cup cooked quinoa
- 1/2 tsp ground cumin
- Salt, to taste
- Pepper, to taste
- 1 tbsp tahini
- 1 tsp lemon juice
- 1/2 tsp garlic powder
- Water to thin

**Directions:**
Preheat the oven to 425 degrees F     Prepare the eggplant by cutting it in half lengthwise and scoop out some of the flesh     Place it on a baking sheet, drizzle with 1 tbsp of oil, sprinkle with salt     Bake for 20 minutes     In the meantime, add the remaining oil in a large skillet     Once heated, add the shallots and mushrooms, sauté until mushrooms have softened, about 5 minutes     Add in the tomatoes, quinoa and spices, cook until the liquid has evaporated     Once the eggplant has cooked, reduce the oven temperature to 350 degrees F     Stuff each half with the tomato-quinoa mixture     Bake for another 10 minutes     Allow to cool completely     Distribute among the containers, store for 2 days     To Serve: Reheat in the microwave for 1-2 minutes or until heated through. Quickly whisk together tahini, lemon, garlic, water and a sprinkle of salt and pepper, drizzle tahini over eggplants and sprinkle with parsley and enjoy.

**Nutrition Info:Per Serving:** Calories:345;Carbs: 38g;Total Fat: 19g;Protein: 9g

## Lasagna

Servings: 8     Cooking Time: 1 Hour 15 Minutes
**Ingredients:**
- Lasagna noodles, oven-ready are the best, easiest, and quickest
- ⅓ cup flour
- 2 tablespoons chives, divided and chopped
- ½ cup white wine
- 2 tablespoons olive oil
- 1 ½ tablespoons thyme
- 1 teaspoon salt
- 1 ¼ cups shallots, chopped
- 1 cup boiled water
- ½ cup Parmigiano-Reggiano cheese
- 3 cups milk, reduced-fat and divided
- 1 tablespoon butter
- ⅓ cup cream cheese, less fat is the best choice
- 6 cloves of garlic, divided and minced
- ½ teaspoon ground black pepper, divided
- 4 ounces dried shiitake mushrooms, sliced
- 1 ounce dried porcini mushrooms, sliced
- 8 ounces cremini mushrooms, sliced

**Directions:**
Keeping your mushrooms separated, drain them all and return them to separate containers.     Bring 1 cup of water to a boil and cook your porcini mushrooms for a half hour.     Preheat your oven to 0 degrees Fahrenheit.     Set a large pan on your stove and turn the burner to medium-high heat.     Add your butter and let it melt.     Combine the olive oil and shallots. Stir the mixture and let it cook for 3 minutes.     Pour half of the pepper, half of the salt, and mushrooms into the pan. Allow the mixture to cook for 6 to minutes. While stirring, add half of the garlic and thyme. Continue to stir for 1 minute.     Pour the wine and turn your burner temperature to high. Let the mixture boil and watch the liquid evaporate for a couple of minutes to reduce it slightly.     Turn off the burner and remove the pan from heat.     Add the cream cheese and chives. Stir thoroughly.     Set a medium-sized skillet on medium-high heat and add 1 tablespoon of oil. Let the oil come to a simmer.     Add the last of the garlic to the pan and saute for 30 seconds.     Pour in 2 ⅓ cup milk and the liquid from the porcini mushrooms. Stir the mixture and allow it to boil.     In a bowl, combine ¼ cup of milk and the flour. Add this mixture to the heated pan. Stir until the mixture starts to thicken.     Grease a pan and add ½ cup of sauce along with a row of noodles.     Spread half of the mushroom mixture on top of the noodles.     Repeat the process, but make sure you top the lasagna with mushrooms and cheese. Turn your timer to 45 minutes and set the pan into the oven.     Remember to garnish the lasagna with chives before enjoying!

**Nutrition Info:**calories: 268, fats: 12.6 grams, carbohydrates: 29 grams, protein: 10 grams.

## Tuna With Vegetable Mix

Servings: 4     Cooking Time: 15 Minutes
**Ingredients:**
- ¼ cup extra-virgin olive oil, divided
- 1 tablespoon rice vinegar
- 1 teaspoon kosher salt, divided
- ¾ teaspoon Dijon mustard
- ¾ teaspoon honey
- 4 ounces baby gold beets, thinly sliced
- 4 ounces fennel bulb, trimmed and thinly sliced
- 4 ounces baby turnips, thinly sliced
- 6 ounces Granny Smith apple, very thinly sliced
- 2 teaspoons sesame seeds, toasted
- 6 ounces tuna steaks
- ½ teaspoon black pepper
- 1 tablespoon fennel fronds, torn

**Directions:**
In a large bowl, add 2 tablespoons of oil, ½ a teaspoon of salt, honey, vinegar, and mustard.    Give the mixture a nice mix.    Add fennel, beets, apple, and turnips; mix and toss until everything is evenly coated. Sprinkle with sesame seeds and toss well.    In a cast-iron skillet, heat 2 tablespoons of oil over high heat. Carefully season the tuna with ½ a teaspoon of salt and pepper    Place the tuna in the skillet and cook for about 3 minutes total, giving 1½ minutes per side. Remove the tuna and slice it up.    Place in containers with the vegetable mix.    Serve with the fennel mix, and enjoy!
**Nutrition Info:Per Serving:**Calories: 443, Total Fat: 17.1 g, Saturated Fat: 2.6 g, Cholesterol: 21 mg, Sodium: 728 mg, Total Carbohydrate: 62.5 g, Dietary Fiber: 12.3 g, Total Sugars: 45 g, Protein: 16.5 g, Vitamin D: 0 mcg, Calcium: 79 mg, Iron: 4 mg, Potassium: 1008 mg

## Mixed Spice Burgers

Servings: 6/2 Chops Each     Cooking Time: 25-30 Minutes
**Ingredients:**
- Medium onion (1)
- Fresh parsley (3 tbsp.)
- Clove of garlic (1)
- Ground allspice (.75 tsp.)
- Pepper (.75 tsp.)
- Ground nutmeg (.25 tsp.)
- Cinnamon (.5 tsp.)
- Salt (.5 tsp.)
- Fresh mint (2 tbsp.)
- 90% lean ground beef (1.5 lb.)
- Optional: Cold Tzatziki sauce

**Directions:**
Finely chop/mince the parsley, mint, garlic, and onions. Whisk the nutmeg, salt, cinnamon, pepper, allspice, garlic, mint, parsley, and onion.    Add the beef and prepare six (6 2x4-inch oblong patties.    Use the medium temperature setting to grill the patties or broil them four inches from the heat source for four to six minutes per side.    When they're done, the meat

thermometer will register 160° Fahrenheit. Serve with the sauce if desired.
**Nutrition Info:**Calories: 231;Protein: 32 grams;Fat: 9 grams

## Tuna Bowl With Kale

Servings: 6     Cooking Time: 15 To 20 Minutes
**Ingredients:**
- 3 tablespoons extra virgin olive oil
- 1 ½ teaspoons minced garlic
- ¼ cup of capers
- 2 teaspoons sugar
- 15 ounce can of drained and rinsed great northern beans
- 1 pound chopped kale with the center ribs removed
- ½ teaspoon ground black pepper
- 1 cup chopped onion
- 2 ½ ounces of drained sliced olives
- ¼ teaspoon sea salt
- ¼ teaspoon crushed red pepper
- 6 ounces of tuna in olive oil, do not drain

**Directions:**
Place a large pot, like a stockpot, on your stove and turn the burner to high heat.    Fill the pot about 3-quarters of the way full with water and let it come to a boil. Add the kale and cook for 2 minutes.    Drain the kale and set it aside.    Turn the heat down to medium and place the empty pot back on the burner.    Add the oil and onion. Saute for 3 to 4 minutes.    Combine the garlic into the oil mixture and saute for another minute. Add the capers, olives, and red pepper.    Cook the ingredients for another minute while stirring.    Pour in the sugar and stir while you toss in the kale. Mix all the ingredients thoroughly and ensure the kale is thoroughly coated.    Cover the pot and set the timer for 8 minutes.    Turn off the heat and add in the tuna, pepper, beans, salt, and any other herbs that will make this one of the best Mediterranean dishes you've ever made.
**Nutrition Info:**calories: 265, fats: 12 grams, carbohydrates: 26 grams, protein: 16 grams.

## Tomato Soup

Servings: 8     Cooking Time: 30 Minutes
**Ingredients:**
- 4 tablespoons olive oil
- 2 medium yellow onions, thinly sliced
- 1 teaspoon salt (extra for taste if needed)
- 2 teaspoons curry powder
- 1 teaspoon red curry powder
- 1 teaspoon ground coriander
- 1 teaspoon ground cumin
- 1/4-1/2 teaspoon red pepper flakes
- 1 15-ounce can diced tomatoes, undrained
- 1 28-ounce can diced or plum tomatoes, undrained
- 5½ cups water (vegetable broth or chicken broth also usable)
- 1 14-ounce can coconut milk
- optional add-ins: cooked brown rice, lemon wedges, fresh thyme, etc.

**Directions:**
Heat oil in a medium-sized pot over medium heat. Add onions and salt and cook for about 10-1minutes until browned.     Stir in curry powder, coriander, red pepper flakes, cumin, and cook for     seconds, being sure to keep stirring well.     Add tomatoes and water (or broth if you prefer).     Simmer the mixture for 1minutes.     Take an immersion blender and puree the mixture until a soupy consistency is achieved.     Enjoy as it is, or add some extra add-ins for a more flavorful experience.

**Nutrition Info:Per Serving:**Calories: 217, Total Fat: 19.3 g, Saturated Fat: 11.5 g, Cholesterol: 0 mg, Sodium: 40 mg, Total Carbohydrate: 12.1 g, Dietary Fiber: 3.3 g, Total Sugars: 7.1 g, Protein: 3 g, Vitamin D: 0 mcg, Calcium: 58 mg, Iron: 2 mg, Potassium: 570 mg

## Cheese Onion Soup

Servings: 4     Cooking Time: 25 Minutes
**Ingredients:**
- 2 large onions, finely sliced
- 2 cups vegetable stock
- 1 teaspoon brown sugar
- 1 cup red wine
- 1 measure of brandy
- 1 teaspoon herbs de Provence
- 4 slices stale bread
- 4 ounces grated strong cheese
- 1-ounce grated parmesan
- 1 tablespoon plain flour
- 2 tablespoons olive oil
- 1-ounce butter
- salt
- pepper

**Directions:**
Heat oil and butter in a pan over medium-high heat. Add onions and brown sugar.     Cook until the onions are golden brown.     Pour brandy and flambé, making sure to keep stirring until the flames are out.     Add plain flour and herbs de Provence and keep stirring well.     Slowly add the stock and red wine.     Season well and simmer for 20 minutes, making sure to add water if the soup becomes too thick.     Ladle the soup into jars.     Before serving, place rounds of stale bread on top.     Add strong cheese.     Garnish with some parmesan.     Place the bowls under a hot grill or in an oven until the cheese has melted.

**Nutrition Info:Per Serving:**Calories: 403, Total Fat: 22.4 g, Saturated Fat: 10.9 g, Cholesterol: 41 mg, Sodium: 886 mg, Total Carbohydrate: 24.9 g, Dietary Fiber: 3.6 g, Total Sugars: 7 g, Protein: 16.2 g, Vitamin D: 4 mcg, Calcium: 371 mg, Iron: 1 mg, Potassium: 242 mg

## Carrot Soup With Parmesan Croutons

Servings: 4     Cooking Time: 25 To 30 Minutes
**Ingredients:**
- 2 cups vegetable broth, no salt added, and low sodium is best
- 1 teaspoon dried thyme
- 1/4 teaspoon sea salt
- 1 ounce grated parmesan cheese
- 2 pounds of carrots, unpeeled
- 2 tablespoons extra virgin olive oil
- 1/2 chopped onion
- 2 1/2 cups water
- 1/4 teaspoon crushed red pepper
- 4 slices of whole-grain bread

**Directions:**
Cut your carrots into 1/2-inch slices     Take one rack from your oven and place it four inches from the broiler heating element. One either rack, place two large-rimmed baking sheets and turn your oven to 450 degrees Fahrenheit.     Add 1 tablespoon of oil and carrots into a large bowl. Stir the carrots around so they become coated with the oil.     Using oven mitts, remove the baking pans and distribute the carrots onto them.     Place the pans back into the oven and turn your timer on for 20 minutes or until the carrots become tender.     Take the carrots out of the oven. Turn your oven to broiler mode.     Set a large stockpot on your stove and turn the range to medium-high. Pour in the remaining olive oil and the onion. Let it cook for 5 minutes while stirring occasionally.     Pour in the broth, thyme, water, crushed red pepper, and sea salt. Stir well.     Let the mixture cook until the ingredients come to a boil.     Once the carrots are done in the oven, add them to the pot.     Remove the pot from the heat and carefully pour the soup into a blender. You will want to pour it in batches and remember to hold the lid of the blender with a rag and release the steam after 30 seconds, so it doesn't explode. Once all the soup is mixed, add it all back into the pot and turn the range heat to medium. Cook until the soup is warm again.     Spread a piece of parchment paper on top of a baking sheet, set the four pieces of bread on the paper.     Sprinkle cheese across the slices and set them on the top rack in your oven.     Turn your oven to broil and let the slices of bread roast for a couple of minutes. Once the cheese is melted, remove the bread from the oven so they don't burn.     Chop the bread into croutons.     Divide the soup into serving bowls, add the croutons, and enjoy!

**Nutrition Info:**calories: 272, fats: 10 grams, carbohydrates: 38 grams, protein: 10 grams.

## Greek Baked Cod

Servings: 4     Cooking Time: 12 Minutes
**Ingredients:**
- 1 ½ lb Cod fillet pieces (4–6 pieces)
- 5 garlic cloves, peeled and minced
- 1/4 cup chopped fresh parsley leaves
- Lemon Juice Mixture:
- 5 tbsp fresh lemon juice
- 5 tbsp extra virgin olive oil
- 2 tbsp melted vegan butter
- For Coating:
- 1/3 cup all-purpose flour
- 1 tsp ground coriander
- 3/4 tsp sweet Spanish paprika
- 3/4 tsp ground cumin
- 3/4 tsp salt
- 1/2 tsp black pepper

**Directions:**
Preheat oven to 400 degrees F     In a bowl, mix together lemon juice, olive oil, and melted butter, set aside     In another shallow bowl, mix all-purpose flour, spices, salt and pepper, set next to the lemon bowl to create a station     Pat the fish fillet dry, then dip the fish in the lemon juice mixture then dip it in the flour mixture, shake off excess flour     In a cast iron skillet over medium-high heat, add 2 tbsp olive oil     Once heated, add in the fish and sear on each side for color, but do not fully cook (just couple minutes on each side), remove from heat     With the remaining lemon juice mixture, add the minced garlic and mix     Drizzle all over the fish fillets     Bake for 10 minutes, for until the it begins to flake easily with a fork     allow the dish to cool completely     Distribute among the containers, store for 2-3 days     To Serve: Reheat in the microwave for 1-2 minutes or until heated through. Sprinkle chopped parsley. Enjoy!
**Nutrition Info:Per Serving:** Calories:321;Carbs: 16g;Total Fat: 18g;Protein: 23g

## Pistachio Sole Fish

Servings: 4     Cooking Time: 10 Minutes
**Ingredients:**
- 4 (5 ounces boneless sole fillets
- Salt and pepper as needed
- ½ cup pistachios, finely chopped
- Zest of 1 lemon
- Juice of 1 lemon
- 1 teaspoon extra virgin olive oil

**Directions:**
Pre-heat your oven to 350 degrees Fahrenheit     Line a baking sheet with parchment paper and keep it on the side     Pat fish dry with kitchen towels and lightly season with salt and pepper     Take a small bowl and stir in pistachios and lemon zest     Place sol on the prepped sheet and press 2 tablespoons of pistachio mixture on top of each fillet     Drizzle fish with lemon juice and olive oil     Bake for 10 minutes until the top is golden and fish flakes with a fork     Serve and enjoy!

Meal Prep/Storage Options: Store in airtight containers in your fridge for 1-2 days.
**Nutrition Info:**Calories: 166;Fat: 6g;Carbohydrates: 2g;Protein: 26g

## Beef Tomato Soup

Servings: 6     Cooking Time: 1 Hour
**Ingredients:**
- 1 pound lean ground beef
- 1 medium onion, chopped
- 1 large green pepper, chopped
- 2 minced garlic cloves
- 1 large tomato, chopped
- 2 tablespoons tomato paste
- 2 tablespoons all-purpose flour
- ¼ cup uncooked rice
- 2 tablespoons fresh chopped parsley (additional for garnish)
- 4 cups beef broth
- 2 tablespoons olive oil
- salt
- pepper

**Directions:**
Add oil to large pot and heat over medium heat.     Add flour and keep whisking until thick paste forms.     Keep whisking for 4 minutes while it bubbles and begins to thin.     Add onions and sauté for 3-minutes.     Stir in tomato paste and ground beef, breaking up ground beef with a wooden spoon.     Cook for about 5 minutes. Add garlic, peppers, and tomatoes.     Mix well until thoroughly combined.     Add broth and bring the mixture to a light boil.     Reduce heat to low, cover, and simmer for 30 minutes, making sure to stir from time to time.     Add rice and parsley and cook for another 15 minutes.     Once the soup has achieved its desired consistency, serve with a garnish of parsley.     This soup is best enjoyed with some crispy bread or boiled potatoes.
**Nutrition Info:Per Serving:**Calories: 268, Total Fat: 10.6 g, Saturated Fat: 2.8 g, Cholesterol: 68 mg, Sodium: 568 mg, Total Carbohydrate: 3 g, Dietary Fiber: 1.7 g, Total Sugars: 3.4 g, Protein: 28 g, Vitamin D: 0 mcg, Calcium: 25 mg, Iron: 15 mg, Potassium: 665 mg

## Baked Tilapia

Servings: 4     Cooking Time: 15 Minutes
**Ingredients:**
- 1 lb tilapia fillets (about 8 fillets)
- 1 tsp olive oil
- 1 tbsp vegan butter
- 2 shallots finely chopped
- 3 garlic cloves minced
- 1 1/2 tsp ground cumin
- 1 1/2 tsp paprika
- 1/4 cup capers
- 1/4 cup fresh dill finely chopped
- Juice from 1 lemon
- Salt & Pepper to taste

**Directions:**
Preheat oven to 375 degrees F     Line a rimmed baking sheet with parchment paper or foil     Lightly mist with cooking spray, arrange the fish fillets evenly on baking sheet     In a small bowl, combine the cumin, paprika, salt and pepper     Season both sides of the fish fillets with the spice mixture     In a small bowl, whisk together the melted butter, lemon juice, shallots, olive oil, and garlic, and brush evenly over fish fillets     Top with the capers     Bake in the oven for 10-15 minutes, until cook through, but not overcooked     Remove from oven and allow the dish to cool completely     Distribute among the containers, store for 2-3 days     To Serve: Reheat in the microwave for 1-2 minutes or until heated through. Top with fresh dill. Serve!
**Nutrition Info:Per Serving:** Calories:;Total Fat: 5g;Protein: 21g

## Herbal Lamb Cutlets With Roasted Veggies

Servings: 6     Cooking Time: 45 Minutes
**Ingredients:**
- 2 deseeded peppers, cut up into chunks
- 1 large sweet potato, peeled and chopped
- 2 sliced courgettes
- 1 red onion, cut into wedges
- 1 tablespoon olive oil
- 8 lean lamb cutlets
- 1 tablespoon thyme leaf, chopped
- 2 tablespoons mint leaves, chopped

**Directions:**
Preheat oven to 390degrees F.     In a large baking dish, place peppers, courgettes, sweet potatoes, and onion. Drizzle all with oil and season with ground pepper. Roast for about 25 minutes     Trim as much fat off the lamb as possible.     Mix in herbs with a few twists of ground black pepper.     Take the veggies out of the oven and push to one side of a baking dish.     Place lamb cutlets on another side, return to oven, and roast for another 10 minutes.     Turn the cutlets over, cook for another 10 minutes, and until the veggies are ready (lightly charred and tender).     Mix everything on the tray and spread over containers.
**Nutrition Info:Per Serving:** Calories: 268, Total Fat: 9.2 g, Saturated Fat: 3 g, Cholesterol: 100 mg, Sodium: mg, Total Carbohydrate: 10.7 g, Dietary Fiber: 2.4 g, Total Sugars: 4.1 g, Protein: 32.4 g, Vitamin D: 0 mcg, Calcium: 20 mg, Iron: 4 mg, Potassium: 365 mg

## A Great Mediterranean Snapper

Servings: 2     Cooking Time: 10 Minutes
**Ingredients:**
- 2 tablespoons extra virgin olive oil
- 1 medium onion, chopped
- 2 garlic cloves, minced
- 1 teaspoon oregano
- 1 can (14 ounces tomatoes, diced with juice
- 1/2 cup black olives, sliced
- 4 red snapper fillets (each 4 ounce
- Salt and pepper as needed
- Garnish
- 1/4 cup feta cheese, crumbled
- 1/4 cup parsley, minced

**Directions:**
Pre-heat your oven to a temperature of 425-degree Fahrenheit     Take a 13x9 inch baking dish and grease it up with non-stick cooking spray     Take a large sized skillet and place it over medium heat     Add oil and heat it up     Add onion, oregano and garlic     Saute for 2 minutes     Add diced tomatoes with juice alongside black olives     Bring the mix to a boil     Remove the heat     Place the fish on the prepped baking dish     Season both sides with salt and pepper     Spoon the tomato mix over the fish     Bake for 10 minutes     Remove the oven and sprinkle a bit of parsley and feta     Enjoy!     Meal Prep/Storage Options: Store in airtight containers in your fridge for 1-3 days.
**Nutrition Info:**Calories: 269;Fat: 13g;Carbohydrates: 10g;Protein: 27g

## Mediterranean Snapper

Servings: 4     Cooking Time: 12 Minutes
**Ingredients:**
- non-stick cooking spray
- 2 tablespoons extra virgin olive oil
- 1 medium onion, chopped
- 2 garlic cloves, minced
- 1 teaspoon oregano
- 1 14-ounce can diced tomatoes, undrained
- 1/2 cup black olives, sliced
- 4 4-ounce red snapper fillets
- salt
- pepper
- 1/4 cup crumbled feta cheese
- 1/4 cup fresh parsley, minced

**Directions:**
Preheat oven to 425 degrees Fahrenheit.     Grease a 13x9 baking dish with non-stick cooking spray.     Heat oil in a large skillet over medium heat.     Add onion, oregano, garlic, and sauté for 2 minutes.     Add can of tomatoes and olives, and bring mixture to a boil; remove from heat.     Season both sides of fillets with salt and pepper and place in the baking dish.     Spoon the tomato mixture evenly over the fish.     Bake for 10 minutes.     Remove from oven and sprinkle with parsley and feta.     Enjoy!
**Nutrition Info:Per Serving:**Calories: 257, Total Fat: g, Saturated Fat: 1.7 g, Cholesterol: 53 mg, Sodium: 217 mg, Total Carbohydrate: 8.2 g, Dietary Fiber: 2.5 g, Total Sugars: 3.8 g, Protein: 31.3 g, Vitamin D: 0 mcg, Calcium: 85 mg, Iron: 1 mg, Potassium: 881 mg

## Italian Skillet Chicken With Mushrooms And Tomatoes

Servings: 4    Cooking Time: 20 Minutes
**Ingredients:**
- 4 large chicken cutlets, boneless skinless chicken breasts cut into 1/4-inch thin cutlets
- 1 tbsp dried oregano, divided
- 1/2 cup all-purpose flour, more for later
- 8 oz Baby Bella mushrooms, cleaned, trimmed, and sliced
- 14 oz grape tomatoes, halved
- 2 tbsp chopped fresh garlic
- Extra Virgin Olive Oil
- 1/2 cup white wine
- 1 tbsp freshly squeezed lemon juice, juice of 1/2 lemon
- 1 tsp salt, divided
- 1 tsp black pepper, divided
- 3/4 cup chicken broth
- Handful baby spinach, optional

**Directions:**
Pat the chicken cutlets dry, season both sides with 2 tsp salt, 1/2 tsp black pepper, 1/2 tbsp dried oregano, Coat the chicken cutlets with the flour, gently dust-off excess and set aside    In a large cast iron skillet with a lid, heat 2 tbsp olive oil    Once heated, brown the chicken cutlets on both sides, for about 3 minutes, then transfer the chicken cutlets to plate    In the same skillet, add more olive oil if needed,    Once heated, add in the mushrooms and sauté on medium-high for about 1 minute    Then add the tomatoes, garlic, the remaining 1/2 tbsp oregano, 1/2 tsp salt, and 1/2 tsp pepper, and 2 tsp flour, cook for 3 minutes or so, stirring regularly    Add in the white wine, cook briefly to reduce, then add the lemon juice and chicken broth Bring the liquid to a boil, then transfer the chicken back into the skillet, cook over high heat for 3-4 minutes, then reduce the heat to medium-low, cover and cook for another 8 minutes or until the chicken is cooked through    Allow the dish to cool completely Distribute among the containers, store for 3 days    To Serve: Reheat in the microwave for 1-2 minutes or until heated through. Serve with baby spinach, your favorite small pasta and a crusty Italian bread!
**Nutrition Info:Per Serving:** Calories:218;Carbs: 16g;Total Fat: 6g;Protein: 23g

## Red Wine–braised Pot Roast With Carrots And Mushrooms

Servings: 4    Cooking Time: 25 Minutes
**Ingredients:**
- 1 pound tri-tip roast
- 1/4 teaspoon kosher salt
- 1 tablespoon olive oil
- 2 cups chopped onion
- 1 teaspoon chopped garlic
- 3 medium carrots, cut into 1/2-inch pieces (2 cups)
- 2 large celery stalks, cut into 1/2-inch pieces (1 cup)
- 8 ounces button or cremini mushrooms, halved
- 1/2 teaspoon fennel seed
- 1/2 teaspoon dried thyme
- 1/2 teaspoon dried oregano
- 1 (14.5-ounce) can no-salt-added diced tomatoes
- 1 cup dry red wine, such as red zinfandel or cabernet sauvignon
- 1 cup reduced-sodium beef broth

**Directions:**
Preheat the oven to 325°F.    Season the roast with the salt.    Heat the oil in a Dutch oven or heavy-bottomed soup pot over high heat. Once the oil is hot, add the roast and brown for minutes on each side. Remove the roast to a plate.    Add the onion, garlic, carrots, celery, and mushrooms to the pot and cook for 5 minutes. Add the fennel seed, thyme, oregano, tomatoes, red wine, and broth and bring to a simmer. Cover the pot with a tight-fitting lid or foil and place in the oven. Cook until the meat is very tender, about 3 hours.    Remove the roast to a plate and spoon the vegetables into a bowl with a slotted spoon. Place the pot on high heat and reduce the liquid by half, about 10 minutes. If your pot is extra wide, it will take less time for the liquid to reduce. Add more salt if needed.    After the meat has cooled, cut 12 slices against the grain. Place 3 slices, 3/4 cup of vegetables, and 1/3 cup of sauce in each of 4 containers.    STORAGE: Store covered containers in the refrigerator for up to 5 days.
**Nutrition Info:Per Serving:** Total calories: 366; Total fat: 14g; Saturated fat: 4g; Sodium: 468mg; Carbohydrates: 23g; Fiber: 6g; Protein: 28g

## Zoodles With Turkey Meatballs

Servings: 4-6    Cooking Time: 30 Minutes
**Ingredients:**
- 2 lbs (3 medium-sized) zucchini, spiralized
- 2 cups marinara sauce, store-bought
- 1/4 cup freshly grated Parmesan cheese
- 2 tsp salt
- For The Meatballs:
- 1 ½ lbs ground turkey
- 1/2 cup Panko
- 1/4 cup freshly grated Parmesan cheese
- 2 large egg yolks
- 1 tsp dried oregano
- 1 tsp dried basil
- 1/2 tsp dried parsley
- 1/4 tsp garlic powder
- 1/4 tsp crushed red pepper flakes
- Kosher salt, to taste
- Freshly ground black pepper, to taste

**Directions:**
Preheat oven to 400 degrees F    Lightly oil a 9×13 baking dish or spray with nonstick spray    In a large bowl, combine the ground turkey, egg yolks, oregano, basil, Panko, Parmesan, parsley, garlic powder and red pepper flakes, season the mixture with salt and pepper, to taste    Use a wooden spoon or clean hands, stir well to combined    Roll the mixture into 1 1/2-to-2-inch meatballs, forming about 24 meatballs    Place the meatballs onto the prepared baking dish    Bake for 18-20 minutes, or until browned and the meatballs are cooked through, set aside    Place the zucchini in a colander over the sink, add the salt and gently toss to combine, allow to sit for 10 minutes    In a large pot of boiling water, cook zucchini for 30 seconds to 1 minute, drain well    Allow to cool, then distribute the zucchini into the containers, top with the meatballs, marinara sauce and the Parmesan. Store in the fridge for up to 4 days    To Serve: Reheat in the microwave for 1-2 minutes or until heated through and enjoy!
**Nutrition Info:Per Serving:** Calories:279;Total Fat: 13g;Total Carbs: ;Fiber: 3g;Protein: 31g

## Italian Platter

Servings: 2    Cooking Time: 45 Minutes
**Ingredients:**
- 1 garlic clove, minced
- 5-ounce fresh button mushrooms, sliced
- 1/8 cup unsalted butter
- ¼ teaspoon dried thyme
- 1/3 cup heavy whipping cream
- Salt and black pepper, to taste
- 2 (6-ounce grass-fed New York strip steaks

**Directions:**
Preheat the grill to medium heat and grease it. Season the steaks with salt and black pepper, and transfer to the grill.    Grill steaks for about 10 minutes on each side and dish out in a platter.    Put butter, mushrooms, salt and black pepper in a pan and cook for about 10 minutes.    Add thyme and garlic and thyme and sauté for about 1 minute.    Stir in the cream and let it simmer for about 5 minutes.    Top the steaks with mushroom sauce and serve hot immediately. Meal Prep Tip: You can store the mushroom sauce in refrigerator for about 2 days. Season the steaks carefully with salt and black pepper to avoid low or high quantities.
**Nutrition Info:**Calories: 332 ;Carbohydrates: 3.2g;Protein: 41.8g;Fat: 20.5g ;Sugar: 1.3g;Sodium: 181mg

## Mediterranean Pizza

Servings: 4 To 8    Cooking Time: 20 Minutes
**Ingredients:**
- 1/2 cup artichoke hearts
- Whole-wheat premade pizza crust
- 1 cup pesto sauce
- 1 cup spinach leaves
- 3 to 4 ounces of feta cheese
- 1 cup sun-dried tomatoes
- 3 ounces of mozzarella cheese
- ½ cup of olives
- Olive oil
- ½ cup bell peppers
- Chopped chicken, pepperoni, or salami

**Directions:**
Turn the temperature of your oven to 350 degrees Fahrenheit.    Use olive oil to brush the top of the whole wheat pizza crust.    Brush the pesto sauce on the pizza crust.    Top with all of the ingredients. You can start with the cheese or mix the ingredients in any way you wish. You can even get a little creative and have fun.    Set your pizza on a pizza pan or directly on your oven rack.    Set your timer to 10 minutes, but watch the pizza carefully so you do not burn the cheese. Remove the pizza and let it cool down for a couple of minutes, then enjoy!
**Nutrition Info:**calories: 300, fats: 11 grams, carbohydrates: 29 grams, protein: 14 grams.

## Roasted Vegetable Quinoa Bowl

Servings: 2     Cooking Time: 20 Minutes
**Ingredients:**
- Quinoa:
- ¾ cup quinoa, rinsed
- 1 ½ cups
- vegetable broth
- Chili-Lime Kale
- 1/2 tsp chili powder
- pinch salt
- pinch pepper
- 2 cups packed kale, de-stemmed and chopped
- 1 tsp olive, coconut or canola oil
- Juice of 1/4 lime
- Garlic Roasted Broccoli:
- 2 cups broccoli,
- 2 tsp olive or canola oil
- 2 cloves garlic, minced
- Pinch of salt
- Black pepper
- Curry Roasted Sweet Potatoes:
- 1 small sweet potato
- 1 tsp olive or canola oil
- 1 tsp curry powder
- 1 tsp sriracha
- Pinch salt
- Spicy Roasted Chickpeas:
- 1 ½ cups (cooked) chickpeas
- 1 tsp olive or canola oil
- 2 tsp sriracha
- 2 tsp soy sauce
- Optional:
- Lime
- Avocado
- Hummus
- Red pepper flakes
- Guacamole

**Directions:**
Preheat the oven to 400-degree F     Line a large baking sheet with parchment paper     Prepare the vegetables by chopping the broccoli into medium sized florets, de-stemming and chopping the kale, scrubbing and slicing the sweet potato into ¼" wide rounds     Take the broccoli florets and massage with oil, garlic, salt and pepper - making sure to work the ingredients into the tops of each florets - Place the florets in a row down in the center third of a large baking sheet     Using the same bowl, the broccoli in, mix together the chickpeas, oil, sriracha and soy sauce, then spread them out in a row next to the broccoli     In the same bowl combine the oil, curry powder, salt, and sriracha, add the sliced sweet potato and toss to coat, then lay the rounds on the remaining third of the baking tray     Bake for 10 minutes, flip the sweet potatoes and broccoli, and redistribute the chickpeas to cook evenly Bake for another 8-12 minutes     For the Quinoa: Prepare the quinoa by rinsing and draining it. Add the rinsed quinoa and vegetable broth to a small saucepan and bring to a boil over high heat. Turn the heat down to medium-low, cover and allow to simmer for about 15 minutes. Once cooked, fluff with a fork and set aside In the meantime, place a large skillet with 1 tsp oil, add in the kale and cook for about 5 minutes, or until nearly tender     Add in the salt, chili powder, and lime juice, toss to coat and cook for another 2-3 minutes     Allow all the ingredient to cool     Distribute among the containers – Add ½ to 1 cup of quinoa into each bowl, top with ½ of the broccoli, ½ kale, ½ the chickpeas and ½ sweet potatoes     To Serve: Reheat in the microwave for 1-2 minutes or until heated through. Enjoy
**Nutrition Info:Per Serving:** Calories:611;Carbs: 93g;Total Fat: 17g;Protein: 24g

## Mediterranean Salmon

Servings: 4     Cooking Time: 15 Minutes
**Ingredients:**
- ½ cup of olive oil
- ¼ cup balsamic vinegar
- 4 garlic cloves, pressed
- 4 pieces salmon fillets
- 1 tablespoon fresh cilantro, chopped
- 1 tablespoon fresh basil, chopped
- 1½ teaspoons garlic salt

**Directions:**
Combine olive oil and balsamic vinegar.     Add salmon fillets to a shallow baking dish.     Rub the garlic onto the fillets.     Pour vinegar and oil all over, making sure to turn them once to coat them.     Season with cilantro, garlic salt, and basil.     Set aside and allow to marinate for about 10 minutes.     Preheat the broiler to your oven.     Place the baking dish with the salmon about 6 inches from the heat source.     Broil for 15 minutes until both sides are evenly browned and can be flaked with a fork.     Make sure to keep brushing with sauce from the pan.     Enjoy!
**Nutrition Info:Per Serving:** Calories: 459, Total Fat: 36.2 g, Saturated Fat: 5.2 g, Cholesterol: 78 mg, Sodium: 80 mg, Total Carbohydrate: 1.2 g, Dietary Fiber: 0.1 g, Total Sugars: 0.1 g, Protein: 34.8 g, Vitamin D: 0 mcg, Calcium: 71 mg, Iron: 1 mg, Potassium: 710 mg

## Heartthrob Mediterranean Tilapia

Servings: 4     Cooking Time: 15 Minutes
**Ingredients:**
- 3 tablespoons sun-dried tomatoes, packed in oil, drained and chopped
- 1 tablespoon capers, drained
- 2 tilapia fillets
- 1 tablespoon oil from sun-dried tomatoes
- 1 tablespoon lemon juice
- 2 tablespoons kalamata olives, chopped and pitted

**Directions:**
Pre-heat your oven to 372-degree Fahrenheit     Take a small sized bowl and add sun-dried tomatoes, olives, capers and stir well     Keep the mixture on the side Take a baking sheet and transfer the tilapia fillets and arrange them side by side     Drizzle olive oil all over them     Drizzle lemon juice     Bake in your oven for 10-15 minutes     After 10 minutes, check the fish for a "Flaky" texture     Once cooked properly, top the fish with tomato mix and serve!     Meal Prep/Storage Options: Store in airtight containers in your fridge for 1-3 days.
**Nutrition Info:** Calories: 183;Fat: 8g;Carbohydrates: 18g;Protein:183g

## Garlic And Cajun Shrimp Bowl With Noodles

Servings: 2    Cooking Time: 15 Minutes
**Ingredients:**
- 1 sliced onion
- 1 tablespoon almond butter, but you can use regular butter as well
- 1 teaspoon onion powder
- ½ teaspoon salt
- 1 sliced red pepper
- 3 cloves of minced garlic
- 1 teaspoon paprika
- 20 jumbo shrimp, deveined and shells removed
- 3 tablespoons of ghee
- 2 zucchini, 3 if they are smaller in size, cut into noodles
- Red pepper flakes and cayenne pepper, as desired

**Directions:**
In a small bowl, mix the pepper flakes, paprika, onion powder, salt, and cayenne pepper.    Toss the shrimp into the cajun mixture and coat the seafood thoroughly. Add the ghee to a medium or large skillet and place on medium-low heat.    Once the ghee is melted, add the garlic and saute for minutes.    Carefully add the shrimp into the skillet and cook until they are opaque. Set the pan aside.    In a new pan, add the butter and allow it to melt.    Combine the zucchini noodles and cook on medium-low heat for 3 to 4 minutes.    Turn off the heat and place the zucchini noodles on serving dishes. Add the shrimp to the top and enjoy.

**Nutrition Info:**calories: 712, fats: 30 grams, carbohydrates: 20.1 grams, protein: grams.

## Garlic Marinated Chicken

Servings: 3    Cooking Time: 15 Minutes
**Ingredients:**
- 1 ½ lbs. boneless skinless chicken breasts,
- 1/4 cup olive oil
- 1/4 cup lemon juice
- 3 cloves garlic, minced
- 1/2 tbsp dried oregano
- 1/2 tsp salt
- Freshly cracked pepper
- To Serve:
- Rice or cauliflower rice
- Roasted vegetables, such as carrots, asparagus, or green beans

**Directions:**
In a large Ziplock bag or dish, add in the olive oil, lemon juice, garlic, oregano, salt, and pepper    Close the bag and shake the ingredients to combine, or stir the ingredients in the dish until well combined    Filet each chicken breast into two thinner pieces and place the pieces in the bag or dish - make sure the chicken is completely covered in marinade and allow to marinate for up to    minutes up to 8 hours, turn occasionally to maximize the marinade flavors    Once ready, heat a large skillet over medium heat    Once heated, transfer the chicken from the marinade to the hot skillet and cook on each side cooked through, about 7 minutes each side, depending on the size - Discard of any excess marinade    Transfer the cooked chicken from the skillet to a clean cutting board, allow to rest for five minutes before slicing    Distribute the chicken, cooked rice and vegetables among the containers. Store in the fridge for up to 4 days.    To Serve: Reheat in the microwave for 1-2 minutes or until heated through and enjoy!

**Nutrition Info:Per Serving:** Calories:446;Total Fat: 24g;Total Carbs: 4g;Fiber: 0g;Protein: 52g

## Tabouli Salad

Servings: 6    Cooking Time:30 Minutes
**Ingredients:**
- ½ cup extra fine bulgar wheat
- 4 firm Roma tomatoes, finely chopped, juice drained
- 1 English cucumber, finely chopped
- 2 bunches fresh parsley, stems removed, finely chopped
- 12-15 fresh mint leaves, finely chopped
- 4 green onions, finely chopped (white and green)
- salt
- 3-4 tablespoons lime juice
- 3-4 tablespoons extra virgin olive oil
- Romaine lettuce leaves
- pita bread

**Directions:**
Wash bulgur wheat thoroughly and allow it to soak under water for 5 minutes.    Drain bulgur wheat well and set aside.    Add all vegetables, green onions, and herbs to a dish.    Add bulgur and season the mixture with salt.    Add limejuice and olive oil. Mix well.    Put to the jars and refrigerate.    Transfer to a serving platter and serve with sides of pita and romaine lettuce.

**Nutrition Info:Per Serving:**Calories: 136, Total Fat: 7.6 g, Saturated Fat: 1.1 g, Cholesterol: 0 mg, Sodium: 72 mg, Total Carbohydrate: 15.6 g, Dietary Fiber: 3.7 g, Total Sugars: 3.6 g, Protein: 3.4 g, Vitamin D: 0 mcg, Calcium: 71 mg, Iron: 3 mg, Potassium: 439 mg

## Mediterranean Flounder

Servings: 4     Cooking Time: 45 Minutes
**Ingredients:**
- Roma or plum tomatoes (5)
- Extra-virgin olive oil (2 tbsp.)
- Spanish onion (half of 1)
- Garlic (2 cloves)
- Italian seasoning (1 pinch)
- Kalamata olives (24)
- White wine (.25 cup)
- Capers (.25 cup)
- Lemon juice (1 tsp.)
- Chopped basil (6 leaves)
- Freshly grated parmesan cheese (3 tbsp.)
- Flounder fillets (1 lb.)
- Freshly torn basil (6 leaves)

**Directions:**
Set the oven to reach 425° Fahrenheit. Remove the pit and chop the olives (set aside.     Pour water into a saucepan and bring to boiling. Plunge the tomatoes into the water and remove immediately. Add to a dish of ice water and drain. Remove the skins, chop, and set to the side for now.     Heat a skillet with the oil using the medium temperature heat setting. Chop and toss in the onions. Sauté them for around four minutes.     Dice and add the garlic, tomatoes, and seasoning. Simmer for five to seven minutes.     Stir in the capers, wine, olives, half of the basil, and freshly squeezed lemon juice.     Lower the heat setting and blend in the cheese. Simmer it until the sauce is thickened (15 min..     Arrange the flounder into a shallow baking tin. Add the sauce and garnish with the remainder of the basil leaves.     Set the timer to bake it for 12 minutes until the fish is easily flaked.
**Nutrition Info:** Calories: 282;Protein: 24.4 grams;Fat: 15.4 grams

## Greek Lemon Chicken Soup

Servings: 8     Cooking Time: 20 Minutes
**Ingredients:**
- 10 cups chicken broth
- 3 tbsp olive oil
- 8 cloves garlic, minced
- 1 sweet onion
- 1 large lemon, zested
- 2 boneless skinless chicken breasts
- 1 cup Israeli couscous (pearl)
- 1/2 tsp crushed red pepper
- 2 oz crumbled feta
- 1/3 cup chopped chive
- Salt, to taste
- Pepper, to taste

**Directions:**
In a large 6-8-quart sauce pot over medium-low heat, add the olive oil     Once heated, sauté the onion and minced the garlic for 3-4 minutes to soften     Then add in the chicken broth, raw chicken breasts, lemon zest, and crushed red pepper to the pot Raise the heat to high, cover, and bring to a boil     Once boiling, reduce the heat to medium, then simmer for 5 minutes     Stir in the couscous, 1 tsp salt, and black pepper to taste Simmer another 5 minute, then turn the heat off Using tongs, remove the two chicken breasts from the pot and transfer to a plate     Use a fork and the tongs to shred the chicken, then return to the pot     Stir in the crumbled feta cheese and chopped chive     Season to taste with salt and pepper as needed     Allow the soup to cool completely     Distribute among the containers, store for 2-3 days     To Serve: Reheat in the microwave for 1-2 minutes or until heated through, or reheat on the stove
**Nutrition Info:Per Serving:** Calories:2Carbs: 23g;Total Fat: g;Protein: 11g

## Mediterranean Steamed Salmon With Fresh Herbs And Lemon

Servings: 4     Cooking Time: 15 Minutes
**Ingredients:**
- 1 yellow onion, halved and sliced
- 4 green onions spring onions, trimmed and sliced lengthwise, divided
- 1 lb skin-on salmon fillet (such as wild Alaskan), cut into 4 portions
- 1/2 tsp Aleppo pepper
- 4 to 5 garlic cloves, chopped
- Extra virgin olive oil
- A large handful fresh parsley
- 1 lemon, thinly sliced
- 1 tsp ground coriander
- 1 tsp ground cumin
- 1/2 cup white wine (or you can use water or low-sodium broth, if you prefer)
- Kosher salt, to taste
- Black pepper, to taste

**Directions:**
Prepare a large piece of wax paper or parchment paper (about 2 feet long) and place it right in the center of a - inch deep pan or braiser     Place the sliced yellow onions and a sprinkle a little bit of green onions the onions on the bottom of the braiser     Arrange the salmon, skin-side down, on top, season with kosher salt and black pepper     In a small bowl, mix together the coriander, cumin, and Aleppo pepper, coat top of salmon with the spice mixture, and drizzle with a little bit of extra virgin olive oil     Then add garlic, parsley and the remaining green onions on top of the salmon (make sure that everything is arrange evenly over the salmon portions.)     Arrange the lemon slices on top of the salmon     Add another drizzle of extra virgin olive oil, then add the white wine     Fold the parchment paper over to cover salmon, secure the edges and cover the braiser with the lid     Place the braising pan over medium-high heat, cook for 5 minutes     Lower the heat to medium, cook for another 8 minutes, covered still     Remove from heat and allow to rest undisturbed for about 5 minutes.     Remove the lid and allow the salmon to cool completely     Distribute among the containers, store for 2-3 days     To Serve: Reheat in the microwave for 1-2 minutes or until heated through. Recipe Notes: The pan or braiser you use needs to have a lid to allow the steamed salmon.
**Nutrition Info:Per Serving:** Calories:321;Carbs: g;Total Fat: 18g;Protein: 28g

## Beef Sausage Pancakes

Servings: 2    Cooking Time: 30 Minutes
**Ingredients:**
- 4 gluten-free Italian beef sausages, sliced
- 1 tablespoon olive oil
- 1/3 large red bell peppers, seeded and sliced thinly
- 1/3 cup spinach
- ¾ teaspoon garlic powder
- 1/3 large green bell peppers, seeded and sliced thinly
- ¾ cup heavy whipped cream
- Salt and black pepper, to taste

**Directions:**
Mix together all the ingredients in a bowl except whipped cream and keep aside.     Put butter and half of the mixture in a skillet and cook for about 6 minutes on both sides.     Repeat with the remaining mixture and dish out.     Beat whipped cream in another bowl until smooth.     Serve the beef sausage pancakes with whipped cream.     For meal prepping, it is compulsory to gently slice the sausages before mixing with other ingredients.

**Nutrition Info:**Calories: 415 ;Carbohydrates: ;Protein: 29.5g;Fat: 31.6g ;Sugar: 4.3g;Sodium: 1040mg

## Grilled Salmon Tzatziki Bowl

Servings: 2    Cooking Time: 15 Minutes
**Ingredients:**
- 8–10 ounces salmon, serves 2
- Olive oil for brushing
- Salt and pepper
- 1 lemon- sliced in half
- Tzatziki:
- ½ cup plain yogurt
- ½ cup sour cream
- 1 garlic clove- finely minced
- 1 tbsp lemon juice, more to taste
- 1 tbsp olive oil
- ½ tsp kosher salt
- ¼ tsp white pepper or black
- ⅛ cup fresh chopped dill (or mint, cilantro or Italian parsley – or a mix)
- 1 ½ cups finely sliced or diced cucumber
- Optional Bowl Additions:
- Cooked Quinoa or rice
- Arugula or other greens
- Grilled veggies like eggplant, peppers, tomatoes, or zucchini
- Fresh veggies of your choice - radishes, cucumber, tomatoes, sprouts
- Garnish with olive oil, lemon, and fresh herbs

**Directions:**
Preheat heat grill to medium high     Cook 1 cup quinoa or rice on the stove, according to directions, allow to cool     Brush the salmon with olive oil, season with salt and pepper, set aside     Create the Tzatziki, by adding plain yogurt, sour cream, garlic clove, lemon juice, olive oil, kosher salt, and white pepper in a bowl, taste and add more lemon juice if desired, store in fridge     Place the salmon on the grill, along with the veggies of you choose to grill, brushing all with olive oil, salt and pepper     Grill the salmon on both sides for 3-4 minutes, or until cooked through     Then grill the lemon, open side down, until good grill marks appear     Once the veggies and salmon are done, allow them to cool     Distribute among the containers - Divide quinoa among the containers, arrange the grilled vegetables and salmon over top.     To Serve: Reheat in the microwave for 1 minute or until heated through. Top with the greens and the fresh veggies, then drizzle a little olive oil on top and season with salt, squeeze the grilled lemon over the whole bowl, spoon the tzatziki over top the salmon, sprinkle with the fresh dill or other herbs. Enjoy with a glass of wine.

**Nutrition Info:Per Serving:** Calories:458;Carbs: 29g;Total Fat: 24g;Protein: 30g

## Smoky Chickpea, Chard, And Butternut Squash Soup

Servings: 8    Cooking Time: 35 Minutes
**Ingredients:**
- 2 slices bacon (about 1 ounce), chopped
- 1 cup chopped onion
- 1 teaspoon chopped garlic
- 1 teaspoon smoked paprika
- ½ teaspoon kosher salt
- 2 teaspoons fresh thyme leaves, roughly chopped
- 1½ pounds butternut squash, peeled, seeded, and cut into 1-inch cubes
- 1 large bunch chard, stems and leaves chopped
- 2 (15.5-oz) cans low-sodium chickpeas, drained and rinsed
- 32 ounces low-sodium chicken broth
- 1 tablespoon freshly squeezed lemon juice
- 8 teaspoons grated Parmesan or Pecorino Romano cheese for garnish

**Directions:**
Place a soup pot, at least 4½ quarts in size, on the stove over medium heat. Add the chopped bacon and cook until the fat has rendered and the bacon is crisp. Remove the bacon pieces to a plate.     Add the chopped onion and garlic to the same pot. Sauté in the bacon fat until the onion is soft, about 5 minutes. Add the paprika, salt, and thyme. Stir to coat the onion well. Add the squash, chard, chickpeas, and broth to the pot. Turn the heat to high, bring the soup to a boil, then turn the heat down to low and simmer until the squash is tender, about 20 minutes.     Add the lemon juice. If necessary, add another pinch of salt to taste.     Place 2 cups of cooled soup in each of 4 containers and top each serving with 2 teaspoons of cheese. Store the remaining 4 Servings: in the freezer to eat later.     STORAGE: Store covered containers in the refrigerator for up to 5 days. If frozen, soup will last 4 months.

**Nutrition Info:Per Serving:** Total calories: 194; Total fat: 2g; Saturated fat: 1g; Sodium: 530mg; Carbohydrates: 34g; Fiber: 11g; Protein: 12g

## Herbed Tuna Salad Wraps

Servings: 4     Cooking Time: 15 Minutes
**Ingredients:**
- 1 (11-ounce) pouch tuna in water
- 1 cup parsley leaves, chopped
- ¼ cup mint leaves, chopped
- ¼ cup minced shallot
- 1½ teaspoons sumac
- 1 teaspoon Dijon mustard
- 1 tablespoon olive oil
- 1 tablespoon freshly squeezed lemon juice
- ¼ cup unsalted sunflower seeds
- 16 large or medium romaine or bibb lettuce leaves
- 1 red bell pepper, cut into thin sticks (3 to 4 inches long)
- 3 Persian cucumbers, cut into thin sticks (3 to 4 inches long)

**Directions:**
In a large bowl, mix together the tuna, parsley, mint, shallot, sumac, mustard, oil, lemon juice, and sunflower seeds.     Place ¾ cup of tuna salad in each of 4 containers. Place 4 lettuce leaves, one quarter of the peppers, and one quarter of the cucumbers in each of 4 separate containers so that they don't get soggy from the tuna salad.     STORAGE: Store covered containers in the refrigerator for up to 4 days.     TIP Tuna in pouches is preferable to cans, because pouches don't need to be drained and the tuna isn't soggy. You can substitute canned salmon, canned sardines, or even shredded rotisserie chicken for the tuna in this salad.
**Nutrition Info:Per Serving:** Total calories: 223; Total fat: 9g; Saturated fat: 1g; Sodium: 422mg; Carbohydrates: 12g; Fiber: 4g; Protein: 24g

## Mediterranean Potato Salad

Servings: 6     Cooking Time: 30 Minutes
**Ingredients:**
- 3 tablespoons extra virgin olive oil
- ½ cup of sliced olives
- 1 tablespoon olive juice
- 3 tablespoons lemon juice, freshly squeezed is best
- 2 tablespoons of mint, fresh and torn
- ¼ teaspoon sea salt
- 2 stalks of sliced celery
- 2 pounds baby potatoes
- 2 tablespoons of chopped oregano, fresh is best

**Directions:**
Cut the potatoes into inch cubes.     Toss the potatoes into a medium saucepan and cover them with water. Place the saucepan on the stove over high heat.     Once the potatoes start to boil, bring the heat down to medium-low.     Let the potatoes simmer for 13 to 1minutes. When you poke the potatoes with a fork and they feel tender, they are done.     As the potatoes are simmering, grab a small bowl and mix the oil, olive juice, lemon juice, and salt. Whisk the ingredients together well.     Once the potatoes are done, drain them and pour the potatoes into a bowl.     Take the juice mixture and pour 3 tablespoons over the potatoes right away.     Combine the potatoes with the celery and olives.     Prior to serving, sprinkle the potatoes with the mint, oregano, and rest of the dressing.
**Nutrition Info:**calories: 175, fats: 7 grams, carbohydrates: 27 grams, protein: 3 grams.

## Mediterranean Zucchini Noodles

Servings: 2     Cooking Time: 10 Minutes
**Ingredients:**
- 2 large zucchini or 1 package of store-bought zucchini noodles
- 1 tsp olive oil
- 4 cloves garlic diced
- 10 oz cherry tomatoes cut in half
- 2-4 oz plain hummus
- 1 tsp oregano
- 1/2 tsp red wine vinegar plus more to taste
- 1/2 cup jarred artichoke hearts, drained and chopped
- 1/4 cup sun-dried tomatoes, drained and chopped
- Salt, to taste
- Pepper to taste
- Parmesan and fresh basil for topping

**Directions:**
Prepare the zucchini by cutting of the ends off zucchini and spiralize, set aside     In a pan over medium heat, add in olive oil     Then add in the garlic and cherry tomatoes to the pan, sauté until tomatoes begin to burst, about to 4 minutes     Add in the zucchini noodles, sun-dried tomatoes, hummus, oregano, artichoke hearts and red wine vinegar to the pan, sauté for 1-2 minutes, or until zucchini is tender-crisp and heated through     Season to taste with salt and pepper as needed     Allow the zoodle to cool     Distribute among the containers, store in the fridge for 2-3 days To Serve: Reheat in the microwave for 30 seconds or until heated through, serve immediately with parmesan and fresh basil. Enjoy
**Nutrition Info:Per Serving:** Calories:241;Carbs: 8g;Total Fat: 37g;Protein: 10g

## Lobster Salad

Servings: 2     Cooking Time: 15 Minutes
**Ingredients:**
- ¼ yellow onion, chopped
- ¼ yellow bell pepper, seeded and chopped
- ¾ pound cooked lobster meat, shredded
- 1 celery stalk, chopped
- Black pepper, to taste
- ¼ cup avocado mayonnaise

**Directions:**
Mix together all the ingredients in a bowl and stir until well combined.     Refrigerate for about 3 hours and serve chilled.     Put the salad into a container for meal prepping and refrigerate for about 2 days.
**Nutrition Info:**Calories: 336 ;Carbohydrates: 2g;Protein: 27.2g;Fat: 25.2g ;Sugar: 1.2g;Sodium: 926mg

## Mediterranean-style Pesto Chicken

Servings: 4    Cooking Time: 40 Minutes
**Ingredients:**
- 1 pound chicken breasts (2 large breasts), butterflied and cut in half to make 4 pieces
- 1 (6-ounce) jar prepared pesto
- 1 teaspoon olive oil
- 12 ounces baby spinach leaves
- Chunky Roasted Cherry Tomato and Basil Sauce

**Directions:**
Place the chicken and pesto in a gallon-size resealable bag. Marinate for at least hour.    Preheat the oven to 350°F and rub a 13-by-9-inch glass or ceramic baking dish with the oil, or spray with cooking spray.    Place the spinach in the pan, then place the chicken on top of the spinach. Pour the pesto from the bag into the dish. Cover the pan with aluminum foil and bake for 20 minutes. Remove the foil and bake for another 15 to 20 minutes. Cool.    Place 1 piece of chicken, one quarter of the spinach, and ⅓ cup of chunky tomato sauce in each of separate containers.    STORAGE: Store covered containers in the refrigerator for up to days.

**Nutrition Info:Per Serving:** Total calories: 531; Total fat: 43g; Saturated fat: 7g; Sodium: 1,243mg; Carbohydrates: 13g; Fiber: 4g; Protein: 29g

## Crispy Baked Chicken

Servings: 2    Cooking Time: 40 Minutes
**Ingredients:**
- 2 chicken breasts, skinless and boneless
- 2 tablespoons butter
- ¼ teaspoon turmeric powder
- Salt and black pepper, to taste
- ¼ cup sour cream

**Directions:**
Preheat the oven to 360 degrees F and grease a baking dish with butter.    Season the chicken with turmeric powder, salt and black pepper in a bowl.    Put the chicken on the baking dish and transfer it in the oven. Bake for about 10 minutes and dish out to serve topped with sour cream.    Transfer the chicken in a bowl and set aside to cool for meal prepping. Divide it into 2 containers and cover the containers. Refrigerate for up to 2 days and reheat in microwave before serving.

**Nutrition Info:**Calories: 304 ;Carbohydrates: 1.4g;Protein: 21g;Fat: 21.6g ;Sugar: 0.1g;Sodium: 137mg

## Vegetarian Lasagna Roll-ups

Servings: 14    Cooking Time: 1 Hour 10 Minutes
**Ingredients:**
- 1 pound lasagna noodles
- 3 thinly sliced zucchini, if your vegetables are smaller make it 4
- ½ cup water
- 3 tablespoons olive oil
- Parmesan cheese and salt to taste
- 24-ounce jar of pasta sauce, you can use any type but the best for the recipes is basil or tomato
- Enough crushed red pepper flakes for your taste buds, this is also optional
- For the cheese filling:
- 6 ounces goat cheese
- 20 ounces of ricotta cheese
- 2 ounces mozzarella cheese
- 1 cup of parsley leaves, chopped
- Dash of salt and pepper
- 3 tablespoons of chopped garlic
- Olive oil

**Directions:**
Set the temperature of your oven to 450 degrees Fahrenheit.    Grease a baking sheet or lay a piece of parchment paper on top.    Slice the zucchini and place them on the baking sheet.    Brush each side of the vegetable with oil and then sprinkle with salt.    Place the baking sheet into the oven and set a timer for 10 minutes.    While the zucchini is baking, start boiling the lasagna noodles. Drain the noodles when they are done cooking and then let them dry on a piece of parchment paper.    Remove the zucchini from the oven and set aside to allow them to cool down a bit. Change the heat of your oven to 350 degrees Fahrenheit.    To make the cheese filling, combine all of the ingredients and drizzle with a little olive oil. Mix well.    Pour a spoonful or two on each of the lasagna noodles.    Set a slice of baked zucchini on top of the cheese mixture.    Roll up the noodles.    In a 9 x inch baking pan, pour the water and ¾ cup of the pasta sauce on the bottom. Stir the ingredients gently so they become mixed.    Place the lasagna roll-ups in the upright position on top of the sauce.    Pour the remaining sauce on the noodles.    If you want a little extra cheese, sprinkle some on top of the lasagna roll-ups.    Set your timer for 40 minutes, but remember to check the liquid half-way through cooking to make sure it does not become too dry. If it does, add a little more water. You can try adding some water to the pasta sauce jar and shaking it up a bit as this will give the water a little sauce flavor.    When the lasagna is cooked, remove it and garnish with basil leaves. Allow it to cool for a couple of minutes and admire your Mediterranean cooking skills before serving.

**Nutrition Info:**calories: 282, fats: 11 grams, carbohydrates: 29 grams, protein: 14.3 grams.

## Milano Chicken

Servings: 6    Cooking Time: 30 Minutes
**Ingredients:**
- 4 skinless and boneless chicken breast halves
- 1 tablespoon vegetable oil
- 2 garlic cloves, crushed
- 1 teaspoon Italian style seasoning
- 1 teaspoon crushed red pepper flakes
- salt
- pepper
- 1 28-ounce can stewed drained tomatoes
- 1 9-ounce package frozen green beans

**Directions:**
Heat oil in a large skillet over medium-high heat. Add chicken to the skillet and season with garlic, red pepper, Italian seasoning, salt, and pepper.    Saute for about 5 minutes.    Add tomatoes and cook for 5 minutes more.    Add green beans and give the whole mixture a gentle stir.    Reduce heat, cover, and simmer for about 15-20 minutes.    Enjoy!
**Nutrition Info:Per Serving:**Calories: 244, Total Fat: 4.9 g, Saturated Fat: 0.5 g, Cholesterol:   mg, Sodium: 399 mg, Total Carbohydrate: 14.1 g, Dietary Fiber: 4.6 g, Total Sugars: 6.4 g, Protein: 38.2 g, Vitamin D: 0 mcg, Calcium: 48 mg, Iron: 3 mg, Potassium: 662 mg

## Tuna Celery Salad

Servings: 4    Cooking Time: 30 Minutes
**Ingredients:**
- 3 5-ounce cans Genova tuna dipped in olive oil
- 2½ celery stalks, chopped
- ½ English cucumber, chopped
- 4-5 small radishes, stems removed, chopped
- 3 green onions, chopped (white and green)
- ½ medium red onion, finely chopped
- ½ cup pitted Kalamata olives, halved
- 1 bunch parsley, stems removed, finely chopped
- 10-15 sprigs fresh mint leaves, stems removed, finely chopped
- 6 slices heirloom tomatoes
- pita chips or pita bread
- 2½ teaspoons high-quality Dijon mustard
- zest of 1 lime
- lime juice, 1½ limes
- 1/3 cup olive oil
- ½ teaspoon sumac
- salt
- pepper
- ½ teaspoon crushed red pepper flakes

**Directions:**
Prepare the vinaigrette by combining and whisking all zesty Dijon mustard vinaigrette Ingredients: in a small bowl.    For the tuna salad, add all base recipe Ingredients: to a large bowl, and mix well with a spoon. Dress the tuna salad with the prepared vinaigrette, and mix again until the tuna salad is coated correctly. Cover, refrigerate and allow to chill for 30 minutes. Once chilled, give the salad a toss and serve with a side of pita chips or pita bread and some sliced up heirloom tomatoes.    Enjoy!
**Nutrition Info:Per Serving:**Calories: 455, Total Fat: 33.8 g, Saturated Fat: 5.9 g, Cholesterol: 3mg, Sodium: 832 mg, Total Carbohydrate: 20.1 g, Dietary Fiber: 6.3

g, Total Sugars: 4 g, Protein: 24.3 g, Vitamin D: 0 mcg, Calcium: 155 mg, Iron: 7 mg, Potassium: 604 mg

## Chicken With Herbed Butter

Servings: 2    Cooking Time: 35 Minutes
**Ingredients:**
- 1/3 cup baby spinach
- 1 tablespoon lemon juice
- ¾ pound chicken breasts
- 1/3 cup butter
- ¼ cup parsley, chopped
- Salt and black pepper, to taste
- 1/3 teaspoon ginger powder
- 1 garlic clove, minced

**Directions:**
Preheat the oven to 450 degrees F and grease a baking dish.    Mix together parsley, ginger powder, lemon juice, butter, garlic, salt and black pepper in a bowl. Add chicken breasts in the mixture and marinate well for about   minutes.    Arrange the marinated chicken in the baking dish and transfer in the oven.    Bake for about 2minutes and dish out to serve immediately. Place chicken in 2 containers and refrigerate for about 3 days for meal prepping. Reheat in microwave before serving.
**Nutrition Info:**Calories: 568 ;Carbohydrates: 1.6g;Protein: 44.6g;Fat: 42.1g;Sugar: 0.3g;Sodium: 384mg

## Italian Tuna Sandwiches

Servings: 4    Cooking Time: 10 Minutes
**Ingredients:**
- 3 tablespoons lemon juice, freshly squeezed
- ½ teaspoon of minced garlic
- 5 ounces tuna, drained
- ½ cup of sliced olives
- 8 slices whole-grain bread
- 2 tablespoons extra virgin olive oil
- ½ teaspoon black pepper
- 1 celery stalk, chopped

**Directions:**
Add the oil, pepper, lemon juice, and garlic to a bowl. Whisk the ingredients well.    Combine the olives, chopped celery, and tuna.    Use a fork to break apart the tuna into chunks.    Stir all of the ingredients until they are well combined.    Set four slices of bread on serving plates or a platter.    Divide the tuna salad equally among the four slices of bread.    Top the tuna salad with the remaining bread to make a sandwich. You'll get the best taste when you let the tuna sandwich sit for about 5 or more minutes before you serve. The salad will start to soak into the bread, and it makes for one tasty meal!
**Nutrition Info:**calories: 347, fats: 17 grams, carbohydrates: 27 grams, protein: 25 grams.

## Mediterranean Baked Sole Fillet

Servings: 6      Cooking Time: 15 Minutes
**Ingredients:**
- 1 lime or lemon, juice of
- 1/2 cup extra virgin olive oil
- 3 tbsp unsalted melted vegan butter
- 2 shallots, thinly sliced
- 3 garlic cloves, thinly-sliced
- 2 tbsp capers
- 1.5 lb Sole fillet, about 10–12 thin fillets
- 4–6 green onions, top trimmed, halved lengthwise
- 1 lime or lemon, sliced (optional)
- 3/4 cup roughly chopped fresh dill for garnish
- 1 tsp seasoned salt, or to your taste
- 3/4 tsp ground black pepper
- 1 tsp ground cumin
- 1 tsp garlic powder

**Directions:**
Preheat over to 375-degree F      In a small bowl, whisk together olive oil, lime juice, and melted butter with a sprinkle of seasoned salt, stir in the garlic, shallots, and capers.      In a separate small bowl, mix together the pepper, cumin, seasoned salt, and garlic powder, season the fish fillets each on both sides      On a large baking pan or dish, arrange the fish fillets and cover with the buttery lime      Arrange the green onion halves and lime slices on top      Bake in 375 degrees F for 10-15 minutes, do not overcook      Remove the fish fillets from the oven      Allow the dish to cool completely Distribute among the containers, store for 2-3 days To Serve: Reheat in the microwave for 1-2 minutes or until heated through. Garnish with the chopped fresh dill. Serve with your favorite and a fresh salad      Recipe Notes: If you can't get your hands on a sole fillet, cook this recipe with a different white fish. Just remember to change the baking time since it will be different.
**Nutrition Info:Per Serving:** Calories:350;Carbs:7 g;Total Fat: 26g;Protein: 23g

## Baked Chicken Breast

Servings: 2      Cooking Time: 50 Minutes
**Ingredients:**
- 2 skinless and boneless chicken breasts (about 8 ounces each)
- salt
- ground black pepper
- 1/4 cup olive oil
- 1/4 cup freshly squeezed lemon juice
- 1 garlic clove, minced
- 1/2 teaspoon dried oregano
- 1/4 teaspoon dried thyme

**Directions:**
Preheat oven to a temperature of 400 degrees F. Season the chicken breasts carefully with salt and pepper on all sides.      Place the chicken in a bowl. Take another bowl and add olive oil, lemon juice, oregano, garlic, and thyme. Mix well to make the

marinade.      Pour the marinade on top of chicken breasts and allow to marinate for 10 minutes.      Set an oven rack about inches above the heat source.      Place the chicken breasts into a baking pan and pour extra marinade on top.      Bake for about 35-45 minutes until the center is no longer pink and the juices run clear. Move the baking dish to top rack and broil for about 5 minutes.      Cool, spread over containers with some side dish and enjoy!
**Nutrition Info:Per Serving:**Calories: 467, Total Fat: 28.5 g, Saturated Fat: 3.9 g, Cholesterol: 130 mg, Sodium: 158 mg, Total Carbohydrate: 1.5 g, Dietary Fiber: 0.4 g, Total Sugars: 0.7 g, Protein: 52.4 g, Vitamin D: 0 mcg, Calcium: 14 mg, Iron: 2 mg, Potassium: 52 mg

## Grilled Lemon Fish

Servings: 4      Cooking Time: 15 Minutes
**Ingredients:**
- 1/4 teaspoon sea salt
- 3 to 4 lemons
- 1/4 teaspoon ground black pepper
- 4 ounces any fish fillets, such as salmon or cod
- 1 tablespoon olive oil

**Directions:**
Ensure that the fish fillets are dry. If you know or feel they are a bit damp, take a paper towel and pat them dry.      Leave the fish fillets on the counter for 10 minutes so they can stand at room temperature. Turn on your grill to medium-high heat or set the temperature to 400 degrees Fahrenheit.      Using nonstick cooking spray, coat the grill so the fish won't stick.      Take one lemon and cut it in half. Set one of the halves aside and cut the remaining half into 1/4-inch thick slices.      Now, take the other half of the lemon and squeeze at least 1 tablespoon of juice out into a small bowl.      Add oil into the small bowl and whisk the ingredients together.      Brush the fish with the lemon and oil mixture. Make sure you get both sides of the fish.      Arrange the lemon slices on the grill in the shape of the fish, it might take about 3 to 4 slices for one fish.      Place the fish on top of the lemon slices and grill the ingredients together. If you don't have a lid for your grill, cover it with a different lid that will fit or use aluminum foil.      When the fish is about half-way done, turn it over so the other side is laying on top of the lemon slices.      You will know the fish is done when it starts to look flaky and separates easily, which you can check by gently pressing a fork onto the fish.
**Nutrition Info:**calories: 147, fats: 5 grams, carbohydrates: 4 grams, protein: 22 grams.

## Italian Baked Beans

Servings: 6     Cooking Time: 15 To 20 Minutes.
**Ingredients:**
- ½ cup chopped onion
- ¼ cup red wine vinegar
- ¼ tablespoon ground cinnamon
- 15 ounces or 2 cans of great northern beans, do not drain
- 2 teaspoons extra virgin olive oil
- 12 ounces tomato paste, low sodium
- ½ cup water

**Directions:**
Turn a burner to medium heat and add oil to a saucepan.     Add the onion and cook for 4 to 5 minutes. Stir well.     Combine the vinegar, tomato paste, cinnamon, and water. Mix until all the ingredients are well combined.     Switch the heat to a low setting. Using a colander, drain one can of beans and pour into the pan.     Open the second can of beans and pour all of it, including the liquid, into the saucepan and stir. Continue to cook the beans for 10 minutes while stirring frequently.     Serve and enjoy!
**Nutrition Info:**calories: 236, fats: 3 grams, carbohydrates: 42 grams, protein: 10 grams.

## Tomato Tilapia

Servings: 4     Cooking Time: 15 Minutes
**Ingredients:**
- 3 tablespoons sun-dried tomatoes packed in oil, drained (juice/oil reserved) and chopped
- 1 tablespoon capers, drained
- 2 pieces tilapia
- 1 tablespoon oil from sun-dried tomatoes
- 1 tablespoon lemon juice
- 2 tablespoons Kalamata olives, pitted and chopped

**Directions:**
Preheat oven to 375 degrees F.     Add sun-dried tomatoes, capers, and olives to a bowl; stir well and set aside.     Place the tilapia fillets side by side on a baking sheet.     Drizzle with oil and lemon juice.     Bake for about 10-1minutes.     Check the fish after 10 minutes to see if they are flakey.     Once done, top the fish with tomato mixture.
**Nutrition Info:Per Serving:**Calories: , Total Fat: 4.4 g, Saturated Fat: 0.8 g, Cholesterol: 28 mg, Sodium: 122 mg, Total Carbohydrate: 0.8 g, Dietary Fiber: 0.3 g, Total Sugars: 0.3 g, Protein: 10.7 g, Vitamin D: 0 mcg, Calcium: 16 mg, Iron: 1 mg, Potassium: 26 mg

## Chicken Lentil Soup

Servings: 4     Cooking Time: 45 Minutes
**Ingredients:**
- 1 pound dried lentils
- 12 ounces boneless chicken thigh meat

- 7 cups water
- 1 small onion, diced
- 2 scallions, chopped
- ¼ cup chopped cilantro
- 3 cloves garlic
- 1 medium tomato, diced
- 1 teaspoon garlic powder
- 1 teaspoon cumin
- ¼ teaspoon oregano
- ½ teaspoon paprika
- ½ teaspoon kosher salt

**Directions:**
Add all of the listed Ingredients: to your Instant Pot. Set your pot to SOUP mode and cook for 30 minutes. Allow the pressure to release naturally.     Take the chicken out and shred.     Place the chicken back in the pot and stir.     Pour to the jars.     Enjoy!
**Nutrition Info:Per Serving:**Calories: 1144, Total Fat: 52.5 g, Saturated Fat: 15.2 g, Cholesterol: 2 mg, Sodium: 558 mg, Total Carbohydrate: 73.2 g, Dietary Fiber: 35.9 g, Total Sugars: 4.3 g, Protein: 90.3 g, Vitamin D: 0 mcg, Calcium: 148 mg, Iron: 13 mg, Potassium: 1241 mg

## Bacon Wrapped Asparagus

Servings: 2     Cooking Time: 30 Minutes
**Ingredients:**
- 1/3 cup heavy whipping cream
- 2 bacon slices, precooked
- 4 small spears asparagus
- Salt, to taste
- 1 tablespoon butter

**Directions:**
Preheat the oven to 360 degrees F and grease a baking sheet with butter.     Meanwhile, mix cream, asparagus and salt in a bowl.     Wrap the asparagus in bacon slices and arrange them in the baking dish.     Transfer the baking dish in the oven and bake for about 20 minutes.     Remove from the oven and serve hot. Place the bacon wrapped asparagus in a dish and set aside to cool for meal prepping. Divide it in 2 containers and cover the lid. Refrigerate for about 2 days and reheat in the microwave before serving.
**Nutrition Info:**Calories: 204 ;Carbohydrates: 1.4g;Protein: 5.9g;Fat: 19.3g;Sugar: 0.5g;Sodium: 291mg

## Cool Mediterranean Fish

Servings: 8     Cooking Time: 30 Minutes
**Ingredients:**
- 6 ounces halibut fillets
- 1 tablespoon Greek seasoning
- 1 large tomato, chopped
- 1 onion, chopped
- 5 ounces kalamata olives, pitted
- ¼ cup capers
- ¼ cup olive oil
- 1 tablespoon lemon juice
- Salt and pepper as needed

**Directions:**
Pre-heat your oven to 350-degree Fahrenheit
Transfer the halibut fillets on a large aluminum foil
Season with Greek seasoning     Take a bowl and add
tomato, onion, olives, olive oil, capers, pepper, lemon
juice and salt     Mix well and spoon the tomato mix
over the halibut     Seal the edges and fold to make a
packet     Place the packet on a baking sheet and bake
in your oven for 30-40 minutes     Serve once the fish
flakes off and enjoy!     Meal Prep/Storage Options:
Store in airtight containers in your fridge for 1-2 days.
**Nutrition Info:**Calories: 429;Fat:
26g;Carbohydrates: ;Protein:36g

## Luncheon Fancy Salad

Servings: 2     Cooking Time: 40 Minutes
**Ingredients:**
- 6-ounce cooked salmon, chopped
- 1 tablespoon fresh dill, chopped
- Salt and black pepper, to taste
- 4 hard-boiled grass-fed eggs, peeled and cubed
- 2 celery stalks, chopped
- ½ yellow onion, chopped
- ¾ cup avocado mayonnaise

**Directions:**
Put all the ingredients in a bowl and mix until well
combined.     Cover with a plastic wrap and refrigerate
for about 3 hours to serve.     For meal prepping, put
the salad in a container and refrigerate for up to days.
**Nutrition Info:**Calories: 303 ;Carbohydrates:
1.7g;Protein: 10.3g;Fat: 30g ;Sugar: 1g;Sodium: 31g

## Moroccan Spiced Stir-fried Beef With Butternut Squash And Chickpeas

Servings: 4     Cooking Time: 15 Minutes
**Ingredients:**
- 1 tablespoon olive oil, plus 2 teaspoons
- 1 pound precut butternut squash cut into ½-inch cubes
- 3 ounces scallions, white and green parts chopped (1 cup)
- 1 tablespoon water
- ¼ teaspoon baking soda
- ¾ pound flank steak, sliced across the grain into ⅛-inch thick slices
- ½ teaspoon garlic powder
- ¼ teaspoon ground ginger
- ¼ teaspoon turmeric
- ¼ teaspoon ground cumin
- ¼ teaspoon ground coriander
- ⅛ teaspoon cayenne pepper
- ⅛ teaspoon ground cinnamon
- ½ teaspoon kosher salt, divided
- 1 (14-ounce) can chickpeas, drained and rinsed
- ½ cup dried apricots, quartered
- ½ cup cilantro leaves, chopped
- 2 teaspoons freshly squeezed lemon juice
- 8 teaspoons sliced almonds

**Directions:**
Heat tablespoon of oil in a 12-inch skillet. Once the oil is
hot, add the squash and scallions, and cook until the
squash is tender, about 10 to 12 minutes.     Mix the
water and baking soda together in a small prep bowl.
Place the beef in a medium bowl, pour the baking-soda
water over it, and mix to combine. Let it sit for 5
minutes.     In a small bowl, combine the garlic powder,
ginger, turmeric, cumin, coriander, cayenne, cinnamon,
and ¼ teaspoon of salt, then add the mixture to the
beef. Stir to combine.     When the squash is tender,
turn the heat off and add the remaining ¼ teaspoon of
salt and the chickpeas, dried apricots, cilantro, and
lemon juice to taste. Stir to combine. Place the contents
of the pan in a bowl to cool.     Clean out the skillet and
heat the remaining 2 teaspoons of oil over high heat.
When the oil is hot, add the beef and cook until it is no
longer pink, about 2 to 3 minutes.     Place 1¼ cups of
the squash mixture and one quarter of the beef slices in
each of 4 containers. Sprinkle 2 teaspoons of sliced
almonds over each container.     STORAGE: Store
covered containers in the refrigerator for up to 5 days.
**Nutrition Info:Per Serving:** Total calories: 404;
Total fat: 14g; Saturated fat: 1g; Sodium: 355mg;
Carbohydrates: 46g; Fiber: 12g; Protein: 27g

## North African–inspired Sautéed Shrimp With Leeks And Peppers

Servings: 4     Cooking Time: 20 Minutes
**Ingredients:**
- 2 tablespoons olive oil, divided
- 1 large leek, white and light green parts, halved lengthwise, sliced ¼-inch thick
- 2 teaspoons chopped garlic
- 1 large red bell pepper, chopped into ¼-inch pieces
- 1 cup chopped fresh parsley leaves (1 small bunch)
- ½ cup chopped fresh cilantro leaves (½ small bunch)
- ¼ teaspoon ground cumin
- ¼ teaspoon ground coriander
- 1 teaspoon smoked paprika
- 1 pound uncooked peeled, deveined large shrimp (20 to 25 per pound), thawed if frozen, blotted with paper towels
- 1 tablespoon freshly squeezed lemon juice
- ⅛ teaspoon kosher salt

**Directions:**
Heat 2 teaspoons of oil in a -inch skillet over medium heat. Once the oil is hot, add the leeks and garlic and sauté for 2 minutes. Add the peppers and cook for 10 minutes, or until the peppers are soft, stirring occasionally.     Add the chopped parsley and cilantro and cook for 1 more minute. Remove the mixture from the pan and place in a medium bowl.     Mix the cumin, coriander, and paprika in a small prep bowl.     Add 2 teaspoons of oil to the same skillet and increase the heat to medium-high. Add the shrimp in a single layer, sprinkle the spice mixture over the shrimp, and cook for about 2 minutes. Flip the shrimp over and cook for 1 more minute. Add the leek and herb mixture, stir, and cook for 1 more minute.     Turn off the heat and add the remaining 2 teaspoons of oil and the lemon juice. Taste to see whether you need the salt. Add if necessary. Place ¾ cup of couscous or other grain (if using) and 1 cup of the shrimp mixture in each of 4 containers. STORAGE: Store covered containers in the refrigerator for up to 4 days.
**Nutrition Info:Per Serving:** Total calories: 1; Total fat: 9g; Saturated fat: 1g; Sodium: 403mg; Carbohydrates: 9g; Fiber: 2g; Protein: 19g

## Italian Chicken With Sweet Potato And Broccoli

Servings: 8     Cooking Time: 30 Minutes
**Ingredients:**
- 2 lbs boneless skinless chicken breasts, cut into small pieces
- 5-6 cups broccoli florets
- 3 tbsp Italian seasoning mix of your choice
- a few tbsp of olive oil
- 3 sweet potatoes, peeled and diced
- Coarse sea salt, to taste
- Freshly cracked pepper, to taste
- Toppings:
- Avocado
- Lemon juice
- Chives

- Olive oil, for serving
**Directions:**
Preheat the oven to 425 degrees F     Toss the chicken pieces with the Italian seasoning mix and a drizzle of olive oil, stir to combine then store in the fridge for about 30 minutes     Arrange the broccoli florets and sweet potatoes on a sheet pan, drizzle with the olive oil, sprinkle generously with salt     Arrange the chicken on a separate sheet pan     Bake both in the oven for 12-1minutes     Transfer the chicken and broccoli to a plate, toss the sweet potatoes and continue to roast for another 15 minutes, or until ready     Allow the chicken, broccoli, and sweet potatoes to cool     Distribute among the containers and store for 2-3 days     To Serve: Reheat in the microwave for 1 minute or until heated through, top with the topping of choice. Enjoy Recipe Notes: Any kind of vegetables work will with this recipe! So, add favorites like carrots, brussels sprouts and asparagus.
**Nutrition Info:Per Serving:** Calories:222;Total Fat: 4.9g;Total Carbs: 15.3g;Protein: 28g

## Vegetable Soup

Servings: 6     Cooking Time: 20 Minutes
**Ingredients:**
- 1 15-ounce can low sodium cannellini beans, drained and rinsed
- 1 tablespoon olive oil
- 1 small onion, diced
- 2 carrots, diced
- 2 stalks celery, diced
- 1 small zucchini, diced
- 1 garlic clove, minced
- 1 tablespoon fresh thyme leaves, chopped
- 2 teaspoons fresh sage, chopped
- ½ teaspoon salt
- ¼ teaspoon freshly ground black pepper
- 32 ounces low sodium chicken broth
- 1 14-ounce can no-salt diced tomatoes, undrained
- 2 cups baby spinach leaves, chopped
- 1/3 cup freshly grated parmesan

**Directions:**
Mash half of the beans in a small bowl using the back of a spoon and put it to the side.     Add the oil to a large soup pot and place over medium-high heat.     Add carrots, onion, celery, garlic, zucchini, thyme, salt, pepper, and sage.     Cook well for about 5 minutes until the vegetables are tender.     Add broth and tomatoes and bring the mixture to a boil.     Add beans (both mashed and whole) and spinach.     Cook for 3 minutes until the spinach has wilted.     Pour the soup into the jars.     Before serving, top with parmesan.     Enjoy!
**Nutrition Info:Per Serving:**Calories: 359, Total Fat: 7.1 g, Saturated Fat: 2.7 g, Cholesterol: 10 mg, Sodium: 854 mg, Total Carbohydrate: 51.1 g, Dietary Fiber: 20 g, Total Sugars: 5.7 g, Protein: 25.8 g, Vitamin D: 0 mcg, Calcium: 277 mg, Iron: 7 mg, Potassium: 1497 mg

## Greek Chicken Wraps

Servings: 2     Cooking Time: 15 Minutes
**Ingredients:**
- Greek Chicken Wrap Filling:
- 2 chicken breasts 14 oz, chopped into 1-inch pieces
- 2 small zucchinis, cut into 1-inch pieces
- 2 bell peppers, cut into 1-inch pieces
- 1 red onion, cut into 1-inch pieces
- 2 tbsp olive oil
- 2 tsp oregano
- 2 tsp basil
- 1/2 tsp garlic powder
- 1/2 tsp onion powder
- 1/2 tsp salt
- 2 lemons, sliced
- To Serve:
- 1/4 cup feta cheese crumbled
- 4 large flour tortillas or wraps

**Directions:**
Pre-heat oven to 425 degrees F     In a bowl, toss together the chicken, zucchinis, olive oil, oregano, basil, garlic, bell peppers, onion powder, onion powder and salt     Arrange lemon slice on the baking sheet(s), spread the chicken and vegetable out on top (use 2 baking sheets if needed)     Bake for 15 minutes, until veggies are soft and the chicken is cooked through     Allow to cool completely     Distribute the chicken, bell pepper, zucchini and onions among the containers and remove the lemon slices     Allow the dish to cool completely     Distribute among the containers, store for 3 days     To Serve: Reheat in the microwave for 1-2 minutes or until heated through. Wrap in a tortila and sprinkle with feta cheese. Enjoy!

**Nutrition Info:Per Serving:** (1 wrap): Calories:356;Total Fat: 14g;Total Carbs: 26g;Protein: 29g

## Garbanzo Bean Soup

Servings: 4     Cooking Time: 20 Minutes
**Ingredients:**
- 14 ounces diced tomatoes
- 1 teaspoon olive oil
- 1 15-ounce can garbanzo beans
- salt
- pepper
- 2 sprigs fresh rosemary
- 1 cup acini di pepe pasta

**Directions:**
Take a large saucepan and add tomatoes and   ounces of the beans.     Bring the mixture to a boil over medium-high heat.     Puree the remaining beans in a blender/food processor.     Stir the pureed mixture into the pan.     Add the sprigs of rosemary to the pan. Add acini de Pepe pasta and simmer until the pasta is soft, making sure to stir it from time to time.     Remove the rosemary.     Season with pepper and salt.     Enjoy!

**Nutrition Info:Per Serving:**Calories: 473, Total Fat: 8.6 g, Saturated Fat: 1.1 g, Cholesterol: 18 mg, Sodium: 66 mg, Total Carbohydrate: 78.8 g, Dietary Fiber: 19.9 g, Total Sugars: 14 g, Protein: 23.7 g, Vitamin D: 0 mcg, Calcium: 131 mg, Iron: 8 mg, Potassium: 1186 mg

## Spinach And Beans Mediterranean Style Salad

Servings: 4     Cooking Time: 30 Minutes
**Ingredients:**
- 15 ounces drained and rinsed cannellini beans
- 14 ounces drained, rinsed, and quartered artichoke hearts
- 6 ounces or 8 cups baby spinach
- 14 ½ ounces undrained diced tomatoes, no salt is best
- 1 tablespoon olive oil and any additional if you prefer
- ¼ teaspoon salt
- 2 minced garlic cloves
- 1 chopped onion, small in size
- ¼ teaspoon pepper
- ⅛ teaspoon crushed red pepper flakes
- 2 tablespoons Worcestershire sauce

**Directions:**
Place a saucepan on your stovetop and turn the temperature to medium-high.     Let the pan warm up for a minute before you pour in the tablespoon of oil. Continue to let the oil heat up for another minute or two.     Toss in your chopped onion and stir so all the pieces are bathed in oil. Saute the onions for minutes. Add the garlic to the saucepan. Stir and saute the ingredients for another minute.     Combine the salt, red pepper flakes, pepper, and Worcestershire sauce. Mix well and then add the tomatoes to the pan. Stir the mixture constantly for about minutes.     Add the artichoke hearts, spinach, and beans. Saute and stir occasionally to get the taste throughout the dish. Once the spinach starts to wilt, take the salad off of the heat. Serve and enjoy immediately to get the best taste.

**Nutrition Info:**calories: 1, fats: 4 grams, carbohydrates: 30 grams, protein: 8 grams.

## Salmon Skillet Dinner

Servings: 4    Cooking Time: 15 To 20 Minutes
**Ingredients:**
- 1 teaspoon minced garlic
- 1 ½ cup quartered cherry tomatoes
- 1 tablespoon water
- ¼ teaspoon sea salt
- 1 tablespoon lemon juice, freshly squeezed is best
- 1 tablespoon extra virgin olive oil
- 12 ounces drained and chopped roasted red peppers
- 1 teaspoon paprika
- ¼ teaspoon black pepper
- 1 pound salmon fillets

**Directions:**
Remove the skin from your salmon fillets and cut them into 8 pieces.    Turn your stove burner on medium heat and set a skillet on top.    Pour the olive oil into the skillet and let it heat up for a couple of minutes. Add the minced garlic and paprika. Saute the ingredients for 1 minute.    Combine the roasted peppers, black pepper, tomatoes, water, and salt.    Set the heat to medium-high and bring the ingredients to a simmer. This should take 3 to 4 minutes. Remember to stir the ingredients occasionally so the tomatoes don't burn.    Add the salmon and take some of the sauce from the skillet to spoon on top of the fish so it is all covered in the mixture.    Cover the skillet and set a timer for 10 minutes. When the fish reaches 145 degrees Fahrenheit, it is cooked thoroughly.    Turn off the heat and drizzle lemon juice over the fish.    Break up the salmon into chunks and gently mix the pieces of fish with the sauce.    Serve and enjoy!
**Nutrition Info:**calories: 289, fats: 13 grams, carbohydrates: 10 grams, protein: 31 grams.

## Herb-crusted Halibut

Servings: 4    Cooking Time: 25 Minutes
**Ingredients:**
- Fresh parsley (.33 cup)
- Fresh dill (.25 cup)
- Fresh chives (.25 cup)
- Lemon zest (1 tsp.)
- Panko breadcrumbs (.75 cup)
- Olive oil (1 tbsp.)
- Freshly cracked black pepper (.25 tsp.)
- Sea salt (1 tsp.)
- Halibut fillets (4 - 6 oz.)

**Directions:**
Chop the fresh dill, chives, and parsley. Prepare a baking tray using a sheet of foil. Set the oven to reach 400° Fahrenheit.    Combine the salt, pepper, lemon zest, olive oil, chives, dill, parsley, and the breadcrumbs in a mixing bowl.    Rinse the halibut thoroughly. Use paper towels to dry it before baking.    Arrange the fish on the baking sheet. Spoon the crumbs over the fish and press it into each of the fillets.    Bake it until the top is browned and easily flaked or about 10 to 1minutes.

**Nutrition Info:**Calories: 273;Protein: 38 grams;Fat: 7 grams

## Syrian Spiced Lentil, Barley, And Vegetable Soup

Servings: 5    Cooking Time: 40 Minutes
**Ingredients:**
- 1 tablespoon olive oil
- 1 small onion, chopped (about 2 cups)
- 2 medium carrots, peeled and chopped (about 1 cup)
- 1 celery stalk, chopped (about ½ cup)
- 1 teaspoon chopped garlic
- 1 teaspoon ground cumin
- 1 teaspoon ground coriander
- 1 teaspoon turmeric
- ⅛ teaspoon ground cinnamon
- 2 tablespoons tomato paste
- ¾ cup green lentils
- ¾ cup pearled barley
- 8 cups water
- ¾ teaspoon kosher salt
- 1 (5-ounce) package baby spinach leaves
- 2 teaspoons red wine vinegar

**Directions:**
Heat the oil in a soup pot on medium-high heat. When the oil is shimmering, add the onion, carrots, celery, and garlic and sauté for 8 minutes. Add the cumin, coriander, turmeric, cinnamon, and tomato paste and cook for 2 more minutes, stirring frequently.    Add the lentils, barley, water, and salt to the pot and bring to a boil. Turn the heat to low and simmer for    minutes. Add the spinach and continue to simmer for 5 more minutes.    Add the vinegar and adjust the seasoning if needed.    Spoon 2 cups of soup into each of 5 containers.    STORAGE: Store covered containers in the refrigerator for up to    days.
**Nutrition Info:Per Serving:** Total calories: 273; Total fat: 4g; Saturated fat: 1g; Sodium: 459mg; Carbohydrates: 50g; Fiber: 1; Protein: 12g

## Spinach Chicken

Servings: 2     Cooking Time: 20 Minutes
**Ingredients:**
- 2 garlic cloves, minced
- 2 tablespoons unsalted butter, divided
- ¼ cup parmesan cheese, shredded
- ¾ pound chicken tenders
- ¼ cup heavy cream
- 10 ounce frozen spinach, chopped
- Salt and black pepper, to taste

**Directions:**
Heat tablespoon of butter in a large skillet and add chicken, salt and black pepper.    Cook for about 3 minutes on both sides and remove the chicken in a bowl.    Melt remaining butter in the skillet and add garlic, cheese, heavy cream and spinach.    Cook for about 2 minutes and transfer the chicken in it.    Cook for about minutes on low heat and dish out to immediately serve.    Place chicken in a dish and set aside to cool for meal prepping. Divide it in 2 containers and cover them. Refrigerate for about 3 days and reheat in microwave before serving.

**Nutrition Info:**Calories: 288 ;Carbohydrates: 3.6g;Protein: 27g;Fat: 18.3g;Sugar: 0.3g;Sodium: 192mg

## Niçoise-style Tuna Salad With Olives & White Beans

Servings: 4     Cooking Time: 20-30 Minutes
**Ingredients:**
- Green beans (.75 lb.)
- Solid white albacore tuna (12 oz. can)
- Great Northern beans (16 oz. can)
- Sliced black olives (2.25 oz.)
- Thinly sliced medium red onion (¼ of 1)
- Hard-cooked eggs (4 large)
- Dried oregano (1 tsp.)
- Olive oil (6 tbsp.)
- Black pepper and salt (as desired)
- Finely grated lemon zest (.5 tsp.)
- Water (.33 cup)
- Lemon juice (3 tbsp.)

**Directions:**
Drain the can of tuna, Great Northern beans, and black olives. Trim and snap the green beans into halves. Thinly slice the red onion. Cook and peel the eggs until hard-boiled.    Pour the water and salt into a skillet and add the beans. Place a top on the pot and switch the temperature setting to high. Wait for it to boil.    Once the beans are cooking, set a timer for five minutes. Immediately, drain and add the beans to a cookie sheet with a raised edge on paper towels to cool.    Combine the onion, olives, white beans, and drained tuna. Mix them with the zest, lemon juice, oil, and oregano. Dump the mixture over the salad and gently toss. Adjust the seasonings to your liking. Portion the tuna-bean salad with the green beans and eggs to serve.

**Nutrition Info:**Calories: 548;Protein: 36.3 grams;Fat: 30.3 grams

## Whole-wheat Pasta With Roasted Red Pepper Sauce And Fresh Mozzarella

Servings: 4     Cooking Time: 40 Minutes
**Ingredients:**
- 3 large red bell peppers, seeds removed and cut in half
- 1 (10-ounce) container cherry tomatoes
- 2 teaspoons olive oil, plus 2 tablespoons
- 8 ounces whole-wheat penne or rotini
- 1 tablespoon plus 1 teaspoon apple cider vinegar
- 1 teaspoon chopped garlic
- 1½ teaspoons smoked paprika
- ¼ teaspoon kosher salt
- ½ cup packed fresh basil leaves, chopped
- 1 (8-ounce) container fresh whole-milk mozzarella balls (ciliegine), quartered

**Directions:**
Preheat the oven to 400°F and line a sheet pan with a silicone baking mat or parchment paper.    Place the peppers and tomatoes on the pan and toss with teaspoons of oil. Roast for 40 minutes.    While the peppers and tomatoes are roasting, cook the pasta according to the instructions on the box. Drain and place the pasta in a large mixing bowl.    When the peppers are cool enough to handle, peel the skin and discard. It's okay if you can't remove all the skin. Place the roasted peppers, vinegar, garlic, paprika, and salt and the remaining 2 tablespoons of oil in a blender and blend until smooth.    Add the pepper sauce, whole roasted tomatoes, basil, and mozzarella to the pasta and stir to combine.    Place a heaping 2 cups of pasta and sauce in each of 4 containers.    STORAGE: Store covered containers in the refrigerator for up to 5 days.

**Nutrition Info:Per Serving:** Total calories: 463; Total fat: 20g; Saturated fat: 7g; Sodium: 260mg; Carbohydrates: 54g; Fiber: 9g; Protein: 1

## Greek Turkey Meatball Gyro With Tzatziki

Servings: 4     Cooking Time: 16 Minutes
**Ingredients:**
- Turkey Meatball:
- 1 lb. ground turkey
- 1/4 cup finely diced red onion
- 2 garlic cloves, minced
- 1 tsp oregano
- 1 cup chopped fresh spinach
- Salt, to taste
- Pepper, to taste
- 2 tbsp olive oil
- Tzatziki Sauce:
- 1/2 cup plain Greek yogurt
- 1/4 cup grated cucumber
- 2 tbsp lemon juice
- 1/2 tsp dry dill
- 1/2 tsp garlic powder
- Salt, to taste
- 1/2 cup thinly sliced red onion
- 1 cup diced tomato
- 1 cup diced cucumber
- 4 whole wheat flatbreads

**Directions:**
In a large bowl, add in ground turkey, diced red onion, oregano, fresh spinach minced garlic, salt, and pepper Using your hands mix all the ingredients together until the meat forms a ball and sticks together     Then using your hands, form meat mixture into 1″ balls, making about 12 meatballs     In a large skillet over medium high heat, add the olive oil and then add the meatballs, cook each side for 3-minutes until they are browned on all sides, remove from the pan and allow it to rest Allow the dish to cool completely     Distribute in the container, store for 2-3 days     To Serve: Reheat in the microwave for 1-2 minutes or until heated through. In the meantime, in a small bowl, combine the Greek yogurt, grated cucumber, lemon juice, dill, garlic powder, and salt to taste Assemble the gyros by taking the toasted flatbread, add 3 meatballs, sliced red onion, tomato, and cucumber. Top with Tzatziki sauce and serve!
**Nutrition Info:Per Serving:** Calories:429;Carbs: 3;Total Fat: 19g;Protein: 28g

## Grilled Mediterranean Chicken Kebabs

Servings: 10     Cooking Time: 10 Minutes
**Ingredients:**
- Chicken Kebabs:
- 3 chicken fillets, cut in 1-inch cubes
- 2 red bell peppers
- 2 green bell peppers
- 1 red onion
- Chicken Kebab Marinade:
- 2/3 cup extra virgin olive oil, divided
- Juice of 1 lemon, divided
- 6 clove of garlic, chopped, divided
- 4 tsp salt, divided
- 2 tsp freshly ground black pepper, divided
- 2 tsp paprika, divided
- 2 tsp thyme, divided
- 4 tsp oregano, divided

**Directions:**

In a bowl, mix 2 of all ingredients for the marinade-olive oils, lemon juice, garlic, salt, pepper, paprika, thyme and oregano in small bowl     Place the chicken in a ziplock bag and pour marinade over it, marinade in the fridge for about 30 minutes     In a separate ziplock bag, mix the other half of the marinade ingredients - olive oils, lemon juice, garlic, salt, pepper, paprika, thyme and oregano - add the vegetables and marinade for at least  minutes     If you are using wood skewers, soak the skewers in water for about 20-30 minutes Once done, thread the chicken and peppers and onions on the skewers in a pattern about 6 pieces of chicken with peppers and onion in between     Over an outdoor grill or indoor grill pan over medium-high heat, spray the grates lightly with oil     Grill the chicken for about 5 minutes on each side, or until cooked through, then allow to cool completely     Distribute among the containers, store for 2-3 days     To Serve: Reheat in the microwave for 1-2 minutes or until heated through, or cover in foil and reheat in the oven at 375 degrees F for 5 minutes     Recipe Notes: You can also bake the Mediterranean chicken skewers in the oven. Just preheat the oven to 425 F and place the chicken skewers on roasting racks that are over two foil-lined baking sheets. Bake for 15 minutes, turn over and bake for an additional 10 - 15 minutes on the other side, or until cooked through
**Nutrition Info:Per Serving:** Calories:228;Carbs: 5g;Total Fat: 17g;Protein: 14g

## Kidney Beans Cilantro Salad

Servings: 6     Cooking Time: 30 Minutes
**Ingredients:**
- 1 15-ounce can kidney beans, rinsed and drained
- ½ English cucumber, chopped
- 1 medium heirloom tomato, chopped
- 1 bunch fresh cilantro, stems removed and chopped (about 1¼ cups)
- 1 red onion, chopped
- lime juice, 1 large lime
- 3 tablespoons Dijon mustard
- ½ teaspoon fresh garlic paste
- 1 teaspoon sumac
- salt
- pepper

**Directions:**
Place kidney beans, vegetables, and cilantro in a serving bowl.     Cover, refrigerate and allow it to chill.
Before serving, in a small bowl, make the vinaigrette by adding limejuice, oil, fresh garlic, pepper, mustard, and sumac.     Pour the vinaigrette over the salad and give it a gentle stir.     Add some salt and pepper.     Serve!
**Nutrition Info:Per Serving:**Calories: 269, Total Fat: 1.3 g, Saturated Fat: 0.2 g, Cholesterol: 0 mg, Sodium: 112 mg, Total Carbohydrate: 49.3 g, Dietary Fiber: 12.g, Total Sugars: 3.9 g, Protein: 17.6 g, Vitamin D: 0 mcg, Calcium: 94 mg, Iron: 6 mg, Potassium: 1258 mg

## Barley And Mushroom Soup

Servings: 6     Cooking Time: 30 Minutes
**Ingredients:**
- 2 tablespoons of olive oil
- 1 cup chopped carrots
- 6 cups vegetable broth, no salt added, and low sodium is best
- ¼ cup red wine
- 5 tablespoons parmesan cheese, grated
- ½ teaspoon thyme
- 1 cup chopped onion
- 5 cups chopped mushrooms
- 1 cup pearled barley, uncooked
- 2 tablespoons tomato paste

**Directions:**
Place a stockpot on your stove and turn the temperature of the range to medium heat.     Pour in the oil and let it warm up and start to simmer.     Combine the carrots and onion. Let them cook for 5 to 8 minutes while frequently stirring the ingredients together.     Add the mushroom and turn the heat up to medium-high. Stir and cook for a few minutes.     Pour in the broth and stir the ingredients for a few seconds.     Add in the wine, barley, thyme, and tomato paste. Stir everything together and then set the cover on the pot.     When the soup starts to boil, stir and reduce the heat to medium-low.     Cover the soup again and set your timer for 15 minutes, but don't leave it alone. You will want to stir a few times, so all ingredients become well incorporated. Once the dish becomes fragrant and the barley is completely cooked, turn off the heat and serve in bowls. Sprinkle the cheese on top for added taste and enjoy!
**Nutrition Info:** calories: 236, fats: 7 grams, carbohydrates: 35 grams, protein: 8 grams.

## Pan-seared Scallops With Pepper & Onions In Anchovy Oil

Servings: 4     Cooking Time: 45 Minutes
**Ingredients:**
- Olive oil (.33 cup)
- Anchovy fillets (2 oz. can)
- Jumbo sea scallops (1 lb.)
- Orange & red bell pepper (1 large of each)
- Red onion (1)
- Garlic (2 cloves)
- Lime zest (1 tsp.)
- Lemon zest (1.5 tsp.)
- Kosher salt & pepper (1 pinch of each)
- Garnish: Fresh parsley (8 sprigs)

**Directions:**
Coarsely chop the peppers and onions. Mince the garlic and anchovy fillet. Zest/mince the lime and lemon.
Heat the oil and anchovies in a large skillet using a med-high temperature setting.     After the anchovies are sizzling, toss in the scallops, and simmer them for about two minutes - without stirring.     Toss the bell peppers, garlic, red onion, lime zest, lemon zest, salt, and pepper

into a mixing container. Sprinkle the mixture over the scallops. Cook until they have browned (2 min..)     Flip the scallops, stir, and continue cooking until the scallops have browned thoroughly (4-min..)     Top it off using sprigs of parsley before serving.
**Nutrition Info:** Calories: 368; Protein: 24.2 grams; Fat: 23.9 grams

## Chicken Sausage, Artichoke, Kale, And White Bean Gratin

Servings: 8     Cooking Time: 45 Minutes
**Ingredients:**
- 2 teaspoons olive oil, plus 2 tablespoons
- 1 small yellow onion, chopped (about 2 cups)
- 1 (12-ounce) package fully cooked chicken-apple sausage, sliced
- 1 bunch kale, stemmed and chopped (6 to 7 cups)
- ½ cup dry white wine, such as sauvignon blanc
- 4 ounces soft goat cheese
- 2 (15.5-ounce) cans cannellini or great northern beans, drained and rinsed
- 1 (14-ounce) can quartered artichoke hearts
- 1 (14.5-ounce) can no-salt-added diced tomatoes
- 1 teaspoon herbes de Provence
- ¼ teaspoon kosher salt
- 1 cup panko bread crumbs
- 1 teaspoon garlic powder

**Directions:**
Preheat the oven to 350°F. Lightly oil a -by-9-inch glass or ceramic baking dish.     Heat teaspoons of oil in a 12-inch skillet over medium-high heat. When the oil is shimmering, add the onion and cook for 2 minutes. Add the sausage and brown for 3 minutes. Add the kale and cook until wilted, about 3 more minutes. Add the wine and cook for 1 additional minute.     Add the goat cheese and stir until it is melted and the mixture looks creamy.     Add the beans, artichokes, tomatoes, herbes de Provence, and salt, and stir to combine. Transfer the contents of the pan to the baking dish.     Mix the bread crumbs, the garlic powder, and the remaining 2 tablespoons of oil in a small bowl. Spread the bread crumbs evenly across the top of the casserole.     Cover the dish with foil and bake for 30 minutes. Remove the foil and bake for 15 more minutes, until the bread crumbs are lightly browned. Cool.     Place about 1½ cups of casserole in each of 8 containers.     STORAGE: Store covered containers in the refrigerator for up to 5 days. Gratin can be frozen for up to 3 months.
**Nutrition Info: Per Serving:** Total calories: 367; Total fat: 14g; Saturated fat: 5g; Sodium: 624mg; Carbohydrates: 40g; Fiber: 10g; Protein: 1

## Spinach Salad With Blood Orange Vinaigrette

Servings: 6     Cooking Time: 10 Minutes
**Ingredients:**
- ½ cup fresh blood orange juice
- 1/3 cup extra-virgin olive oil
- 2 tablespoons sherry reserve vinegar
- 1 tablespoon fresh grated ginger
- 1 teaspoon garlic powder
- 1 teaspoon ground sumac
- salt
- pepper
- 1/3 cup dried apricots, chopped
- 2 tablespoons sherry reserve vinegar
- 2 loaves pita bread
- 2/3 cup vegetable oil
- 1/3 cup raw unsalted almonds
- 1/3 cup raw sliced almonds
- ½ teaspoon sumac
- ½ teaspoon paprika
- salt
- 4 cups baby spinach
- 3 cups frisee lettuce, chopped
- 2 shallots, thinly sliced
- 1-2 blood oranges, peeled and sliced crosswise

**Directions:**
In a small bowl, soak the dried apricots in the sherry-reserved vinegar for about 5 minutes.     Drain apricots and set aside.     Toast pita bread until crispy and break into pieces.     Heat vegetable oil in a frying pan over medium-high heat.     Add broken pitas and almonds and fry them for a while.     Add sliced up almonds, sumac, and paprika, and toss everything well. Remove from heat once the almonds show a golden brown color.     Place on paper towels and allow to drain.     In a mixing bowl, add baby spinach, shallots, apricots, frisee lettuce.     Prepare the vinaigrette by taking a bowl and whisking in all blood orange vinaigrette Ingredients: listed above.     Before serving, dress the salad with the prepared orange vinaigrette and toss well.     Add fried pita chips and almonds and toss again.     Serve into individual bowls with a garnish of two blood orange slices.     Enjoy!
**Nutrition Info:Per Serving:**Calories: 462, Total Fat: 41.2 g, Saturated Fat: 6.9 g, Cholesterol: 0 mg, Sodium: 110 mg, Total Carbohydrate: 22.6 g, Dietary Fiber: 6.8 g, Total Sugars: 6.8 g, Protein: 6.1 g, Vitamin D: 0 mcg, Calcium: 163 mg, Iron: 3 mg, Potassium: 702 mg

## Lasagna Tortellini Soup

Servings: 6     Cooking Time: 6 Hours
**Ingredients:**
- 1 lb extra lean ground beef
- 1 package (16 oz) frozen cheese filled tortellini
- 3 cups beef broth
- 1/2 cup yellow onion, chopped
- 2 cloves garlic, minced
- 1 can (28 oz) crushed tomatoes
- 1 can (14.5 oz) petite diced tomatoes
- 1 can (6 oz) tomato paste
- 1 can (10.75 oz) tomato condensed soup
- 1 tsp white sugar
- 1 ½ tsp dried basil
- 1 tsp Italian seasoning
- 1/2 tbsp salt, to taste
- 1/4 tsp pepper
- Optional:
- 4 tbsp fresh parsley
- 1/2 tsp fennel seeds
- Toppings:
- Freshly grated Parmesan cheese
- Large spoonful of ricotta cheese

**Directions:**
In a large skillet over medium heat, brown the ground beef until cooked through     Add the onion and garlic in the last few minutes of the cooking     While the beef is cooking, pour in the crushed tomatoes, petite diced tomatoes, tomato paste, and tomato condensed soup in the slow cooker. - Don't drain the cans!     Add in the sugar, the dried basil, fennel, Italian seasoning, salt, and pepper, adjust to taste     Stir in the cooked ground beef with onions and garlic     Add in the beef broth – or dissolved beef bouillon cubes into boiling water     Cook on high for 3-4 hours or low for 5-hours.     15-20 minutes before you are ready to serve the soup, add in the frozen tortellini     Set the slow cooker to high and allow the tortellini to heat through     Allow to cool, then distribute the soup into the container and store in the fridge for up to 3 days     To Serve: Reheat in the microwave or on the stove top, top with freshly grated Parmesan cheese, a large spoonful of ricotta cheese, extra seasonings and freshly chopped parsley.
**Nutrition Info:Per Serving:** Calories:499;Total Fat: 17g;Total Carbs: 53g;Fiber: 8g;Protein: 34g

# Greek Quinoa Bowls

Servings: 2     Cooking Time: 12 Minutes

**Ingredients:**
- 1 cup quinoa
- 1 ½ cups water
- 1 cup chopped green bell pepper
- 1 cup chopped red bell pepper
- 1/3 cup crumbled feta cheese
- 1/4 cup extra virgin olive oil
- 2-3 tbsp apple cider vinegar
- Salt, to taste
- Pepper, to taste
- 1-2 tbsp fresh parsley
- To Serve:
- Hummus
- Pita wedges
- Olives
- Fresh tomatoes
- Sliced or chopped avocado
- Lemon wedges

**Directions:**
Rinse and drain the quinoa using a mesh strainer or sieve. Place a medium saucepan to medium heat and lightly toast the quinoa to remove any excess water. Stir as it toasts for just a few minutes, to add a nuttiness and fluff to the quinoa     Then add the water, set burner to high, and bring to a boil.     Once boiling, reduce heat to low and simmer, covered with the lid slightly ajar, for 12-1minutes or until quinoa is fluffy and the liquid have been absorbed     In the meantime, mix whisk together olive oil, apple cider vinegar, salt, and pepper to make the dressing, store in the fridge until ready to serve     Add in the red bell peppers, green bell peppers, and parsley     Give the quinoa a little fluff with a fork, remove from the pot     Allow to cool completely     Distribute among the containers, store for 2-3 days     To Serve: Reheat in the microwave for 1-2 minutes or until heated through.     Pour the dressing over the quinoa bowl, toss add the feta cheese. Season with additional salt and pepper to taste, if desired. Enjoy!

**Nutrition Info:Per Serving:** Calories:645;Carbs: 61g;Total Fat: 37g;Protein: 16g

# Salmon Stew

Servings: 2     Cooking Time: 20 Minutes

**Ingredients:**
- 1 pound salmon fillet, sliced
- 1 onion, chopped
- Salt, to taste
- 1 tablespoon butter, melted
- 1 cup fish broth
- ½ teaspoon red chili powder

**Directions:**
Season the salmon fillets with salt and red chili powder. Put butter and onions in a skillet and sauté for about 3 minutes.     Add seasoned salmon and cook for about 2 minutes on each side.     Add fish broth and secure the lid.     Cook for about 7 minutes on medium heat and open the lid.     Dish out and serve immediately. Transfer the stew in a bowl and keep aside to cool for meal prepping. Divide the mixture into 2 containers. Cover the containers and refrigerate for about 2 days. Reheat in the microwave before serving.

**Nutrition Info:**Calories: 272 ;Carbohydrates: 4.4g;Protein: 32.1g;Fat: 14.2g ;Sugar: 1.9g;Sodium: 275mg

# Balsamic Chicken And Veggie Skewers

Servings: 4     Cooking Time: 25 Minutes

**Ingredients:**
- 1 pound boneless, skinless chicken breasts, cut into 1-inch cubes
- ⅓ cup balsamic vinegar
- 4 tablespoons olive oil, divided
- 4 teaspoons dried Italian herbs, divided
- 2 teaspoons garlic powder, divided
- 2 teaspoons onion powder, divided
- 8 ounces whole button or cremini mushrooms, stems removed
- 1 large red bell pepper, cut into 1-inch squares
- 1 small red onion, quartered and layers pulled apart
- 1 large zucchini, sliced into ½-inch rounds
- ¾ teaspoon kosher salt
- 8 (11¾-inch) wooden or metal skewers, soaked in water for at least 1 hour if wooden

**Directions:**
Preheat the oven to 450°F. Line a sheet pan with aluminum foil.     Place the chicken in a gallon-size resealable bag along with the balsamic vinegar, tablespoons of oil, 2 teaspoons of Italian herbs, 1 teaspoon of garlic powder, and 1 teaspoon of onion powder. Seal the bag and make sure all the pieces of chicken are coated with marinade.     In a second resealable bag, place the mushrooms, bell pepper, onion, and zucchini and the remaining 2 tablespoons of oil, 2 teaspoons of Italian herbs, 1 teaspoon of garlic powder, and 1 teaspoon of onion powder. Seal the bag and shake to make sure the veggies are coated. Refrigerate both bags and marinate for at least 2 hours. Thread the chicken and veggies on 8 skewers, alternating both chicken and veggies on each skewer. Place 6 skewers vertically in the center of the pan, 1 horizontally at the top, and 1 at the bottom. Sprinkle half the salt over the skewers, then flip over and sprinkle the skewers with the remaining salt.     Bake for 15 minutes, carefully flip the skewers, then bake for another 10 minutes. Cool.     If you have containers long enough to fit the skewers, place 2 skewers directly in each of 4 containers. If not, break the skewers in half or slide the meat and veggies off the skewers.

STORAGE: Store covered containers in the refrigerator for up to 5 days.

**Nutrition Info:Per Serving:** Total calories: 224; Total fat: 10g; Saturated fat: 2g; Sodium: 631mg; Carbohydrates: 11g; Fiber: 3g; Protein: 27g

## Pesto Chicken And Tomato Zoodles

Servings: 4     Cooking Time: 15 Minutes
**Ingredients:**
- 3 Zucchini, inspiralized
- 2 boneless skinless chicken breasts
- 1 1/2 cup cherry tomatoes
- 2 tsp olive oil
- 1/2 tsp salt
- Store brought Pesto or Homemade Basil Pesto
- Salt, to taste
- Pepper, to taste

**Directions:**
Preheat grill to medium high heat     Season both sides of the chicken with salt and pepper     Place cherry tomatoes in a small bowl, add the olive oil and 1/2 tsp salt, and toss the tomatoes     In the meantime, inspiralize the zucchini, set aside     Pour the pesto over the zucchini noodles, using salad toss or tongs, mix the pesto in with the zoodles until it is completely combined Place the chicken on the grill and grill each side for 5-7 minutes, or until cooked through     Place cherry tomatoes in a grill basket and grill for 5 minutes, until tomatoes burst     Remove the tomatoes and chicken from the grill, slice the chicken and place both sliced chicken and tomatoes into the pesto zoodles bowl allow the dish to cool completely     Distribute among the containers, store for 2-3 days     To Serve: Reheat in the microwave for 1-2 minutes or until heated through. Enjoy
**Nutrition Info:Per Serving:** Calories:396;Carbs: 8g;Total Fat: 30g;Protein: 18g

## Broiled Herb Sole With Cauliflower Mashed Potatoes

Servings: 4     Cooking Time: 16 Minutes
**Ingredients:**
- 12 ounces cauliflower florets, cut into 1-inch pieces
- 1 (12-ounce) Yukon Gold potato, cut into ¾-inch pieces (do not peel)
- 2 tablespoons olive oil
- ¼ teaspoon kosher salt
- 2 teaspoons olive oil, plus more to grease the pan
- 3 tablespoons chopped parsley
- 3 tablespoons chopped fresh dill
- 1 tablespoon freshly squeezed lemon juice
- ½ teaspoon chopped garlic
- 1¼ pounds boneless, skinless sole or tilapia
- ¼ teaspoon kosher salt
- 4 lemon wedges, for serving

**Directions:**
TO MAKE THE CAULIFLOWER MASHED POTATOES     Pour enough water into a saucepan that it reaches ½ inch up the side of the pan. Turn the heat to high and bring the water to a boil. Add the cauliflower and potatoes, and cover the pan. Steam for 10 minutes or until the veggies are very tender.     Drain the vegetables if water remains in the pan. Transfer the

veggies to a large bowl and add the olive oil and salt. Taste and add an additional pinch of salt if you need it. Once the veggies have cooled, scoop ¾ cup of cauliflower mashed potatoes into each of containers. TO MAKE THE SOLE     Preheat the oven to the high broiler setting. Line a sheet pan with foil and lightly grease the pan with oil or cooking spray.     Mix the oil, parsley, dill, lemon juice, and garlic in a small bowl. Pat the fish with paper towels to remove excess moisture and place on the lined sheet pan. Sprinkle the salt over the fish, then spread the herb mixture over the fish. Broil for about 6 minutes or until the fish is flaky. If your fish is very thin, broil for 5 minutes.     When everything has cooled, place one quarter of the fish in each of the 4 cauliflower containers. Serve with lemon wedges.     STORAGE: Store covered containers in the refrigerator for up to 4 days.
**Nutrition Info:Per Serving:** Total calories: 291; Total fat: 11g; Saturated fat: 1g; Sodium: 423mg; Carbohydrates: 20g; Fiber: 2g; Protein: 29g

## Citrus Poached Lovely Salmon

Servings: 4     Cooking Time: 40 Minutes
**Ingredients:**
- 6 cups water
- ½ cup freshly squeezed lemon juice
- Juice of 1 lime
- Zest of 1 lime
- 1 sweet onion, thinly sliced
- 1 cup celery leaves, coarsely chopped
- 1 tablespoon fresh dill, chopped
- 1 tablespoon fresh thyme, chopped
- 2 dried bay leaves
- ½ teaspoon black peppercorns
- ½ teaspoon sea salt
- 1 (24 ounce) salmon side, skinned and deboned, cut into 4 pieces

**Directions:**
Take a large saucepan and place it over medium-high heat     Stir water, lemon, lime juice, lemoon juice, lime zest, onion, celery, greens, thyme, dill and bay leaves Strain the liquid through fine mesh sieve, discard any solids     Pour strained poaching liquid into large skillet over low heat     Bring to a simmer     Add fish and cover skillet, poach for 10 minutes until opaque Remove salmon from liquid and serve     Enjoy! Meal Prep/Storage Options: Store in airtight containers in your fridge for 1-3 days.
**Nutrition Info:**Calories: 248;Fat: 11g;Carbohydrates: 4g;Protein: 34g

## Bean Lettuce Wraps

Servings: 4     Cooking Time: 20 Minutes
**Ingredients:**
- 8 Romaine lettuce leaves
- ½ cup Garlic hummus or any prepared hummus
- ¾ cup chopped tomatoes
- 15 ounce can great northern beans, drained and rinsed
- ½ cup diced onion
- 1 tablespoon extra virgin olive oil
- ¼ cup chopped parsley
- ¼ teaspoon black pepper

**Directions:**
Set a skillet on top of the stove range over medium heat. In the skillet, warm the oil for a couple of minutes. Add the onion into the oil. Stir frequently as the onion cooks for a few minutes.     Combine the pepper and tomatoes and cook for another couple of minutes. Remember to stir occasionally.     Add the beans and continue to stir and cook for 2 to 3 minutes.     Turn the burner off, remove the skillet from heat, and add the parsley.     Set the lettuce leaves on a flat surface and spread 1 tablespoon of hummus on each leaf.     Divide the bean mixture onto the leaves.     Spread the bean mixture down the center of the leaves.     Fold the leaves by starting lengthwise on one side.     Fold over the other side so the leaf is completely wrapped. Serve and enjoy!
**Nutrition Info:** calories: 211, fats: 8 grams, carbohydrates: 28 grams, protein: 10 grams.

## Greek Chicken Shish Kebab

Servings: 6     Cooking Time: 10 Minutes
**Ingredients:**
- ¼ cup olive oil
- ¼ cup lemon juice
- ¼ cup white vinegar
- 2 garlic cloves, minced
- 1 teaspoon ground cumin
- 1 teaspoon dried oregano
- ½ teaspoon dried thyme
- ¼ teaspoon salt
- ¼ teaspoon ground black pepper
- 2 pounds boneless and skinless chicken breasts, cut up into 1½inch pieces
- 6 wooden skewers
- 2 large green or red bell peppers, cut up into 1inch pieces
- 12 cherry tomatoes
- 12 fresh mushrooms

**Directions:**
In a large bowl, whisk in olive oil, vinegar, garlic, lemon juice, cumin, thyme, oregano, salt, and black pepper. Mix well.     Add the chicken to the bowl and coat it thoroughly by tossing it.     Cover the bowl with plastic wrap, refrigerate, and allow it to marinate for 2 hours. Soak your wooden skewers in water for about 30 minutes.     Preheat grill to medium-high heat and lightly oil the grate.     Remove the chicken from your marinade and shake off any extra liquid.     Discard the remaining marinade.     Thread pieces of chicken with bits of onion, bell pepper, cherry tomatoes, and mushrooms alternating between them.     Cook on grill for 10 minutes each side until browned on all sides. Chill, place to containers.     Pre-heat before eating. Enjoy!
**Nutrition Info:Per Serving:** Calories: 183, Total Fat: 9.8 g, Saturated Fat: 1.4 g, Cholesterol: 22 mg, Sodium: 141 mg, Total Carbohydrate: 14.1 g, Dietary Fiber: 4.4 g, Total Sugars: 8.5 g, Protein: 6 g, Vitamin D: 130 mcg, Calcium: 42 mg, Iron: 3 mg, Potassium: 821 mg

## Skillet Shrimp With Summer Squash And Chorizo

Servings: 8     Cooking Time: 20 Minutes
**Ingredients:**
- 1 lb large shrimp or prawns, peeled and deveined, tail can remain or frozen frozen, thawed
- 7 oz Spanish Chorizo, or mild Chorizo or hot Chorizo, sliced
- Extra virgin olive oil
- Juice of 1/2 lemon
- 1 summer squash, halved then sliced, half moons
- 1 small hot pepper such as jalapeno pepper, optional
- 1/2 medium red onion, sliced
- Fresh parsley for garnish
- 3/4 tsp smoked paprika
- 3/4 tsp ground cumin
- 1/2 tsp garlic powder
- Salt, to taste
- Pepper, to taste

**Directions:**
Pat shrimp dry, then season with salt, pepper, paprika, cumin, and garlic powder, toss to coat, set aside     In a large cast iron skillet over medium-high, add the Chorizo and brown on both sides, about 4 minutes or until the Chorizo is cooked, transfer to a plate     In the same skillet, add a drizzle of extra virgin olive oil if needed     Add the summer squash, and a sprinkle of salt and pepper and sear undisturbed for about 3 to minutes on one side. turnover and sear another 2 minutes on the other side until nicely colored, transfer the squash to the plate with Chorizo     In the same skillet, now add a little extra virgin olive oil and tilting to make sure the bottom is well coated     Once heated, add the shrimp and cook, stirring frequently, until the shrimp flesh starts to turn a little pink, but still not quite fully cooked, about 3 minutes     Return the Chorizo and squash to the skillet, toss to combine, cook another 3 minutes or until shrimp is cooked – its pink and the tails turn a bright red     Transfer the shrimp skillet to a large serving platter, allow to cool     Distribute among the containers, store for 2-3 days     To Serve: Reheat on the stove for 1-2 minutes or until heated through. Squeeze 1/2 lemon on top, and sliced red onions and hot peppers.
**Nutrition Info:Per Serving:** Calories:192;Carbs: 4g;Total Fat: ;Protein: 17g

## Shrimp & Penne

Servings: 8    Cooking Time: 35 Minutes
**Ingredients:**
- Penne pasta (16 oz. pkg.)
- Salt (.25 tsp.)
- Olive oil (2 tbsp.)
- Diced tomatoes (2 - 14.5 oz. cans)
- Garlic (1 tbsp.)
- Red onion (.25 cup)
- White wine (.25 cup)
- Shrimp (1 lb.)
- Grated parmesan cheese (1 cup)

**Directions:**
Dice the red onion and garlic. Peel and devein the shrimp.    Add salt to a large soup pot of water and set it on the stovetop to boil. Add the pasta and cook for nine to ten minutes. Drain it thoroughly in a colander. Empty oil into a skillet. Warm it using the medium temperature setting.    Toss in the garlic and onion to sauté until they're tender.    Pour in the tomatoes and wine. Continue cooking for about ten minutes, stirring occasionally.    Fold in the shrimp and continue cooking for about five minutes or until it's opaque. Combine the pasta and shrimp and top it off with the cheese to serve.
**Nutrition Info:**Calories: 3   ;Fat: 8.5 grams;Protein: 24.5 grams

## Chickpeas And Brussel Sprouts Salad

Servings: 4    Cooking Time: 10 Minutes
**Ingredients:**
- 1 cup roasted chickpeas. To give the dish a saltier taste, you can add sea salt.
- 4 cups kale, chopped
- 9 ounces Brussels sprouts, shredded
- 1 avocado, peeled, pitted, and cut

**Directions:**
Divide the kale and Brussels sprouts into four bowls. Add the chickpeas and the avocado.    You can add a little sea salt and/or pepper to taste. Another tip for more taste is to drizzle a little Vinaigrette dressing or your favorite homemade Mediterranean dressing.
**Nutrition Info:**calories: 337, fats: 20 grams, carbohydrates: 30 grams, protein: 12 grams.

## Meat Loaf

Servings: 12    Cooking Time: 1 Hour 15 Minutes
**Ingredients:**
- 1 garlic clove, minced
- ½ teaspoon dried thyme, crushed
- ½ pound grass-fed lean ground beef
- 1 organic egg, beaten
- Salt and black pepper, to taste
- ¼ cup onions, chopped
- 1/8 cup sugar-free ketchup

- 2 cups mozzarella cheese, freshly grated
- ¼ cup green bell pepper, seeded and chopped
- ½ cup cheddar cheese, grated
- 1 cup fresh spinach, chopped

**Directions:**
Preheat the oven to 350 degrees F and grease a baking dish.    Put all the ingredients in a bowl except spinach and cheese and mix well.    Arrange the meat over a wax paper and top with spinach and cheese.    Roll the paper around the mixture to form a meatloaf. Remove the wax paper and transfer the meat loaf in the baking dish.    Put it in the oven and bake for about 1 hour.    Dish out and serve hot.    Meal Prep Tip: Let the meat loafs cool for about 10 minutes to bring them to room temperature before serving.
**Nutrition Info:**Calories: 43;Carbohydrates: 8g;Protein: 40.8g;Fat: 26g ;Sugar: 1.6g;Sodium: 587mg

## Couscous With Pepperoncini & Tuna

Servings: 4    Cooking Time: 20 Minutes
**Ingredients:**
- The Couscous:
- Chicken broth or water (1 cup)
- Couscous (1.25 cups)
- Kosher salt (.75 tsp.)
- The Accompaniments:
- Oil-packed tuna (2- 5-oz. cans)
- Cherry tomatoes (1 pint - halved)
- Sliced pepperoncini (.5 cup)
- Chopped fresh parsley (.33 cup)
- Capers (.25 cup)
- Olive oil (for serving)
- Black pepper & kosher salt (as desired)
- Lemon (1 quartered)

**Directions:**
Make the couscous in a small saucepan using water or broth. Prepare it using the medium heat temperature setting. Let it sit for about ten minutes.    Toss the tomatoes, tuna, capers, parsley, and pepperoncini into a mixing bowl.    Fluff the couscous when done and dust using the pepper and salt. Spritz it using the oil and serve with the tuna mix and a lemon wedge.
**Nutrition Info:**Calories: 226;Protein: 8 grams;Fat: 1 gram

## Tilapia With Avocado & Red Onion

Servings: 4    Cooking Time: 15 Minutes
**Ingredients:**
- Olive oil (1 tbsp.)
- Sea salt (.25 tsp.)
- Fresh orange juice (1 tbsp.)
- Tilapia fillets (four 4 oz. - more rectangular than square)
- Red onion (.25 cup)
- Sliced avocado (1)
- Also Needed: 9-inch pie plate

**Directions:**
Combine the salt, juice, and oil to add into the pie dish. Work with one fillet at a time. Place it in the dish and turn to coat all sides.    Arrange the fillets in a wagon wheel-shaped formation. (Each of the fillets should be in the center of the dish with the other end draped over the edge.    Place a tablespoon of the onion on top of each of the fillets and fold the end into the center. Cover the dish with plastic wrap, leaving one corner open to vent the steam.    Place in the microwave using the high heat setting for three minutes. It's done when the center can be easily flaked.    Top the fillets off with avocado and serve.
**Nutrition Info:**Calories: 200;Protein: 22 grams;Fat: 11 grams

## Baked Salmon With Dill

Servings: 4    Cooking Time: 15 Minutes
**Ingredients:**
- Salmon fillets (4- 6 oz. portions - 1-inch thickness)
- Kosher salt (.5 tsp.)
- Finely chopped fresh dill (1.5 tbsp.)
- Black pepper (.125 tsp.)
- Lemon wedges (4)

**Directions:**
Warm the oven in advance to reach 350° Fahrenheit. Lightly grease a baking sheet with a misting of cooking oil spray and add the fish. Lightly spritz the fish with the spray along with a shake of salt, pepper, and dill. Bake it until the fish is easily flaked (10 min..)    Serve with lemon wedges.
**Nutrition Info:**Calories: 2;Protein: 28 grams;Fat: 16 grams

## Steak And Veggies

Servings: 6    Cooking Time: 15 Minutes
**Ingredients:**
- 2 lbs baby red potatoes
- 16 oz broccoli florets
- 2 tbsp olive oil
- 3 cloves garlic, minced
- 1 tsp dried thyme
- Kosher salt, to taste
- Freshly ground black pepper, to taste
- 2 lbs (1-inch-thick) top sirloin steak, patted dry

**Directions:**

Preheat oven to broil    Lightly oil a baking sheet or coat with nonstick spray    In a large pot over high heat, boil salted water, cook the potatoes until parboiled for 12-15 minutes, drain well    Place the potatoes and broccoli in a single layer onto the prepared baking sheet    Add the olive oil, garlic and thyme, season with salt and pepper, to taste and then gently toss to combine    Season the steaks with salt and pepper, to taste, and add to the baking sheet in a single layer    Place it into oven and broil until the steak is browned and charred at the edges, about 4-5 minutes per side for medium-rare, or until the desired doneness    Distribute the steak and veggies among the containers. Store in the fridge for up to 3 days    To Serve: Reheat in the microwave for 1-2 minutes. Top with garlic butter and enjoy
**Nutrition Info:Per Serving:** Calories:460;Total Fat: 24g;Total Carbs: 24g;Fiber: 2.6g;Protein: 37g

## Lentil And Roasted Carrot Salad With Herbs And Feta

Servings: 4    Cooking Time: 25 Minutes
**Ingredients:**
- ¾ cup brown or green lentils
- 3 cups water
- 1 pound baby carrots, halved on the diagonal
- 2 teaspoons olive oil, plus 2 tablespoons
- ½ teaspoon kosher salt, divided
- 1 teaspoon garlic powder
- 1 cup packed parsley leaves, chopped
- ½ cup packed cilantro leaves, chopped
- ¼ cup packed mint leaves, chopped
- ½ teaspoon grated lemon zest
- 4 teaspoons freshly squeezed lemon juice
- ¼ cup crumbled feta cheese

**Directions:**
Preheat the oven to 400°F. Line a sheet pan with a silicone baking mat or parchment paper.    Place the lentils and water in a medium saucepan and turn the heat to high. As soon as the water comes to a boil, turn the heat to low and simmer until the lentils are firm yet tender, 10 to   minutes (see tip). Drain and cool. While the lentils are cooking, place the carrots on the sheet pan and toss with 2 tablespoons of oil, ¼ teaspoon of salt, and the garlic powder. Roast the carrots in the oven until firm yet tender, about 20 to 25 minutes. Cool when done.    In a large bowl, mix the cooled lentils, carrots, parsley, cilantro, mint, lemon zest, lemon juice, feta, the remaining 2 tablespoons of oil, and the remaining ¼ teaspoon of salt. Add more lemon juice and/or salt to taste if needed.    Place 1¼ cups of the mixture in each of 4 containers.    STORAGE: Store covered containers in the refrigerator for up to 5 days.
**Nutrition Info:Per Serving:** Total calories: 2; Total fat: 12g; Saturated fat: 3g; Sodium: 492mg; Carbohydrates: 31g; Fiber: 13g; Protein: 12g

## Cinnamon Squash Soup

Servings: 6    Cooking Time: 1 Hour
**Ingredients:**
- 1 small butternut squash, peeled and cut up into 1-inch pieces
- 4 tablespoons extra-virgin olive oil, divided
- 1 small yellow onion
- 2 large garlic cloves
- 1 teaspoon salt, divided
- 1 pinch black pepper
- 1 teaspoon dried oregano
- 2 tablespoons fresh oregano
- 2 cups low sodium chicken stock
- 1 cinnamon stick
- ½ cup canned white kidney beans, drained and rinsed
- 1 small pear, peeled and cored, chopped up into ½ inch pieces
- 2 tablespoons walnut pieces
- ¼ cup Greek yogurt
- 2 tablespoons freshly chopped parsley

**Directions:**
Preheat oven to 425 degrees F.    Place squash in bowl and season with a ½ teaspoon of salt and tablespoons of olive oil.    Spread the squash onto a roasting pan and roast for about 25 minutes until tender.    Set aside squash to let cool.    Heat remaining 2 tablespoons of olive oil in a medium-sized pot over medium-high heat. Add onions and sauté until soft.    Add dried oregano and garlic and sauté for 1 minute and until fragrant. Add squash, broth, pear, cinnamon stick, pepper, and remaining salt.    Bring mixture to a boil.    Once the boiling point is reached, add walnuts and beans. Reduce the heat and allow soup to cook for approximately 20 minutes until flavors have blended well.    Remove the cinnamon stick.    Use an immersion blender and blend the entire mixture until smooth.    Add yogurt gradually while whisking to ensure that you are getting a very creamy soup. Season with some additional salt and pepper if needed. Garnish with parsley and fresh oregano.    Enjoy!
**Nutrition Info:Per Serving:**Calories: 197, Total Fat: 11.6 g, Saturated Fat: 1.7 g, Cholesterol: 0 mg, Sodium: 264 mg, Total Carbohydrate: 20.2 g, Dietary Fiber: 7.1 g, Total Sugars: 4.3 g, Protein: 6.1 g, Vitamin D: 0 mcg, Calcium: 103 mg, Iron: 3 mg, Potassium: 425 mg

## Creamy Chicken

Servings: 2    Cooking Time: 25 Minutes
**Ingredients:**
- ½ small onion, chopped
- ¼ cup sour cream
- Salt and black pepper, to taste
- 1 tablespoon butter
- ¼ cup mushrooms
- ½ pound chicken breasts

**Directions:**

Heat butter in a skillet and add onions and mushrooms. Sauté for about 5 minutes and add chicken breasts and salt.    Secure the lid and cook for about 5 more minutes.    Add sour cream and cook for about 3 minutes.    Open the lid and dish out in a bowl to serve immediately.    Transfer the creamy chicken breasts in a dish and set aside to cool for meal prepping. Divide them in 2 containers and cover their lid. Refrigerate for 2-3 days and reheat in microwave before serving.
**Nutrition Info:**Calories: 335 ;Carbohydrates: 2.9g;Protein: 34g;Fat: 20.2g;Sugar: 0.8g;Sodium: 154mg

## Chicken Drummies With Peach Glaze

Servings: 4    Cooking Time: 25 Minutes
**Ingredients:**
- 2 pounds of chicken drummies, remove the skin
- 15 ounce can of sliced peaches, drain the juice
- ¼ cup cider vinegar
- ½ teaspoon paprika
- ¼ teaspoon black pepper
- ¼ cup honey
- 3 garlic cloves
- ¼ teaspoon sea salt

**Directions:**
Before you turn your oven on, make sure that one rack is 4 inches below the broiler element.    Set your oven's temperature to 500 degrees Fahrenheit.    Line a large baking sheet with a piece of aluminum foil.    Set a wire cooling rack on top of the foil.    Spray the rack with cooking spray.    Add the honey, peaches, garlic, vinegar, salt, paprika, and pepper into a blender. Mix until smooth.    Set a medium saucepan on top of your stove and set the range temperature to medium heat. Pour the mixture into the saucepan and bring it to a boil while stirring constantly.    Once the sauce is done, divide it into two small bowls and set one off to the side. With the second bowl, brush half of the mixture onto the chicken drummies.    Roast the drummies for 10 minutes.    Take the drummies out of the oven and switch to broiler mode.    Brush the drummies with the other half of the sauce from the second bowl.    Again, place the drummies back into the oven and set a timer for 5 minutes.    When the timer goes off, flip the drummies over and broil for another 3 to 4 minutes. Serve the drummies with the reserved sauce and enjoy!
**Nutrition Info:**calories: 291, fats: 5 grams, carbohydrates: 33 grams, protein: 30 grams.

## Berry Compote With Orange Mint Infusion

Servings: 8      Cooking Time: 20 Minutes
**Ingredients:**
- ½ cup water
- 3 orange pekoe tea bags
- 3 sprigs of fresh mint
- 1 cup fresh strawberries, hulled and halved lengthwise
- 1 cup fresh golden raspberries
- 1 cup fresh red raspberries
- 1 cup fresh blueberries
- 1 cup fresh blackberries
- 1 cup fresh sweet cherries, pitted and halved
- 1-milliliter bottle of Sauvignon Blanc
- 2/3 cup sugar
- ½ cup pomegranate juice
- 1 teaspoon vanilla
- fresh mint sprigs

**Directions:**
In a small saucepan, bring water to a boil and add tea bags and 3 mint sprigs.      Stir well, cover, remove from heat, and allow to stand for 10 minutes.      In a large bowl, add strawberries, red raspberries, golden raspberries, blueberries, blackberries, and cherries. Put to the side.      In a medium-sized saucepan, and add the wine, sugar, and pomegranate juice.      Pour the infusion (tea mixture) through a fine-mesh sieve and into the pan with wine.      Squeeze the bags to release the liquid, and then discard bags and mint springs. Cook well until the sugar has completely dissolved; remove from heat.      Stir in vanilla and allow to chill for 2 hours.      Pour the mix over the fruits.      Garnish with mint sprigs and serve.      Enjoy!
**Nutrition Info:Per Serving:**Calories: 119, Total Fat: 0.3 g, Saturated Fat: 0 g, Cholesterol: 0 mg, Sodium: 3 mg, Total Carbohydrate: 31.6 g, Dietary Fiber: 5 g, Total Sugars: 26.2 g, Protein: 1.2 g, Vitamin D: 0 mcg, Calcium: 28 mg, Iron: 1 mg, Potassium: 158 mg

## Quinoa Bruschetta Salad

Servings: 5      Cooking Time: 15 Minutes
**Ingredients:**
- 2 cups water
- 1 cup uncooked quinoa
- 1 (10-ounce) container cherry tomatoes, quartered
- 1 teaspoon chopped garlic
- 1¼ cups thinly sliced scallions, white and green parts (1 small bunch)
- 1 (8-ounce) container fresh whole-milk mozzarella balls (ciliegine), quartered
- 2 tablespoons balsamic vinegar
- 2 tablespoons olive oil
- ½ teaspoon kosher salt
- ½ cup fresh basil leaves, chiffonaded (cut into strips)

**Directions:**
Place the water and quinoa in a saucepan and bring to a boil. Cover, turn the heat to low, and simmer for minutes.      While the quinoa is cooking, place the tomatoes, garlic, scallions, mozzarella, vinegar, and oil

in a large mixing bowl. Stir to combine.      Once the quinoa is cool, add it to the tomato mixture along with the salt and basil. Mix to combine.      Place 1⅓ cups of the mixture in each of 5 containers and refrigerate. Serve at room temperature.      STORAGE: Store covered containers in the refrigerator for up to days.
**Nutrition Info:Per Serving:** Total calories: 323; Total fat: 1; Saturated fat: 6g; Sodium: 317mg; Carbohydrates: 30g; Fiber: 4g; Protein: 14g

## Zesty Lemon Parmesan Chicken And Zucchini Noodles

Servings: 2      Cooking Time: 15 Minutes
**Ingredients:**
- 2 packages Frozen zucchini noodle Spirals
- 1-1/2 lbs. boneless skinless chicken breast, cut into bite-sized pieces
- 1 tsp fine sea salt
- 2 tsp dried oregano
- 1/2 tsp ground black pepper
- 4 garlic cloves, minced
- 2 tbsp vegan butter
- 2 tsp lemon zest
- 2 tsp oil
- 1/3 cup parmesan
- 2/3 cup broth
- Lemon slices, for garnish
- Parsley, for garnish

**Directions:**
Cook zucchini noodles according to package instructions, drain well      In a large skillet over medium heat, add the oil      Season chicken with salt and pepper, brown chicken pieces, for about 4 minutes per side depending on the thickness, or until cooked through – Work in cook in batches if necessary      Transfer the chicken to a pan      In the same skillet, add in the garlic, and cook until fragrant about 30 seconds      Add in the butter, oregano and lemon zest, pour in chicken broth to deglaze making sure to scrape up all the browned bits stuck to the bottom of the pan      Turn the heat up to medium-high, bring sauce and chicken up to a boil, immediately lower the heat and stir in the parmesan cheese      Place the chicken back in pan and allow it to gently simmer for 3-4 minutes, or until sauce has slightly reduced and thickened up      Taste and adjust seasoning, allow the noodles to cool completely      Distribute among the containers, store for 2-3 days      To Serve: Reheat in the microwave for 1-2 minutes or until heated through. Garnish with the fresh parsley and lemon slices and enjoy!
**Nutrition Info:Per Serving:** Calories:633;Carbs: 4g;Total Fat: 35g;Protein: 70g

## Three Citrus Sauce Scallops

Servings: 4     Cooking Time: 15 Minutes
**Ingredients:**
- 2 teaspoons extra virgin olive oil
- 1 shallot, minced
- 20 sea scallops, cleaned
- 1 tablespoon lemon zest
- 2 teaspoons orange zest
- 1 teaspoon lime zest
- 1 tablespoon fresh basil, chopped
- ½ cup freshly squeezed lemon juice
- 2 tablespoons honey
- 1 tablespoon plain Greek yogurt
- Pinch of sea salt

**Directions:**
Take a large skillet and place it over medium-high heat
Add olive oil and heat it up     Add shallots and Saute
for 1 minute     Add scallops in the skillet and sear for 5
minutes, turning once     Move scallops to edge and stir
in lemon, orange, lime zest, basil, orange juice and
lemon juice     Simmer the sauce for 3 minutes
Whisk in honey, yogurt and salt     Cook for 4 minutes
and coat the scallops in the sauce     Serve and enjoy!
Meal Prep/Storage Options: Store in airtight containers
in your fridge for 1-2 days.
**Nutrition Info:**Calories: 207;Fat: 4g;Carbohydrates:
17g;Protein: 26g

## Steamed Mussels Topped With Wine Sauce

Servings: 4     Cooking Time: 15 Minutes
**Ingredients:**
- 2 pounds mussels
- 1 tablespoon extra virgin olive oil
- 1 cup sliced onion
- 1 cup dry white wine
- ¼ teaspoon ground black pepper
- ¼ teaspoon sea salt
- 3 sliced cloves of garlic
- 2 lemon slices
- Optional: lemon wedges for serving

**Directions:**
Set a large colander in the sink and turn your water to
cold.     Run water over the mussels, but do not let them
sit in the water. If you notice any shells that are not
tightly sealed or are cracked, you need to discard them.
All shells need to be closed tightly.     Turn off the water
and leave the mussels in the colander.     Set a large
skillet on your stovetop and turn your range heat to
medium-high.     Pour the olive oil into the skillet and
allow it to heat up before you add the onion.     Saute
the onion for 2 to 3 minutes.     Combine the garlic and
cook the mixture for another minute while stirring
continuously.     Pour in the wine, pepper, lemon slices,
and salt. Stir the ingredients as you bring them to a boil.
Add the mussels and place the lid on the skillet.     Cook
the mixture for 3 to 4 minutes or until the shells begin
to open on the mussels. It will help to gently pick up the
skillet and shake it a couple of times when the mussels

are cooking.     If you notice any shells that did not
open, use a spoon and discard them.     Scoop the
mussels into a serving bowl and pour the mixture over
the top.     If you have lemon wedges, place them on the
top of the steamed mussels before serving. Enjoy!
**Nutrition Info:**calories: 222, fats: 7 grams,
carbohydrates: 11 grams, protein: 18 grams.

## Spice Potato Soup

Servings: 4-6     Cooking Time: 30 Minutes
**Ingredients:**
- 2 tablespoons extra virgin olive oil
- 1 large onion, chopped
- 2 garlic cloves, crushed
- 1 pound sweet potatoes, peeled and cut into
  medium pieces
- ½ teaspoon ground cumin
- ¼ teaspoon ground chili
- ½ teaspoon ground coriander
- ¼ teaspoon ground cinnamon
- ¼ teaspoon salt
- 2 cups chicken stock
- ¼ cup of  low-fat crème Fraiche
- 2 tablespoons freshly chopped parsley
- coriander

**Directions:**
Heat olive oil in a large pan over medium-high heat.
Add onions and sauté until slightly browned.     Reduce
heat to medium, add garlic, and keep cooking for 2-
minutes more.     Add sweet potatoes and sauté for 3-
minutes.     Add the remaining spices and season with
salt.     Cook for 2 minutes.     Add stock, turn the heat
up, and bring the mixture to a boil, stirring occasionally.
Cover and lower heat to a slow simmer.     Cook for 20
minutes until the potatoes are tender.     Remove the
pan from the heat.     Take an immersion blender and
puree the whole mixture.     Add a bit of water if the
soup is too thick.     Check the soup for seasoning.
Ladle the soup into your jars.     Give a swirl of crème
Fraiche.     Sprinkle with chopped parsley.     Enjoy!
**Nutrition Info:Per Serving:**Calories: 176, Total Fat:
8.4 g, Saturated Fat: 0.8 g, Cholesterol: 0 mg, Sodium:
362 mg, Total Carbohydrate: 24.3 g, Dietary Fiber: 3.8
g, Total Sugars: 1.7 g, Protein: 2 g, Vitamin D: 0 mcg,
Calcium: 30 mg, Iron: 1 mg, Potassium: 675 mg

## Spicy Cajun Shrimp

Servings: 2     Cooking Time: 50 Minutes

**Ingredients:**
- 3 cloves garlic, crushed
- 4 tablespoons butter, divided
- 2 large zucchini, spiraled
- 1 red pepper, sliced
- 1 onion, sliced
- 20-30 jumbo shrimp
- 1 teaspoon paprika
- dash cayenne pepper
- ½ teaspoon of sea salt
- dash red pepper flakes
- 1 teaspoon garlic powder
- 1 teaspoon onion powder

**Directions:**
Pass the zucchini through a spiralizer.     Combine the Ingredients: listed under Cajun Seasoning above. Add oil and 2 tablespoons of butter to a pan and allow to heat up over medium heat.     Add onion and red pepper and sauté for minutes.     Add shrimp and cook well.     Place the remaining 2 tablespoons of butter in another pan and allow it to melt over medium heat. Add zucchini noodles and sauté for 3 minutes. Transfer the noodles to a container.     Top with the prepared Cajun shrimp and veggie mix.     Season with salt and enjoy!

**Nutrition Info:Per Serving:**Calories: 734, Total Fat: 24.2 g, Saturated Fat: 14.7 g, Cholesterol: 12mg, Sodium: 6703 mg, Total Carbohydrate: 29.1 g, Dietary Fiber: 7.1 g, Total Sugars: 24.9 g, Protein: 106.8 g, Vitamin D: 16 mcg, Calcium: 694 mg, Iron: 6 mg, Potassium: 1229 mg

## Pan-seared Salmon

Servings: 4     Cooking Time: 20 Minutes

**Ingredients:**
- Salmon fillets (4 @ 6 oz. each)
- Olive oil (2 tbsp.)
- Capers (2 tbsp.)
- Pepper & salt (.125 tsp. each)
- Lemon (4 slices)

**Directions:**
Warm a heavy skillet for about three minutes using the medium heat temperature setting.     Lightly spritz the salmon with oil. Arrange them in the pan and increase the temperature setting to high.     Sear for approximately three minutes. Sprinkle with the salt, pepper, and capers.     Flip the salmon over and continue cooking for five minutes or until browned the way you like it.     Garnish with lemon slices and serve.

**Nutrition Info:**Calories: 371;Protein: 33.7 grams;Fat: 25.1 grams

## Pasta Faggioli Soup

Servings: 8     Cooking Time: 1 Hour

**Ingredients:**
- 1 28-ounce can diced tomatoes
- 1 14-ounce can great northern beans, undrained
- 14 ounces spinach, chopped and drained
- 1 14-ounce can tomato sauce
- 3 cups chicken broth
- 1 tablespoon garlic, minced
- 8 slices bacon, cooked crisp, crumbled
- 1 tablespoon dried parsley
- 1 teaspoon garlic powder
- 1½ teaspoons salt
- ½ teaspoon ground black pepper
- ½ teaspoon dried basil
- ½ pound seashell pasta
- 3 cups water

**Directions:**
Take a large stockpot and add the diced tomatoes, spinach, beans, chicken broth, tomato sauce, water, bacon, garlic, parsley, garlic powder, pepper, salt, and basil.     Put it over medium-high heat and bring the mixture to a boil.     Immediately reduce the heat to low and simmer for 40 minutes, covered.     Add pasta and cook uncovered for about 10 minutes until al dente. Ladle the soup into serving bowls.     Sprinkle some cheese on top.     Enjoy!

**Nutrition Info:Per Serving:**Calories: 23 Total Fat: 2.3 g, Saturated Fat: 0.7 g, Cholesterol: 2 mg, Sodium: 2232 mg, Total Carbohydrate: 40.6 g, Dietary Fiber: 13.1 g, Total Sugars: 6.4 g, Protein: 16.3 g, Vitamin D: 0 mcg, Calcium: 160 mg, Iron: 5 mg, Potassium: 1455 mg

## Fattoush Salad

Servings: 4    Cooking Time: 10 Minutes
**Ingredients:**
- 2 loaves pita bread
- 3 tablespoons extra virgin olive oil
- ½ teaspoon of sumac
- salt
- pepper
- 1 heart romaine lettuce, chopped
- 1 English cucumber, chopped
- 5 Roma tomatoes, chopped
- 5 green onions, chopped
- 5 radishes, stems removed, thinly sliced
- 2 cups fresh parsley leaves, stems removed, chopped
- 1 cup fresh mint leaves, chopped
- lime juice, 1½ limes
- 1/3 bottle extra virgin olive oil
- salt
- pepper
- 1 teaspoon ground sumac
- ¼ teaspoon ground cinnamon
- scant ¼ teaspoon ground allspice

**Directions:**
Toast pita bread until crisp but not browned.    Heat 3 tablespoons of olive oil in a large pan over medium heat. Break the toasted pita into pieces and add them to the oil.    Fry pita bread until browned, making sure to toss them from time to time.    Add salt, ½ a teaspoon of sumac, and pepper.    Remove the pita from the heat and place on a paper towel to drain.    In a large mixing bowl, combine lettuce, tomatoes, cucumber, green onions, parsley, and radish.    Before serving, make the lime vinaigrette by mixing all Ingredients: listed above under vinaigrette in a separate bowl.    Pour the vinaigrette over the Ingredients: in the other bowl and gently toss.    Add pita chips on top and the remaining sumac.    Give it a final toss and enjoy!
**Nutrition Info:Per Serving:**Calories: 200, Total Fat: 11.5 g, Saturated Fat: 1.7 g, Cholesterol: 0 mg, Sodium: 113 mg, Total Carbohydrate: 23.5 g, Dietary Fiber: 5.8 g, Total Sugars: 6.6 g, Protein: 5.2 g, Vitamin D: 0 mcg, Calcium: 145 mg, Iron: 6 mg, Potassium: 852 mg

## Roast Chicken

Servings: 6    Cooking Time: 1 – 1 ½ Hour
**Ingredients:**
- fresh orange juice, 1 large orange
- ¼ cup Dijon mustard
- ¼ cup olive oil
- 4 teaspoons dried Greek oregano
- salt
- ground black pepper
- 12 potatoes, peeled and cubed
- 5 garlic cloves, minced
- 1 whole chicken

**Directions:**
Preheat oven to 375 degrees F.    Take a bowl and whisk in orange juice, Greek oregano, Dijon mustard, salt, and pepper. Mix well.    Add potatoes to the bowl and coat them thoroughly.    Transfer the potatoes to a large baking dish, leaving remaining juice in a bowl. Stuff the garlic cloves into your chicken (under the skin).    Place the chicken into the bowl with the remaining juice and coat it thoroughly.    Transfer chicken to the baking dish, placing it on top of the potatoes.    Pour any extra juice on top of chicken and potatoes.    Bake uncovered until the thickest part of the chicken registers 160 degrees F, and the juices run clear, anywhere from 60 – minutes.    Remove the chicken and cover it with doubled aluminum foil. Allow it to rest for 10 minutes.    Slice, spread over containers and enjoy!
**Nutrition Info:Per Serving:**Calories: 1080, Total Fat: 36.4 g, Saturated Fat: 8.8 g, Cholesterol: 325 mg, Sodium: 458 mg, Total Carbohydrate: 70.5 g, Dietary Fiber: 11.1 g, Total Sugars: 6.3 g, Protein: 16 g, Vitamin D: 0 mcg, Calcium: 120 mg, Iron: 7 mg, Potassium: 2691 mg

## Chicken Eggplant

Servings: 5    Cooking Time: 40 Minutes
**Ingredients:**
- 3 pieces of eggplants, peeled and cut up lengthwise into ½ inch slices
- 3 tablespoons olive oil
- 6 skinless and boneless chicken breast halves, diced
- 1 onion, diced
- 2 tablespoons tomato paste
- ½ cup water
- 2 teaspoons dried oregano
- salt
- pepper

**Directions:**
Place the eggplant strips in a large pot filled with lightly salted water.    Allow them to soak for 30 minutes. Remove the eggplant from the pot and brush thoroughly with olive oil.    Heat a skillet over medium heat.    Add eggplant and sauté for a few minutes. Transfer the sautéed eggplant to a baking dish.    Heat a large skillet over medium heat.    Add chicken, onion, and sauté.    Stir in water and tomato paste.    Reduce heat to low, cover, and simmer for minutes.    Preheat oven to 400 degrees F.    Pour the chicken tomato mix over your eggplant.    Season with oregano, pepper, and salt.    Cover with aluminum foil and bake for 20 minutes.    Cool, place to containers and chill.
**Nutrition Info:Per Serving:**Calories: 319, Total Fat: 11.3 g, Saturated Fat: 1.2 g, Cholesterol: 117 mg, Sodium: 143 mg, Total Carbohydrate: 7.2 g, Dietary Fiber: 3.1 g, Total Sugars: 3.5 g, Protein: 48 g, Vitamin D: 0 mcg, Calcium: 22 mg, Iron: 2 mg, Potassium: 244 mg

## Grilled Steak

Servings: 2      Cooking Time: 15 Minutes
**Ingredients:**
- ¼ cup unsalted butter
- 2 garlic cloves, minced
- ¾ pound beef top sirloin steaks
- ¾ teaspoon dried rosemary, crushed
- 2 oz. parmesan cheese, shredded
- Salt and black pepper, to taste

**Directions:**
Preheat the grill and grease it.      Season the sirloin steaks with salt and black pepper.      Transfer the steaks on the grill and cook for about 5 minutes on each side. Dish out the steaks in plates and keep aside. Meanwhile, put butter and garlic in a pan and heat until melted.      Pour it on the steaks and serve hot.      Divide the steaks in 2 containers and refrigerate for about 3 days for meal prepping purpose. Reheat in microwave before serving.
**Nutrition Info:**Calories: 3 ;Carbohydrates: 1.5g ;Protein: 41.4g;Fat: 23.6g;Sugar: 0g;Sodium: 352mg

## Beef And Veggie Lasagna

Servings: 10      Cooking Time: 1 Hour 10 Minutes
**Ingredients:**
- 3 teaspoons olive oil, divided
- 1 medium zucchini, quartered lengthwise and chopped (about 1⅓ cups)
- 3 cups packed baby spinach
- 1 cup chopped yellow onion
- 1 teaspoon chopped garlic
- 8 ounces button or cremini mushrooms, finely chopped
- 1 cup shredded carrots
- 8 ounces lean (90/10) ground beef
- ½ cup dry red wine
- 1 (28-ounce) can low-sodium or no-salt-added crushed tomatoes
- 1 (15-ounce) can tomato sauce
- ¼ teaspoon kosher salt
- 1 (16-ounce) container low-fat (2%) cottage cheese
- 1 large egg
- 3 tablespoons grated Parmesan cheese
- 2 cups shredded part-skim mozzarella cheese, divided
- ½ cup fresh basil leaves, chopped
- 1 (9-ounce) box oven-ready lasagna noodles

**Directions:**
Preheat the oven to 375°F.      Heat 1 teaspoon of oil in a 1inch skillet over medium-high heat. When the oil is shimmering, add the zucchini and cook for 2 minutes. Add the spinach and continue to cook for 1 more minute. Remove the veggies to a plate.      In the same skillet, heat the remaining 2 teaspoons of oil over medium-high heat. When the oil is hot, add the onion and garlic and cook for 2 minutes. Add the mushrooms and carrots and cook for 4 more minutes. Add the ground beef and continue cooking for 4 more minutes, until the meat has browned. Add the wine and cook for 1 minute. Add the crushed tomatoes, tomato sauce, and salt, stir, and turn off the heat.      In a large mixing bowl, combine the cottage cheese, egg, and Parmesan, ½ cup of shredded cheese, and the basil.      Ladle 2 cups of sauce on the bottom of a 9-by-13-inch glass or ceramic baking dish. Place 4 noodles side by side in the pan. Layer 1 cup of sauce, half of the veggies, and half of the cottage cheese. Repeat with 4 more noodles, 1 cup of sauce, the remaining half of the veggies, and the remaining half of the cottage cheese. Top with 4 more noodles, the remainder of the sauce, and the remaining 1½ cups of shredded cheese.      Cover the pan with foil, trying not to touch the foil to the cheese, and bake for 40 minutes. Remove the foil and bake for 10 to 15 more minutes, until the cheese starts to brown.      When the lasagna cools, cut it into 10 pieces and place 1 piece in each of 10 containers.      STORAGE: Store covered containers in the refrigerator for up to 5 days. Cooked lasagna freezes well and can last for up to 3 months.
**Nutrition Info:Per Serving:** Total calories: 321; Total fat: 11g; Saturated fat: 4g; Sodium: 680mg; Carbohydrates: 34g; Fiber: 5g; Protein: 24g

## Greek Shrimp And Farro Bowls

Servings: 4      Cooking Time: 20 Minutes
**Ingredients:**
- 1 lb peeled and deveined shrimp
- 3 Tbsp. extra virgin olive oil
- 2 cloves garlic, minced
- 2 bell peppers, sliced thick
- 2 medium-sized zucchinis, sliced into thin rounds
- pint cherry tomatoes, halved
- ¼ cup thinly sliced green or black olives
- 4 Tbsp. 2% reduced-fat plain Greek yogurt
- Juice of 1 lemon
- 2 tsp fresh chopped dill
- 1 Tbsp. fresh chopped oregano
- ½ tsp smoked paprika
- ½ tsp sea salt
- ¼ tsp black pepper
- 1 cup dry farro

**Directions:**
In a bowl, add the olive oil, garlic, lemon, dill, oregano, paprika, salt, and pepper, whisk to combine      Pour 3/4 the amount of marinade over shrimp, toss to coat and all to stand 10 minutes      Reserve the rest of the marinade for later      Cook the farro according to package instructions in water or chicken stock      In a grill pan or nonstick skillet over medium heat, add the olive      Once heated, add shrimp, cook for 2-3 minutes per side, until no longer pink, then transfer to a plate Working in batches, cook bell pepper, zucchinis, and cherry tomatoes to the grill pan or skillet, cook for 5-6 minutes, until softened      allow the dish to cool completely      Distribute the farro among the containers, evenly add the shrimp, grilled vegetables, olives, and tomatoes, store for 2 days      To Serve: Reheat in the microwave for 1-2 minutes or until heated through. Drizzle the reserved marinade over top. Top each bowl with 1 tbsp Greek yogurt and extra lemon juice, if desired
**Nutrition Info:Per Serving:** Calories:428;Carbs: 45g;Total Fat: 13g;Protein: 34g

## Asparagus Salmon Fillets

Servings: 2     Cooking Time: 30 Minutes
**Ingredients:**
- 1 teaspoon olive oil
- 4 asparagus stalks
- 2 salmon fillets
- ¼ cup butter
- ¼ cup champagne
- Salt and freshly ground black pepper, to taste

**Directions:**
Preheat the oven to 355 degrees F and grease a baking dish.      Put all the ingredients in a bowl and mix well. Put this mixture in the baking dish and transfer it in the oven.      Bake for about 20 minutes and dish out. Place the salmon fillets in a dish and keep aside to cool for meal prepping. Divide it into 2 containers and close the lid. Refrigerate for 1 day and reheat in microwave before serving.

**Nutrition Info:**Calories: 475 ;Carbohydrates: 1.1g;Protein: 35.2g;Fat: 38g;Sugar: 0.5g;Sodium: 242mg

## Grilled Calamari With Berries

Servings: 4     Cooking Time: 5 Minutes
**Ingredients:**
- ¼ cup olive oil
- ¼ cup extra virgin olive oil
- 1 thinly sliced apple
- ¾ cup blueberries
- ¼ cup sliced almonds
- 1 ½ pounds calamari tube
- ¼ cup dried cranberries
- 6 cups spinach
- 2 tablespoons apple cider vinegar
- 1 tablespoon lemon juice
- Sea salt and pepper to your liking

**Directions:**
Start by making the vinaigrette. Combine apple cider vinegar, lemon juice, extra virgin olive oil, sea salt, and pepper. Whisk well and set aside.      Set your grill to medium heat.      In a separate bowl, add the calamari tube and mix with salt, pepper, and olive oil.      Set the calamari on the grill and cook both sides for 2 to 3 minutes.      In another bowl, mix the salad by adding the spinach, cranberries, almonds, blueberries, and apples. Toss to mix.      Set the cooked calamari onto a cutting board and let it cool for a few minutes. Cut them into ¼-inch thick rings and then toss them into the salad bowl.      Sprinkle the vinaigrette sauce onto the salad. Toss to mix the ingredients and enjoy!

**Nutrition Info:**calories: 567, fats: 24.4 grams, carbohydrates: 30 grams, protein: 55 grams.

## Italian Sausage And Veggie Pizza Pasta

Servings: 8     Cooking Time: 30 Minutes

**Ingredients:**
- 1 tsp olive oil
- 1 (2.25 oz) can of sliced black olives
- 1 (28 oz) can of tomato sauce
- 1 (16 oz) box penne pasta
- 3 cups water
- 3 sweet Italian sausage links, casings removed, around 1 lb of sausage
- 1 cup sliced onions
- 1 cup sliced green bell pepper
- 2-3 garlic cloves, minced or pressed
- 8 oz. sliced mushrooms
- 1/2 cup Pepperoni, cut in half and then each half cut into thirds + a few extra whole pieces for topping
- 1/2 tsp Italian seasoning
- 1/2 tsp salt
- Salt, to taste
- Pepper to taste
- 2 cups shredded mozzarella cheese, divided
- Garnish:
- Chopped fresh parsley and Romano cheese

**Directions:**
In a deep heavy-bottom, oven-safe pot over medium heat, add the oil      Once heated, add in the sausage and break it up with a wooden spoon      Then add in the onions, peppers, garlic and mushrooms, stir to combine, season with salt and pepper to taste. Sauté until the sausage crumbles have browned, stirring frequently for around 10 minutes      Add in the pepperoni and olives to the pan, sauté for 1-2 minutes. Then add in the sauce, water, Italian seasoning, salt and pasta to the pan, stir to combine      Bring the pot to a boil      Once boiling, reduce the heat to medium low, cover and allow to simmer for 10 minutes, stirring occasionally      Remove the cover and continue to simmer for 3-5 minutes, stirring occasionally      Stir in 1/2 cup of shredded Mozzarella cheese, sprinkle the remaining cheese on top      Arrange a few more whole pepperonis on top of the cheese, broil for a few minutes until the cheese is bubbling and melted      Top with the parsley and Romano cheese      Allow to cool and distribute the pasta evenly among the containers. Store in the fridge for 3-4 days or in the freezer for 2 weeks. To Serve: Reheat in the oven at 375 degrees for 1-2 minutes or until heated through.      Recipe Note: If you would like it to be spicy, you can also use hot Italian sausage.

**Nutrition Info:Per Serving:** Calories:450;Total Fat: 21.9g;Total Carbs: 22g;Fiber: 5g;Protein: 43g

## Baked Chicken Thighs With Lemon, Olives, And Brussels Sprouts

Servings: 4     Cooking Time: 40 Minutes
**Ingredients:**
- 2 tablespoons olive oil, divided
- 1 pound Brussels sprouts, stemmed and halved (quartered if the sprouts are extra large)
- 1 pound boneless, skinless chicken thighs
- 2 teaspoons chopped garlic
- 1 teaspoon dried oregano
- ½ teaspoon kosher salt
- 3 tablespoons freshly squeezed lemon juice
- ½ cup pitted kalamata olives

**Directions:**
Preheat the oven to 350°F.     Spread 1 tablespoon of oil over the bottom of a 13-by-9-inch glass or ceramic baking dish. Add the Brussels sprouts to the pan and spread out evenly. Place the chicken on top of the sprouts and rub the garlic and oregano into the top of the chicken.     Sprinkle the salt, the remaining 1 tablespoon of oil, the lemon juice, and the olives over the contents of the pan.     Cover the pan with aluminum foil and bake for 20 minutes. Remove the foil and bake uncovered for 20 more minutes. Cool. Place one quarter of the chicken and ¾ cup of Brussels sprouts in each of 4 containers. Drizzle any remaining juices from the pan over the chicken.     STORAGE: Store covered containers in the refrigerator for 5 days.
**Nutrition Info:Per Serving:** Total calories: 28 Total fat: 18g; Saturated fat: 3g; Sodium: 737mg; Carbohydrates: 14g; Fiber: 5g; Protein: 20g

## Slow Cooker Lamb, Herb, And Bean Stew

Servings: 4     Cooking Time: 15 Minutes
**Ingredients:**
- 3 bunches of parsley (about 6 packed cups of leaves)
- 1 large bunch cilantro (about 1½ packed cups of leaves)
- 1 bunch scallions, sliced (both white and green parts, about 1¼ cups)
- 1 pound leg of lamb, fat trimmed, cut into 1-inch pieces
- 2 tablespoons olive oil, divided
- 1 medium onion, chopped
- 2 teaspoons chopped garlic
- 2 teaspoons turmeric
- ¾ teaspoon kosher salt
- 2 tablespoons tomato paste
- 2½ cups low-sodium chicken broth
- 2 (15.5-ounce) cans low-sodium kidney beans, drained and rinsed
- 2 tablespoons freshly squeezed lemon juice

**Directions:**
Finely chop the parsley leaves, cilantro leaves, and scallions with a knife, or pulse in the food processor until finely chopped but not puréed. With this amount of herbs, you'll need to pulse in two batches.     Pat the lamb cubes with a paper towel. Heat a 1inch skillet over medium-high heat and add 1 tablespoon of oil. Once the oil is shimmering, add the lamb and brown for 5 minutes, flipping after 3 minutes. Place the lamb in the slow cooker.     Turn the heat down to medium and add the remaining 1 tablespoon of oil to the skillet. Once the oil is hot, add the onions and garlic and sauté for minutes. Add the turmeric, salt, and tomato paste and continue to cook for 2 more minutes, stirring frequently.     Add the chopped parsley, cilantro, and scallions. Sauté for 5 minutes, stirring occasionally. While the herbs are cooking, add the broth, beans, and lemon juice to the slow cooker. Add the herb mixture when it's done cooking on the stove. Turn the slow cooker to the low setting and cook for 8 hours.     Taste and add more salt and/or lemon juice if needed. Cool. Scoop 2 cups of stew into each of 4 containers. STORAGE: Store covered containers in the refrigerator for up to 5 days. Stew can be frozen for up to 4 months.
**Nutrition Info:Per Serving:** Total calories: 486; Total fat: 15g; Saturated fat: 5g; Sodium: 6mg; Carbohydrates: 51g; Fiber: 15g; Protein: 41g

## Holiday Chicken Salad

Servings: 2     Cooking Time: 25 Minutes
**Ingredients:**
- 1 celery stalk, chopped
- 1½ cups cooked grass-fed chicken, chopped
- ¼ cup fresh cranberries
- ¼ cup sour cream
- ½ apple, chopped
- ¼ yellow onion, chopped
- 1/8 cup almonds, toasted and chopped
- 2-ounce feta cheese, crumbled
- ¼ cup avocado mayonnaise
- Salt and black pepper, to taste

**Directions:**
Stir together all the ingredients in a bowl except almonds and cheese.     Top with almonds and cheese to serve.     Meal Prep Tip: Don't add almonds and cheese in the salad if you want to store the salad. Cover with a plastic wrap and refrigerate to serve.
**Nutrition Info:**Calories: 336 ;Carbohydrates: 8.8g;Protein: 25g;Fat: 23.2g ;Sugar: 5.4g;Sodium: 383mg

## Costa Brava Chicken

Servings: 4    Cooking Time: 35 Minutes
**Ingredients:**
- 1 20-ounce can pineapple chunks
- 10 skinless and boneless chicken breast halves
- 1 tablespoon vegetable oil
- 1 teaspoon ground cumin
- 1 teaspoon ground cinnamon
- 2 garlic cloves, minced
- 1 onion, quartered
- 1 14-ounce can stewed tomatoes
- 2 cups black olives
- ½ cup salsa
- 2 tablespoons water
- 1 red bell pepper, thinly sliced
- salt

**Directions:**
Drain the pineapple chunks, but be sure to reserve the juice.    Sprinkle pineapples with salt.    Heat oil in a large frying pan over medium heat.    Add the chicken and cook until brown.    Combine the cinnamon and cumin and sprinkle over the chicken.    Add garlic and onion and cook until the onions are tender.    Add reserved pineapple juices, olives, tomatoes, and salsa. Reduce heat, cover, and allow to simmer for 25 minutes.    Combine the cornstarch and water in a bowl.    Add the cornstarch mixture to the pan and stir. Add the bell pepper and simmer for a little longer until the sauce bubbles and thickens.    Stir in pineapple chunks until thoroughly heated.    Enjoy!
**Nutrition Info:Per Serving:**Calories: 651, Total Fat: 16.5 g, Saturated Fat: 1.7 g, Cholesterol: 228 mg, Sodium: 1053 mg, Total Carbohydrate: 34.7 g, Dietary Fiber: 7.2 g, Total Sugars: 20.3 g, Protein: 94.5 g, Vitamin D: 0 mcg, Calcium: 118 mg, Iron: 6 mg, Potassium: 606 mg

## One Skillet Greek Lemon Chicken And Rice

Servings: 5    Cooking Time: 45 Minutes
**Ingredients:**
- Marinade:
- 2 tsp dried oregano
- 1 tsp dried minced onion
- 4-5 cloves garlic, minced
- Zest of 1 lemon
- 1/2 tsp kosher salt
- 1/2 tsp black pepper
- 1-2 Tbsp olive oil to make a loose paste
- 5 bone-in, skin on chicken thighs
- Rice:
- 1 1/2 Tbsp olive oil
- 1 large yellow onion, peeled and diced
- 1 cup dry long-grain white rice (NOT minute or quick cooking varieties)
- 2 cups chicken stock
- 1 1/4 tsp dried oregano
- 5 cloves garlic, minced
- 3/4 tsp kosher salt
- 1/2 tsp black pepper
- Lemon slices, optional
- Fresh minced parsley, for garnish
- Extra lemon zest, for garnish

**Directions:**
In a large resealable plastic bag, add the oregano, dried minced onion, garlic, lemon zest, salt, black pepper, and olive oil, massage to combine    Add chicken thighs, and then turn/massage to coat, refrigerate 15 minutes or overnight    Preheat oven to o F degrees    In a large cast iron or heavy oven safe skillet over medium-high heat, add 1 1/2 Tbsp olive oil to    Remove the chicken thighs from the refrigerator, shake off the excess marinade and add chicken thighs, skin side down, to pan, cook 4-minutes per side    Transfer to a plate and wipe the skillet lightly with a paper towel to remove any burnt bits, reserving chicken grease in pan. Lower the heat to medium and add onion to pan, cook 3-4 minutes, until softened and slightly charred. Add in garlic and cook 1 minute    Then add in the rice, oregano, salt and pepper, stir together and cook for 1 minute    Pour in chicken stock, turn the temperature up to medium-high, bring to a simmer    Once simmering, place the chicken thighs on top of the rice mixture, push down gently    Cover with lid or foil, and bake 35 minutes    Uncover, return to oven and bake an additional 10-15 minutes, until liquid is removed, the rice is tender, and chicken is cooked through    Allow the rice and chicken to cool    Distribute among the containers, store in fridge for 2-3 days    To serve: Reheat in the microwave for 1 minute to 2 minutes or cooked through. Garnish with lemon zest and parsley, and serve!
**Nutrition Info:Per Serving:** Calories:325;Carbs: 35g;Total Fat: 11g;Protein: 21g

## Trout With Wilted Greens

Servings: 4    Cooking Time: 15 Minutes
**Ingredients:**
- 2 teaspoons extra virgin olive oil
- 2 cups kale, chopped
- 2 cups Swiss chard, chopped
- ½ sweet onion, thinly sliced
- 4 (5 ounce boneless skin-on trout fillets)
- Juice of 1 lemon
- Sea salt
- Freshly ground pepper
- Zest of 1 lemon

**Directions:**
Pre-heat your oven to 375-degree Fahrenheit    Lightly grease a 9 by 13-inch baking dish with olive oil    Arrange the kale, Swiss chard, onion in a dish    Top greens with fish, skin side up and drizzle with olive oil and lemon juice    Season fish with salt and pepper Bake for 15 minutes until fish flakes    Sprinkle zest Serve and enjoy!    Meal Prep/Storage Options: Store in airtight containers in your fridge for 1-3 days.
**Nutrition Info:**Calories: 315;Fat: 14g;Carbohydrates: 6g;Protein: 39g

## One Skillet Chicken In Roasted Red Pepper Sauce

Servings: 4     Cooking Time: 20 Minutes
**Ingredients:**
- 4-6 boneless skinless chicken thighs or breasts
- 2/3 cup chopped roasted red peppers (see note)
- 2 tsp Italian seasoning, divided
- 4 tbsp oil
- 1 tbsp minced garlic
- 1/2 tsp salt
- 1/4 tsp black pepper
- 1 cup heavy cream
- 2 tbsp crumbled feta cheese, optional
- Thinly sliced fresh basil, optional

**Directions:**
In a blender or food processer, combine the roasted red peppers, tsp Italian seasoning, oil, garlic, salt, and pepper, pulse until smooth.     In a large skillet over medium heat, add the olive oil and season chicken with remaining 1 tsp Italian seasoning. Cook chicken for 6-8 minutes on each side, or until cooked through and lightly browned on the outside. Then transfer to a plate and cover     Add the red pepper mixture to the pan, stir over medium heat 2-minutes, or until heated throughout. Add the heavy cream, stir until mixture is thick and creamy     Add chicken, toss in the sauce to coat     allow the dish to cool completely     Distribute among the containers, store for 2-3 days     To Serve: Reheat in the microwave for 1-2 minutes or until heated through. Garnish with crumbled feta cheese and fresh basil. Serve with your favorite grain.     Recipe Notes: You can purchase jarred roasted red peppers at most grocery stores around the olives.
**Nutrition Info:Per Serving:** Calories:655;Carbs: 12g;Total Fat: 25g;Protein: 8

## Mediterranean Minestrone Soup

Servings: 4     Cooking Time: 40 Minutes
**Ingredients:**
- 1 large onion, finely chopped
- 4 cups vegetable stock
- 4 cloves crushed garlic
- 1 ounce chopped carrots
- 4 ounces chopped red bell pepper
- 4 ounces chopped celery (keep leaves)
- 1 16-ounce can diced tomatoes
- 1 16-ounce can white beans
- 4 ounces fresh spinach, chopped
- 4 ounces multi-colored pasta
- 2 ounces grated parmesan
- 2 tablespoons olive oil
- bunch of chopped parsley
- 1 teaspoon dried oregano
- salt
- pepper
- 4 ounces salami, finely sliced (if desired)

**Directions:**
Heat oil in a pan over medium heat.     Add chopped onions, red pepper, carrots, and celery.     Saute for about 10 minutes until tender.     Add garlic and cook on low heat for 2 minutes more.     Add your stock and

tomatoes and cook for an additional 10 minutes.     Add pasta and cook for 15 minutes more until al dente. Taste / check your seasoning; add salt and pepper as needed.     Add parsley, beans, celery leaves, spinach, and salami (if using), and stir.     Pour the whole mixture to a boil and stir for about 2 minutes.     Enjoy the soup hot!
**Nutrition Info:Per Serving:**Calories: 888, Total Fat: 19.9 g, Saturated Fat: 6.3 g, Cholesterol: 30 mg, Sodium: 1200 mg, Total Carbohydrate: 139.5 g, Dietary Fiber: 31.8 g, Total Sugars: 14.3 g, Protein: 49.4 g, Vitamin D: 14 mcg, Calcium: 64.3 mg, Iron: 22 mg, Potassium: 3951 mg

## Baked Shrimp Stew

Servings: 4-6     Cooking Time: 25 Minutes
**Ingredients:**
- Greek extra virgin olive oil
- 2 1/2 lb prawns, peeled, deveined, rinsed well and dried
- 1 large red onion, chopped (about two cups)
- 5 garlic cloves, roughly chopped
- 1 red bell pepper, seeded, chopped
- 2 15-oz cans diced tomatoes
- 1/2 cup water
- 1 1/2 tsp ground coriander
- 1 tsp sumac
- 1 tsp cumin
- 1 tsp red pepper flakes, more to taste
- 1/2 tsp ground green cardamom
- Salt and pepper, to taste
- 1 cup parsley leaves, stems removed
- 1/3 cup toasted pine nuts
- 1/4 cup toasted sesame seeds
- Lemon or lime wedges to serve

**Directions:**
Preheat the oven to 375 degrees F     In a large frying pan, add 1 tbsp olive oil     Sauté the prawns for 2 minutes, until they are barely pink, then remove and set aside     In the same pan over medium-high heat, drizzle a little more olive oil and sauté the chopped onions, garlic and red bell peppers for 5 minutes, stirring regularly     Add in the canned diced tomatoes and water, allow to simmer for 10 minutes, until the liquid reduces, stir occasionally     Reduce the heat to medium, add the shrimp back to the pan, stir in the spices the ground coriander, sumac, cumin, red pepper flakes, green cardamom, salt and pepper, then the toasted pine nuts, sesame seeds and parsley leaves, stir to combined     Transfer the shrimp and sauce to an oven-safe earthenware or stoneware dish, cover tightly with foil Place in the oven to bake for minutes, uncover and broil briefly.     allow the dish to cool completely Distribute among the containers, store for 2-3 days To Serve: Reheat on the stove for 1-2 minutes or until heated through. Serve with your favorite bread or whole grain. Garnish with a side of lime or lemon wedges.
**Nutrition Info:Per Serving:**
Calories:377;Carbs: ;Total Fat: 20g;Protein: 41g

## Rainbow Salad With Roasted Chickpeas

Servings: 2-3     Cooking Time: 40 Minutes
**Ingredients:**
- Creamy avocado dressing, store bought or homemade
- 3 large tri-color carrots - one orange, one red, and one yellow
- 1 medium zucchini
- 1/4 cup fresh basil, cut into ribbons
- 1 can chickpeas, rinsed and drained
- 1 tbsp olive oil
- 1 tsp chili powder
- 1/2 tsp cumin
- Salt, to taste
- Pepper, to taste

**Directions:**
Preheat the oven to 400 degrees F     Pat the chickpeas dry with paper towels     Add them to a bowl and toss with the olive oil, chili powder, cumin, and salt and pepper     Arrange the chickpeas on a baking sheet in a single layer     Bake for 30-40 minutes - making sure to shaking the pan once in a while to prevent over browning. The chickpeas will be done when they're crispy and golden brown, allow to cool     With a grater, peeler, mandolin or spiralizer, shred the carrots and zucchini into very thin ribbons     Once the zucchini is shredded, lightly press it with paper towels to remove excess moisture     Add the shredded zucchini and carrots to a bowl, toss with the basil     Add in the roasted chickpeas, too gently to combine     Distribute among the containers, store for 2 days     To Serve: Top with the avocado dressing and enjoy
**Nutrition Info:Per Serving:** (without dressing): Calories:640;Total Fat: 51g;Total Carbs: 9.8g;Protein: 38.8g

## Sour And Sweet Fish

Servings: 2     Cooking Time: 25 Minutes
**Ingredients:**
- 1 tablespoon vinegar
- 2 drops stevia
- 1 pound fish chunks
- 1/4 cup butter, melted
- Salt and black pepper, to taste

**Directions:**
Put butter and fish chunks in a skillet and cook for about 3 minutes.     Add stevia, salt and black pepper and cook for about 10 minutes, stirring continuously. Dish out in a bowl and serve immediately.     Place fish in a dish and set aside to cool for meal prepping. Divide it in 2 containers and refrigerate for up to 2 days. Reheat in microwave before serving.
**Nutrition Info:**Calories: 2 ;Carbohydrates: 2.8g;Protein: 24.5g;Fat: 16.7g;Sugar: 2.7g;Sodium: 649mg

## Papaya Mangetout Stew

Servings: 2     Cooking Time: 5 Minutes
**Ingredients:**
- 2 cups Mangetout
- 2 cups bean sprouts
- 1 tablespoon water
- 1 papaya, peeled, deseeded, and cubed
- 1 lime, juiced
- 2 tablespoon unsalted peanuts
- small handful basil leaves, torn
- small handful mint leaves, chopped

**Directions:**
Take a large frying pan and place it over high heat. Add Mangetout, 1 tablespoon of water, and bean sprouts.     Cook for about 2-minutes.     Remove from heat, add papaya, and lime juice.     Toss everything well.     Spread over containers.     Before eating, garnish with herbs and peanuts.     Enjoy!
**Nutrition Info:Per Serving:**Calories: 283, Total Fat: 6.4 g, Saturated Fat: 0.g, Cholesterol: 0 mg, Sodium: 148 mg, Total Carbohydrate: 42.8 g, Dietary Fiber: 4.9 g, Total Sugars: 21.5 g, Protein: 20.1 g, Vitamin D: 0 mcg, Calcium: 205 mg, Iron: 3 mg, Potassium: 743 mg

## Mediterranean Pork Pita Sandwich

Servings: 6     Cooking Time: 10 Minutes
**Ingredients:**
- 2 teaspoons olive oil, plus 1 tablespoon
- 2 cups packed baby spinach leaves, finely chopped
- 4 ounces mushrooms, finely chopped
- 1 teaspoon chopped garlic
- 1 pound extra-lean ground pork
- 1 large egg
- 1/2 cup panko bread crumbs
- 1/3 cup chopped fresh dill
- 1/4 teaspoon kosher salt
- 6 large romaine lettuce leaves, ripped into pieces to fit pita
- 2 tomatoes, sliced
- 3 whole-wheat pitas, cut in half
- 3/4 cup Garlic Yogurt Sauce

**Directions:**
Heat 2 teaspoons of oil in a -inch skillet over medium heat. Once the oil is shimmering, add the spinach, mushrooms, and garlic and sauté for 3 minutes. Cool for 5 minutes.     Place the mushroom mixture in a large mixing bowl and add the pork, egg, bread crumbs, dill, and salt. Mix with your hands until everything is well combined. Make 6 patties, about 1/2-inch thick and 3 inches in diameter.     Heat the remaining 1 tablespoon of oil in the same 12-inch skillet over medium-high heat. When the oil is hot, add the patties. They should all be able to fit in the pan. If not, cook in 2 batches. Cook for 5 minutes on the first side and 4 minutes on the second side. The outside should be golden brown, and the inside should no longer be pink. Place 1 patty in each of 6 containers. In each of 6 separate containers that will not be reheated, place 1 torn lettuce leaf and 2 tomato slices. Wrap the pita halves in plastic wrap and place one in each veggie container. Spoon 2 tablespoons of yogurt sauce into each of 6 sauce containers.     STORAGE: Store covered containers in the refrigerator for up to days. Uncooked patties can be frozen for up to 4 months, while cooked patties can be frozen for up to 3 months.
**Nutrition Info:Per Serving:** Total calories: 309; Total fat: 11g; Saturated fat: 3g; Sodium: 343mg; Carbohydrates: 22g; Fiber: 3g; Protein: 32g

## Salmon With Warm Tomato-olive Salad

Servings: 4     Cooking Time: 25 Minutes

**Ingredients:**
- Salmon fillets (4/approx. 4 oz./1.25-inches thick)
- Celery (1 cup)
- Medium tomatoes (2)
- Fresh mint (.25 cup)
- Kalamata olives (.5 cup)
- Garlic (.5 tsp.)
- Salt (1 tsp. + more to taste)
- Honey (1 tbsp.)
- Red pepper flakes (.25 tsp.)
- Olive oil (2 tbsp. + more for the pan)
- Vinegar (1 tsp.)

**Directions:**
Slice the tomatoes and celery into inch pieces and mince the garlic. Chop the mint and the olives.     Heat the oven using the broiler setting.     Whisk the oil, vinegar, honey, red pepper flakes, and salt (1 tsp.. Brush the mixture onto the salmon.     Line the broiler pan with a sheet of foil. Spritz the pan lightly with olive oil, and add the fillets (skin side downward.     Broil them for four to six minutes until well done.     Meanwhile, make the tomato salad. Mix ½ teaspoon of the salt with the garlic.     Prepare a small saucepan on the stovetop using the med-high temperature setting. Pour in the rest of the oil and add the garlic mixture with the olives and one tablespoon of vinegar. Simmer for about three minutes.     Prepare the serving dishes. Pour the bubbly mixture into the bowl and add the mint, tomato, and celery. Dust it with the salt as desired and toss.     When the salmon is done, serve with a tomato salad.

**Nutrition Info:**Calories: 433;Protein: 38 grams;Fat: 26 grams

# Sauces and Dressings Recipes

## Pomegranate Vinaigrette

Servings: ½ Cup    Cooking Time: 5 Minutes
**Ingredients:**
- ⅓ cup pomegranate juice
- 1 teaspoon Dijon mustard
- 1 tablespoon apple cider vinegar
- ½ teaspoon dried mint
- 2 tablespoons plus 2 teaspoons olive oil

**Directions:**
Place the pomegranate juice, mustard, vinegar, and mint in a small bowl and whisk to combine.    Whisk in the oil, pouring it into the bowl in a thin steam.    Pour the vinaigrette into a container and refrigerate. STORAGE: Store the covered container in the refrigerator for up to 2 weeks. Bring the vinaigrette to room temperature and shake before serving.
**Nutrition Info:**Per Serving (2 tablespoons): Total calories: 94; Total fat: 10g; Saturated fat: 2g; Sodium: 30mg; Carbohydrates: 3g; Fiber: 0g; Protein: 0g

## Green Olive And Spinach Tapenade

Servings: 1½ Cups    Cooking Time: 20 Minutes
**Ingredients:**
- 1 cup pimento-stuffed green olives, drained
- 3 packed cups baby spinach
- 1 teaspoon chopped garlic
- ½ teaspoon dried oregano
- ⅓ cup packed fresh basil
- 2 tablespoons olive oil
- 2 teaspoons red wine vinegar

**Directions:**
Place all the ingredients in the bowl of a food processor and pulse until the mixture looks finely chopped but not puréed.    Scoop the tapenade into a container and refrigerate.    STORAGE: Store the covered container in the refrigerator for up to 5 days.
**Nutrition Info:**Per Serving (¼ cup): Total calories: 80; Total fat: 8g; Saturated fat: 1g; Sodium: 6mg; Carbohydrates: 1g; Fiber: 1g; Protein: 1g

## Bulgur Pilaf With Almonds

Servings: 4    Cooking Time: 20 Minutes
**Ingredients:**
- ⅔ cup uncooked bulgur
- 1⅓ cups water
- ¼ cup sliced almonds
- 1 cup small diced red bell pepper
- ⅓ cup chopped fresh cilantro
- 1 tablespoon olive oil
- ¼ teaspoon salt

**Directions:**
Place the bulgur and water in a saucepan and bring the water to a boil. Once the water is at a boil, cover the pot with a lid and turn off the heat. Let the covered pot stand for 20 minutes.    Transfer the cooked bulgur to a large mixing bowl and add the almonds, peppers, cilantro, oil, and salt. Stir to combine.    Place about 1 cup of bulgur in each of 4 containers.    STORAGE: Store covered containers in the refrigerator for up to 5 days. Bulgur can be either reheated or eaten at room temperature.
**Nutrition Info:Per Serving:** Total calories: 17 Total fat: 7g; Saturated fat: 1g; Sodium: 152mg; Carbohydrates: 25g; Fiber: 6g; Protein: 4g

## Garlic Yogurt Sauce

Servings: 1 Cup    Cooking Time: 5 Minutes
**Ingredients:**
- 1 cup low-fat (2%) plain Greek yogurt
- ½ teaspoon garlic powder
- 1 tablespoon freshly squeezed lemon juice
- 1 tablespoon olive oil
- ¼ teaspoon kosher salt

**Directions:**
Mix all the ingredients in a medium bowl until well combined.    Spoon the yogurt sauce into a container and refrigerate.    STORAGE: Store the covered container in the refrigerator for up to 7 days.
**Nutrition Info:**Per Serving (¼ cup): Total calories: 75; Total fat: 5g; Saturated fat: 1g; Sodium: 173mg; Carbohydrates: 3g; Fiber: 0g; Protein: 6g.

## Orange And Cinnamon–scented Whole-wheat Couscous

Servings: 4    Cooking Time: 10 Minutes
**Ingredients:**
- 2 teaspoons olive oil
- ¼ cup minced shallot
- ½ cup freshly squeezed orange juice (from 2 oranges)
- ½ cup water
- ⅛ teaspoon ground cinnamon
- ¼ teaspoon kosher salt
- 1 cup whole-wheat couscous

**Directions:**
Heat the oil in a saucepan over medium heat. Once the oil is shimmering, add the shallot and cook for 2 minutes, stirring frequently. Add the orange juice, water, cinnamon, and salt, and bring to a boil.    Once the liquid is boiling, add the couscous, cover the pan, and turn off the heat. Leave the couscous covered for 5 minutes. When the couscous is done, fluff with a fork. Place ¾ cup of couscous in each of 4 containers. STORAGE: Store covered containers in the refrigerator for up to 5 days. Freeze for up to 2 months.
**Nutrition Info:Per Serving:** Total calories: 21 Total fat: 4g; Saturated fat: <1g; Sodium: 147mg; Carbohydrates: 41g; Fiber: 5g; Protein: 8g

## Chunky Roasted Cherry Tomato And Basil Sauce

Servings: 1⅓ Cups    Cooking Time: 40 Minutes
**Ingredients:**
- 2 pints cherry tomatoes (20 ounces total)
- 2 teaspoons olive oil, plus 3 tablespoons
- ¼ teaspoon kosher salt
- ½ teaspoon chopped garlic
- ¼ cup fresh basil leaves

**Directions:**
Preheat the oven to 350°F. Line a sheet pan with a silicone baking mat or parchment paper.    Place the tomatoes on the lined sheet pan and toss with teaspoons of oil. Roast for 40 minutes, shaking the pan halfway through.    While the tomatoes are still warm, place them in a medium mixing bowl and add the salt, the garlic, and the remaining tablespoons of oil. Mash the tomatoes with the back of a fork. Stir in the fresh basil.    Scoop the sauce into a container and refrigerate.    STORAGE: Store the covered container in the refrigerator for up to days.
**Nutrition Info:** Per Serving (⅓ cup): Total calories: 141; Total fat: 13g; Saturated fat: 2g; Sodium: 158mg; Carbohydrates: 7g; Fiber: 2g; Protein: 1g

## Basil, Almond, And Celery Heart Pesto

Servings: 1 Cup    Cooking Time: 10 Minutes
**Ingredients:**
- ½ cup raw, unsalted almonds
- 3 cups fresh basil leaves, (about 1½ ounces)
- ½ cup chopped celery hearts with leaves
- ¼ teaspoon kosher salt
- 1 tablespoon freshly squeezed lemon juice
- ¼ cup olive oil
- 3 tablespoons water

**Directions:**
Place the almonds in the bowl of a food processor and process until they look like coarse sand.    Add the basil, celery hearts, salt, lemon juice, oil and water and process until smooth. The sauce will be somewhat thick. If you would like a thinner sauce, add more water, oil, or lemon juice, depending on your taste preference. Scoop the pesto into a container and refrigerate. STORAGE: Store the covered container in the refrigerator for up to 2 weeks. Pesto may be frozen for up to 6 months.
**Nutrition Info:** Per Serving (¼ cup): Total calories: 231; Total fat: 22g; Saturated fat: 3g; Sodium: 178mg; Carbohydrates: 6g; Fiber: 3g; Protein: 4g

## Sautéed Kale With Garlic And Lemon

Servings: 4    Cooking Time: 7 Minutes
**Ingredients:**
- 1 tablespoon olive oil
- 3 bunches kale, stemmed and roughly chopped
- 2 teaspoons chopped garlic
- ¼ teaspoon kosher salt
- 1 tablespoon freshly squeezed lemon juice

**Directions:**
Heat the oil in a -inch skillet over medium-high heat. Once the oil is shimmering, add as much kale as will fit in the pan. You will probably only fit half the leaves into the pan at first. Mix the kale with tongs so that the leaves are coated with oil and start to wilt. As the kale wilts, keep adding more of the raw kale, continuing to use tongs to mix. Once all the kale is in the pan, add the garlic and salt and continue to cook until the kale is tender. Total cooking time from start to finish should be about 7 minutes.    Mix the lemon juice into the kale. Add additional salt and/or lemon juice if necessary. Place 1 cup of kale in each of 4 containers and refrigerate.    STORAGE: Store covered containers in the refrigerator for up to 5 days.
**Nutrition Info:** Per Serving: Total calories: 8 Total fat: 1g; Saturated fat: <1g; Sodium: 214mg; Carbohydrates: 17g; Fiber: 6g; Protein: 6g

## Creamy Polenta With Chives And Parmesan

Servings: 5    Cooking Time: 15 Minutes
**Ingredients:**
- 1 teaspoon olive oil
- ¼ cup minced shallot
- ½ cup white wine
- 3¼ cups water
- ¾ cup cornmeal
- 3 tablespoons grated Parmesan cheese
- ½ teaspoon kosher salt
- ¼ cup chopped chives

**Directions:**
Heat the oil in a saucepan over medium heat. Once the oil is shimmering, add the shallot and sauté for 2 minutes. Add the wine and water and bring to a boil. Pour the cornmeal in a thin, even stream into the liquid, stirring continuously until the mixture starts to thicken. Reduce the heat to low and continue to cook for 10 to 12 minutes, whisking every 1 to 2 minutes.    Turn the heat off and stir in the cheese, salt, and chives. Cool. Place about ¾ cup of polenta in each of containers. STORAGE: Store covered containers in the refrigerator for up to 5 days.
**Nutrition Info:** Per Serving: Total calories: 110; Total fat: 3g; Saturated fat: 1g; Sodium: 29g; Carbohydrates: 16g; Fiber: 1g; Protein: 3g

## Mocha-nut Stuffed Dates

Servings: 5     Cooking Time: 10 Minutes
**Ingredients:**
- 2 tablespoons creamy, unsweetened, unsalted almond butter
- 1 teaspoon unsweetened cocoa powder
- 3 tablespoons walnut pieces
- 2 tablespoons water
- ¼ teaspoon honey
- ¾ teaspoon instant espresso powder
- 10 Medjool dates, pitted

**Directions:**
In a small bowl, combine the almond butter, cocoa powder, and walnut pieces.     Place the water in a small microwaveable mug and heat on high for 30 seconds. Add the honey and espresso powder to the water and stir to dissolve.     Add the espresso water to the cocoa bowl and combine thoroughly until a creamy, thick paste forms.     Stuff each pitted date with 1 teaspoon of mocha filling.     Place 2 dates in each of small containers.     STORAGE: Store covered containers in the refrigerator for up to 5 days.

**Nutrition Info:Per Serving:** Total calories: 205; Total fat: ; Saturated fat: 1g; Sodium: 1mg; Carbohydrates: 39g; Fiber: 4g; Protein: 3g

## Roasted Eggplant Dip (baba Ghanoush)

Servings: 2 Cups     Cooking Time: 45 Minutes
**Ingredients:**
- 2 eggplants (close to 1 pound each)
- 1 teaspoon chopped garlic
- 3 tablespoons unsalted tahini
- ¼ cup freshly squeezed lemon juice
- 1 tablespoon olive oil
- ½ teaspoon kosher salt

**Directions:**
Preheat the oven to 450°F and line a sheet pan with a silicone baking mat or parchment paper.     Prick the eggplants in many places with a fork, place on the sheet pan, and roast in the oven until extremely soft, about 45 minutes. The eggplants should look like they are deflating.     When the eggplants are cool, cut them open and scoop the flesh into a large bowl. You may need to use your hands to pull the flesh away from the skin. Discard the skin. Mash the flesh very well with a fork.     Add the garlic, tahini, lemon juice, oil, and salt. Taste and adjust the seasoning with additional lemon juice, salt, or tahini if needed.     Scoop the dip into a container and refrigerate.     STORAGE: Store the covered container in the refrigerator for up to 5 days.

**Nutrition Info:**Per Serving (¼ cup): Total calories: 8 Total fat: 5g; Saturated fat: 1g; Sodium: 156mg; Carbohydrates: 10g; Fiber: 4g; Protein: 2g

## Honey-lemon Vinaigrette

Servings: ½ Cup     Cooking Time: 5 Minutes
**Ingredients:**
- ¼ cup freshly squeezed lemon juice
- 1 teaspoon honey
- 2 teaspoons Dijon mustard
- ⅛ teaspoon kosher salt
- ¼ cup olive oil

**Directions:**
Place the lemon juice, honey, mustard, and salt in a small bowl and whisk to combine.     Whisk in the oil, pouring it into the bowl in a thin steam.     Pour the vinaigrette into a container and refrigerate. STORAGE: Store the covered container in the refrigerator for up to 2 weeks. Allow the vinaigrette to come to room temperature and shake before serving.

**Nutrition Info:**Per Serving (2 tablespoons): Total calories: 131; Total fat: 14g; Saturated fat: 2g; Sodium: 133mg; Carbohydrates: 3g; Fiber: <1g; Protein: <1g

## Spanish Romesco Sauce

Servings: 1⅔ Cups     Cooking Time: 10 Minutes
**Ingredients:**
- ½ cup raw, unsalted almonds
- 4 medium garlic cloves (do not peel)
- 1 (12-ounce) jar of roasted red peppers, drained
- ½ cup canned diced fire-roasted tomatoes, drained
- 1 teaspoon smoked paprika
- ½ teaspoon kosher salt
- Pinch cayenne pepper
- 2 teaspoons red wine vinegar
- 2 tablespoons olive oil

**Directions:**
Preheat the oven to 350°F.     Place the almonds and garlic cloves on a sheet pan and toast in the oven for 10 minutes. Remove from the oven and peel the garlic when cool enough to handle.     Place the almonds in the bowl of a food processor. Process the almonds until they resemble coarse sand,     to 45 seconds. Add the garlic, peppers, tomatoes, paprika, salt, and cayenne. Blend until smooth.     Once the mixture is smooth, add the vinegar and oil and blend until well combined. Taste and add more vinegar or salt if needed.     Scoop the romesco sauce into a container and refrigerate. STORAGE: Store the covered container in the refrigerator for up to 7 days.

**Nutrition Info:**Per Serving (⅓ cup): Total calories: 158; Total fat: 13g; Saturated fat: 1g; Sodium: 292mg; Carbohydrates: 10g; Fiber: 3g; Protein: 4g

## Cardamom Mascarpone With Strawberries

Servings: 4    Cooking Time: 10 Minutes
**Ingredients:**
- 1 (8-ounce) container mascarpone cheese
- 2 teaspoons honey
- ¼ teaspoon ground cardamom
- 2 tablespoons milk
- 1 pound strawberries (should be 24 strawberries in the pack)

**Directions:**
Combine the mascarpone, honey, cardamom, and milk in a medium mixing bowl.    Mix the ingredients with a spoon until super creamy, about 30 seconds.    Place 6 strawberries and 2 tablespoons of the mascarpone mixture in each of 4 containers.    STORAGE: Store covered containers in the refrigerator for up to 5 days.
**Nutrition Info:Per Serving:** Total calories: 289; Total fat: 2; Saturated fat: 10g; Sodium: 26mg; Carbohydrates: 11g; Fiber: 3g; Protein: 1g

## Sweet And Spicy Green Pumpkin Seeds

Servings: 2 Cups    Cooking Time: 15 Minutes
**Ingredients:**
- 2 cups raw green pumpkin seeds (pepitas)
- 1 egg white, beaten until frothy
- 3 tablespoons honey
- 1 tablespoon chili powder
- ¼ teaspoon cayenne pepper
- 1 teaspoon ground cinnamon
- ¼ teaspoon kosher salt

**Directions:**
Preheat the oven to 350°F. Line a sheet pan with a silicone baking mat or parchment paper.    In a medium bowl, mix all the ingredients until the seeds are well coated. Place on the lined sheet pan in a single, even layer.    Bake for 15 minutes. Cool the seeds on the sheet pan, then peel clusters from the baking mat and break apart into small pieces.    Place ¼ cup of seeds in each of 8 small containers or resealable sandwich bags.    STORAGE: Store covered containers or resealable bags at room temperature for up to days.
**Nutrition Info:**Per Serving (¼ cup): Total calories: 209; Total fat: 15g; Saturated fat: 3g; Sodium: 85mg; Carbohydrates: 11g; Fiber: 2g; Protein: 10g

## Raspberry Red Wine Sauce

Servings: 1 Cup    Cooking Time: 20 Minutes
**Ingredients:**
- 2 teaspoons olive oil
- 2 tablespoons finely chopped shallot
- 1½ cups frozen raspberries
- 1 cup dry, fruity red wine
- 1 teaspoon thyme leaves, roughly chopped
- 1 teaspoon honey
- ¼ teaspoon kosher salt
- ½ teaspoon unsweetened cocoa powder

**Directions:**
In a -inch skillet, heat the oil over medium heat. Add the shallot and cook until soft, about 2 minutes.    Add the raspberries, wine, thyme, and honey and cook on medium heat until reduced, about 15 minutes. Stir in the salt and cocoa powder.    Transfer the sauce to a blender and blend until smooth. Depending on how much you can scrape out of your blender, this recipe makes ¾ to 1 cup of sauce.    Scoop the sauce into a container and refrigerate.    STORAGE: Store the covered container in the refrigerator for up to 7 days.
**Nutrition Info:**Per Serving (¼ cup): Total calories: 107; Total fat: 3g; Saturated fat: <1g; Sodium: 148mg; Carbohydrates: 1g; Fiber: 4g; Protein: 1g

## Antipasti Shrimp Skewers

Servings: 4    Cooking Time: 10 Minutes
**Ingredients:**
- 16 pitted kalamata or green olives
- 16 fresh mozzarella balls (ciliegine)
- 16 cherry tomatoes
- 16 medium (41 to 50 per pound) precooked peeled, deveined shrimp
- 8 (8-inch) wooden or metal skewers

**Directions:**
Alternate 2 olives, 2 mozzarella balls, 2 cherry tomatoes, and 2 shrimp on 8 skewers.    Place skewers in each of 4 containers.    STORAGE: Store covered containers in the refrigerator for up to 4 days.
**Nutrition Info:Per Serving:** Total calories: 108; Total fat: 6g; Saturated fat: 1g; Sodium: 328mg; Carbohydrates: ; Fiber: 1g; Protein: 9g

## Smoked Paprika And Olive Oil–marinated Carrots

Servings: 4    Cooking Time: 5 Minutes
**Ingredients:**
- 1 (1-pound) bag baby carrots (not the petite size)
- 2 tablespoons olive oil
- 2 tablespoons red wine vinegar
- ¼ teaspoon garlic powder
- ¼ teaspoon ground cumin
- ¼ teaspoon smoked paprika
- ⅛ teaspoon red pepper flakes
- ¼ cup chopped parsley
- ¼ teaspoon kosher salt

**Directions:**
Pour enough water into a saucepan to come ¼ inch up the sides. Turn the heat to high, bring the water to a boil, add the carrots, and cover with a lid. Steam carrots for 5 minutes, until crisp tender.    After the carrots have cooled, mix with the oil, vinegar, garlic powder, cumin, paprika, red pepper, parsley, and salt. Place ¾ cup of carrots in each of 4 containers. STORAGE: Store covered containers in the refrigerator for up to 5 days.
**Nutrition Info:Per Serving:** Total calories: 109; Total fat: 7g; Saturated fat: 1g; Sodium: 234mg; Carbohydrates: 11g; Fiber: 3g; Protein: 2g

## Tzatziki Sauce

Servings: 2½ Cups    Cooking Time: 15 Minutes
**Ingredients:**
- 1 English cucumber
- 2 cups low-fat (2%) plain Greek yogurt
- 1 tablespoon olive oil
- 2 teaspoons freshly squeezed lemon juice
- ½ teaspoon chopped garlic
- ½ teaspoon kosher salt
- ⅛ teaspoon freshly ground black pepper
- 2 tablespoons chopped fresh dill
- 2 tablespoons chopped fresh mint

**Directions:**
Place a sieve over a medium bowl. Grate the cucumber, with the skin, over the sieve. Press the grated cucumber into the sieve with the flat surface of a spatula to press as much liquid out as possible.    In a separate medium bowl, place the yogurt, oil, lemon juice, garlic, salt, pepper, dill, and mint and stir to combine.    Press on the cucumber one last time, then add it to the yogurt mixture. Stir to combine. Taste and add more salt and lemon juice if necessary.    Scoop the sauce into a container and refrigerate.    STORAGE: Store the covered container in the refrigerator for up to days.
**Nutrition Info:**Per Serving (¼ cup): Total calories: 51; Total fat: 2g; Saturated fat: 1g; Sodium: 137mg; Carbohydrates: 3g; Fiber: <1g; Protein: 5g

## Fruit Salad With Mint And Orange Blossom Water

Servings: 5    Cooking Time: 10 Minutes
**Ingredients:**
- 3 cups cantaloupe, cut into 1-inch cubes
- 2 cups hulled and halved strawberries
- ½ teaspoon orange blossom water
- 2 tablespoons chopped fresh mint

**Directions:**
In a large bowl, toss all the ingredients together. Place 1 cup of fruit salad in each of 5 containers. STORAGE: Store covered containers in the refrigerator for up to 5 days.
**Nutrition Info:**Per Serving: Total calories: 52; Total fat: 1g; Saturated fat: <1g; Sodium: 10mg; Carbohydrates: 12g; Fiber: 2g; Protein: 1g

## Roasted Broccoli And Red Onions With Pomegranate Seeds

Servings: 5    Cooking Time: 20 Minutes
**Ingredients:**
- 1 (12-ounce) package broccoli florets (about 6 cups)
- 1 small red onion, thinly sliced
- 2 tablespoons olive oil
- ¼ teaspoon kosher salt
- 1 (5.3-ounce) container pomegranate seeds (1 cup)

**Directions:**
Preheat the oven to 425°F and line 2 sheet pans with silicone baking mats or parchment paper.    Place the broccoli and onion on the sheet pans and toss with the oil and salt. Place the pans in the oven and roast for minutes.    After removing the pans from the oven, cool the veggies, then toss with the pomegranate seeds. Place 1 cup of veggies in each of 5 containers. STORAGE: Store covered containers in the refrigerator for up to days.
**Nutrition Info:Per Serving:** Total calories: 118; Total fat: ; Saturated fat: 1g; Sodium: 142mg; Carbohydrates: 12g; Fiber: 4g; Protein: 2g

## Chermoula Sauce

Servings: 1 Cup    Cooking Time: 10 Minutes
**Ingredients:**
- 1 cup packed parsley leaves
- 1 cup cilantro leaves
- ½ cup mint leaves
- 1 teaspoon chopped garlic
- ½ teaspoon ground cumin
- ½ teaspoon ground coriander
- ½ teaspoon smoked paprika
- ⅛ teaspoon cayenne pepper
- ⅛ teaspoon kosher salt
- 3 tablespoons freshly squeezed lemon juice
- 3 tablespoons water
- ½ cup extra-virgin olive oil

**Directions:**
Place all the ingredients in a blender or food processor and blend until smooth.    Pour the chermoula into a container and refrigerate.    STORAGE: Store the covered container in the refrigerator for up to 5 days.
**Nutrition Info:**Per Serving (¼ cup): Total calories: 257; Total fat: 27g; Saturated fat: ; Sodium: 96mg; Carbohydrates: 4g; Fiber: 2g; Protein: 1g

## Pesto Deviled Eggs With Sun-dried Tomatoes

Servings: 5    Cooking Time: 15 Minutes
**Ingredients:**
- 5 large eggs
- 3 tablespoons prepared pesto
- ¼ teaspoon white vinegar
- 2 tablespoons low-fat (2%) plain Greek yogurt
- 5 teaspoons sliced sun-dried tomatoes

**Directions:**
Place the eggs in a saucepan and cover with water. Bring the water to a boil. As soon as the water starts to boil, place a lid on the pan and turn the heat off. Set a timer for    minutes.    When the timer goes off, drain the hot water and run cold water over the eggs to cool. Peel the eggs, slice in half vertically, and scoop out the yolks. Place the yolks in a medium mixing bowl and add the pesto, vinegar, and yogurt. Mix well, until creamy. Scoop about 1 tablespoon of the pesto-yolk mixture into each egg half. Top each with ½ teaspoon of sun-dried tomatoes.    Place 2 stuffed egg halves in each of separate containers.    STORAGE: Store covered containers in the refrigerator for up to 5 days.
**Nutrition Info:Per Serving:** Total calories: 124; Total fat: 9g; Saturated fat: 2g; Sodium: 204mg; Carbohydrates: 2g; Fiber: <1g; Protein: 8g

## White Bean And Mushroom Dip

Servings: 3 Cups    Cooking Time: 8 Minutes
**Ingredients:**
- 2 teaspoons olive oil, plus 2 tablespoons
- 8 ounces button or cremini mushrooms, sliced
- 1 teaspoon chopped garlic
- 1 tablespoon fresh thyme leaves
- 2 (15.5-ounce) cans cannellini beans, drained and rinsed
- 2 tablespoons plus 1 teaspoon freshly squeezed lemon juice
- ½ teaspoon kosher salt

**Directions:**
Heat 2 teaspoons of oil in a -inch skillet over medium-high heat. Once the oil is shimmering, add the mushrooms and sauté for 6 minutes. Add the garlic and thyme and continue cooking for 2 minutes.    While the mushrooms are cooking, place the beans and lemon juice, the remaining tablespoons of oil, and the salt in the bowl of a food processor. Add the mushrooms as soon as they are done cooking and blend everything until smooth. Scrape down the sides of the bowl if necessary and continue to process until smooth. Taste and adjust the seasoning with lemon juice or salt if needed.    Scoop the dip into a container and refrigerate.    STORAGE: Store the covered container in the refrigerator for up to days. Dip can be frozen for up to 3 months.
**Nutrition Info:**Per Serving (½ cup): Total calories: 192; Total fat: ; Saturated fat: 1g; Sodium: 197mg; Carbohydrates: 25g; Fiber: 7g; Protein: 9g

## North African Spiced Sautéed Cabbage

Servings: 4    Cooking Time: 10 Minutes
**Ingredients:**
- 2 teaspoons olive oil
- 1 small head green cabbage (about 1½ to 2 pounds), cored and thinly sliced
- 1 teaspoon ground coriander
- 1 teaspoon garlic powder
- ½ teaspoon caraway seeds
- ½ teaspoon ground cumin
- ¼ teaspoon kosher salt
- Pinch red chili flakes (optional—if you don't like heat, omit it)
- 1 teaspoon freshly squeezed lemon juice

**Directions:**
Heat the oil in a -inch skillet over medium-high heat. Once the oil is hot, add the cabbage and cook down for 3 minutes. Add the coriander, garlic powder, caraway seeds, cumin, salt, and chili flakes (if using) and stir to combine. Continue cooking the cabbage for about 7 more minutes.    Stir in the lemon juice and cool. Place 1 heaping cup of cabbage in each of 4 containers. STORAGE: Store covered containers in the refrigerator for up to 5 days.
**Nutrition Info:Per Serving:** Total calories: 69; Total fat: 3g; Saturated fat: <1g; Sodium: 178mg; Carbohydrates: 11g; Fiber: 4g; Protein: 3g

## Blueberry, Flax, And Sunflower Butter Bites

Servings: 6    Cooking Time: 10 Minutes
**Ingredients:**
- ¼ cup ground flaxseed
- ½ cup unsweetened sunflower butter, preferably unsalted
- ⅓ cup dried blueberries
- 2 tablespoons all-fruit blueberry preserves
- Zest of 1 lemon
- 2 tablespoons unsalted sunflower seeds
- ⅓ cup rolled oats

**Directions:**
Mix all the ingredients in a medium mixing bowl until well combined.    Form 1balls, slightly smaller than a golf ball, from the mixture and place on a plate in the freezer for about 20 minutes to firm up.    Place 2 bites in each of 6 containers and refrigerate.    STORAGE: Store covered containers in the refrigerator for up to 5 days. Bites may also be stored in the freezer for up to 3 months.
**Nutrition Info:Per Serving:** Total calories: 229; Total fat: 14g; Saturated fat: 1g; Sodium: 1mg; Carbohydrates: 26g; Fiber: 3g; Protein: 7g

## Dijon Red Wine Vinaigrette

Servings: ½ Cup    Cooking Time: 5 Minutes
**Ingredients:**
- 2 teaspoons Dijon mustard
- 3 tablespoons red wine vinegar
- 1 tablespoon water
- ¼ teaspoon dried oregano
- ¼ teaspoon chopped garlic
- ⅛ teaspoon kosher salt
- ¼ cup olive oil

**Directions:**
Place the mustard, vinegar, water, oregano, garlic, and salt in a small bowl and whisk to combine.    Whisk in the oil, pouring it into the mustard-vinegar mixture in a thin steam.    Pour the vinaigrette into a container and refrigerate.    STORAGE: Store the covered container in the refrigerator for up to 2 weeks. Allow the vinaigrette to come to room temperature and shake before serving.
**Nutrition Info:**Per Serving (2 tablespoons): Total calories: 123; Total fat: 14g; Saturated fat: 2g; Sodium: 133mg; Carbohydrates: 0g; Fiber: 0g; Protein: 0g

## Hummus

Servings: 1½ Cups    Cooking Time: 5 Minutes
**Ingredients:**
- 1 (15-ounce) can low-sodium chickpeas, drained and rinsed
- ¼ cup unsalted tahini
- ½ teaspoon chopped garlic
- ¼ cup freshly squeezed lemon juice
- ¼ teaspoon kosher salt
- 3 tablespoons olive oil
- 3 tablespoons cold water

**Directions:**
Place all the ingredients in a food processor or blender and blend until smooth.    Taste and adjust the seasonings if needed.    Scoop the hummus into a container and refrigerate.    STORAGE: Store the covered container in the refrigerator for up to 5 days.
**Nutrition Info:**Per Serving (¼ cup): Total calories: 192; Total fat: 13g; Saturated fat: 2g; Sodium: 109mg; Carbohydrates: 16g; Fiber: ; Protein: 5g

## Candied Maple-cinnamon Walnuts

Servings: 4    Cooking Time: 15 Minutes
**Ingredients:**
- 1 cup walnut halves
- ½ teaspoon ground cinnamon
- 2 tablespoons pure maple syrup

**Directions:**
Preheat the oven to 325°F. Line a baking sheet with a silicone baking mat or parchment paper.    In a small bowl, mix the walnuts, cinnamon, and maple syrup until the walnuts are coated.    Pour the nuts onto the baking sheet, making sure to scrape out all the maple syrup. Bake for 15 minutes. Allow the nuts to cool completely.    Place ¼ cup of nuts in each of containers or resealable sandwich bags.    STORAGE: Store covered containers at room temperature for up to 7 days.
**Nutrition Info:Per Serving:** Total calories: 190; Total fat: 17g; Saturated fat: 2g; Sodium: 2mg; Carbohydrates: 10g; Fiber: 2g; Protein: 4g

## Artichoke-olive Compote

Servings: 1⅓ Cups    Cooking Time: 15 Minutes
**Ingredients:**
- 1 (6-ounce) jar marinated artichoke hearts, chopped
- ⅓ cup chopped pitted green olives (8 to 9 olives)
- 3 tablespoons chopped fresh basil
- ½ teaspoon freshly squeezed lemon juice
- 2 teaspoons olive oil

**Directions:**
Place all the ingredients in a medium mixing bowl and stir to combine.    Place the compote in a container and refrigerate.    STORAGE: Store the covered container in the refrigerator for up to 7 days.
**Nutrition Info:**Per Serving (⅓ cup): Total calories: 8 Total fat: 7g; Saturated fat: 1g; Sodium: 350mg; Carbohydrates: 5g; Fiber: <1g; Protein: <1g

# Soups and Salads Recipes

## Mexican Tortilla Soup

Servings: 4     Cooking Time: 40 Minutes
**Ingredients:**
- 1-pound chicken breasts, boneless and skinless
- 1 can (15 ounces whole peeled tomatoes
- 1 can (10 ounces red enchilada sauce
- 1 and 1/2 teaspoons minced garlic
- 1 yellow onion, diced
- 1 can (4 ounces fire-roasted diced green chile
- 1 can (15 ounces black beans, drained and rinsed
- 1 can (15 ounces fire-roasted corn, undrained
- 1 container (32 ounces chicken stock or broth
- 1 teaspoon ground cumin
- 2 teaspoons chili powder
- 3/4 teaspoons paprika
- 1 bay leaf
- Salt and freshly cracked pepper, to taste
- 1 tablespoon chopped cilantro
- Tortilla strips, Freshly squeezed lime juice, freshly grated cheddar cheese,

**Directions:**
Set your Instant Pot on Sauté mode.     Toss olive oil, onion and garlic into the insert of the Instant Pot. Sauté for 4 minutes then add chicken and remaining ingredients.     Mix well gently then seal and lock the lid.     Select Manual mode for 7 minutes at high pressure.     Once done, release the pressure completely then remove the lid.     Adjust seasoning as needed. Garnish with desired toppings.     Enjoy.
**Nutrition Info:**Calories: 390;Carbohydrate: 5.6g;Protein: 29.5g;Fat: 26.5g;Sugar: 2.1g;Sodium: 620mg

## Chicken Noodle Soup

Servings: 6     Cooking Time: 35 Minutes
**Ingredients:**
- 1 tablespoon olive oil
- 1 1/2 cups peeled and diced carrots
- 1 1/2 cup diced celery
- 1 cup chopped yellow onion
- 3 tablespoons minced garlic
- 8 cups low-sodium chicken broth
- 2 teaspoons minced fresh thyme
- 2 teaspoons minced fresh rosemary
- 1 bay leaf
- salt and freshly ground black pepper
- 2 1/2 lbs. bone-in, skin-on chicken thighs, skinned
- 3 cups wide egg noodles, such as American beauty
- 1 tablespoon fresh lemon juice
- 1/4 cup chopped fresh parsley

**Directions:**
Preheat olive oil in the insert of the Instant Pot on Sauté mode.     Add onion, celery, and carrots and sauté them for minutes.     Stir in garlic and sauté for 1 minute.

Add bay leaf, thyme, broth, rosemary, salt, and pepper. Seal and secure the Instant Pot lid and select Manual mode for 10 minutes at high pressure.     Once done, release the pressure completely then remove the lid. Add noodles to the insert and switch the Instant Pot to sauté mode.     Cook the soup for 6 minutes until noodles are all done.     Remove the chicken and shred it using a fork.     Return the chicken to the soup then add lemon juice and parsley.     Enjoy.
**Nutrition Info:**Calories: 333;Carbohydrate: 3.3g;Protein: 44.7g;Fat: 13.7g;Sugar: 1.1g;Sodium: 509mg

## Turkey Arugula Salad

Servings: 2     Cooking Time: 5 Minutes
**Ingredients:**
- 4 oz turkey breast meat, diced into small pieces
- 3.5 oz arugula leaves
- 10 raspberries
- Juice from ½ a lime
- 2 tablespoons extra virgin olive oil

**Directions:**
Mix together the turkey with the rest of the ingredients in a large bowl until well combined.     Dish out in a glass bowl and serve immediately.
**Nutrition Info:**Calories: 246;Carbs: 15.4g;Fats: 15.9g;Proteins: 12.2g;Sodium: 590mg;Sugar: 7.6g

## Cheesy Broccoli Soup

Servings: 4     Cooking Time: 30 Minutes
**Ingredients:**
- ½ cup heavy whipping cream
- 1 cup broccoli
- 1 cup cheddar cheese
- Salt, to taste
- 1½ cups chicken broth

**Directions:**
Heat chicken broth in a large pot and add broccoli. Bring to a boil and stir in the rest of the ingredients. Allow the soup to simmer on low heat for about 20 minutes.     Ladle out into a bowl and serve hot.
**Nutrition Info:**Calories: 188;Carbs: 2.6g;Fats: 15g;Proteins: 9.8g;Sodium: 514mg;Sugar: 0.8g

## Rich Potato Soup

Servings: 4     Cooking Time: 30 Minutes
**Ingredients:**
- 1 tablespoon butter
- 1 medium onion, diced
- 3 cloves garlic, minced
- 3 cups chicken broth
- 1 can/box cream of chicken soup
- 7-8 medium-sized russet potatoes, peeled and chopped
- 1 1/2 teaspoons salt
- Black pepper to taste
- 1 cup milk
- 1 tablespoon flour
- 2 cups shredded cheddar cheese
- Garnish:
- 5-6 slices bacon, chopped
- Sliced green onions
- Shredded cheddar cheese

**Directions:**
Heat butter in the insert of the Instant Pot on sauté mode.     Add onions and sauté for 4 minutes until soft. Stir in garlic and sauté it for 1 minute.     Add potatoes, cream of chicken, broth, salt, and pepper to the insert. Mix well then seal and lock the lid.     Cook this mixture for 10 minutes at Manual Mode with high pressure. Meanwhile, mix flour with milk in a bowl and set it aside.     Once the instant pot beeps, release the pressure completely.     Remove the Instant Pot lid and switch the instant pot to Sauté mode.     Pour in flour slurry and stir cook the mixture for 5 minutes until it thickens.     Add 2 cups of cheddar cheese and let it melt.     Garnish it as desired.     Serve.
**Nutrition Info:**Calories: 784;Carbohydrate: 54.8g;Protein: 34g;Fat: 46.5g;Sugar: 7.5g;Sodium: 849mg

## Mediterranean Lentil Soup

Servings: 4     Cooking Time: 20 Minutes
**Ingredients:**
- 1 tablespoon olive oil
- 1/2 cup red lentils
- 1 medium yellow or red onion
- 2 garlic cloves, chopped
- 1/2 teaspoon ground cumin
- 1/2 teaspoon ground coriander
- 1/2 teaspoon ground sumac
- 1/2 teaspoon red chili flakes
- 1/2 teaspoon dried parsley
- 3/4 teaspoons dried mint flakes
- pinch of sugar
- 2.5 cups water
- salt, to taste
- black pepper, to taste
- juice of 1/2 lime
- parsley or cilantro, to garnish

**Directions:**
Preheat oil in the insert of your Instant Pot on Sauté mode.     Add onion and sauté until it turns golden brown.     Toss in the garlic, parsley sugar, mint flakes, red chili flakes, sumac, coriander, and cumin.     Stir cook this mixture for 2 minutes.     Add water, lentils, salt, and pepper. Stir gently.     Seal and lock the Instant Pot lid and select Manual mode for 8 minutes at high pressure.     Once done, release the pressure completely then remove the lid.     Stir well then add lime juice. Serve warm.
**Nutrition Info:**Calories: 525;Carbohydrate: 59.8g;Protein: 30.1g;Fat: 19.3g;Sugar: 17.3g;Sodium: 897mg

## Creamy Keto Cucumber Salad

Servings: 2     Cooking Time: 5 Minutes
**Ingredients:**
- 2 tablespoons mayonnaise
- Salt and black pepper, to taste
- 1 cucumber, sliced and quartered
- 2 tablespoons lemon juice

**Directions:**
Mix together the mayonnaise, cucumber slices, and lemon juice in a large bowl.     Season with salt and black pepper and combine well.     Dish out in a glass bowl and serve while it is cold.
**Nutrition Info:**Calories: 8Carbs: 9.3g;Fats: 5.2g;Proteins: 1.2g;Sodium: 111mg;Sugar: 3.8g

## Sausage Kale Soup With Mushrooms

Servings: 6     Cooking Time: 1 Hour 10 Minutes
**Ingredients:**
- 2 cups fresh kale, cut into bite sized pieces
- 6.5 ounces mushrooms, sliced
- 6 cups chicken bone broth
- 1 pound sausage, cooked and sliced
- Salt and black pepper, to taste

**Directions:**
Heat chicken broth with two cans of water in a large pot and bring to a boil.     Stir in the rest of the ingredients and allow the soup to simmer on low heat for about 1 hour.     Dish out and serve hot.
**Nutrition Info:**Calories: 259;Carbs: ;Fats: 20g;Proteins: 14g;Sodium: 995mg;Sugar: 0.6g

## Minestrone Soup

Servings: 6     Cooking Time: 25 Minutes
**Ingredients:**
- 2 tablespoons olive oil
- 3 cloves garlic, minced
- 1 onion, diced
- 2 carrots, peeled and diced
- 2 stalks celery, diced
- 1 1/2 teaspoons dried basil
- 1 teaspoon dried oregano
- 1/2 teaspoon fennel seed
- 6 cups low sodium chicken broth
- 1 (28-ounce can diced tomatoes
- 1 (16-ounce can kidney beans, drained and rinsed
- 1 zucchini, chopped
- 1 (3-inch Parmesan rind
- 1 bay leaf
- 1 bunch kale leaves, chopped
- 2 teaspoons red wine vinegar
- Kosher salt and black pepper, to taste
- 1/3 cup freshly grated Parmesan
- 2 tablespoons chopped fresh parsley leaves

**Directions:**
Preheat olive oil in the insert of the Instant Pot on Sauté mode.     Add carrots, celery, and onion, sauté for 3 minutes.     Stir in fennel seeds, oregano, and basil. Stir cook for 1 minute.     Add stock, beans, tomatoes, parmesan, bay leaf, and zucchini.     Secure and seal the Instant Pot lid then select Manual mode to cook for minutes at high pressure.     Once done, release the pressure completely then remove the lid.     Add kale and let it sit for 2 minutes in the hot soup.     Stir in red wine, vinegar, pepper, and salt.     Garnish with parsley and parmesan.     Enjoy.
**Nutrition Info:**Calories: 805;Carbohydrate: 2.5g;Protein: 124.1g;Fat: 34g;Sugar: 1.4g;Sodium: 634mg

## Kombu Seaweed Salad

Servings: 6     Cooking Time: 40 Minutes
**Ingredients:**
- 4 garlic cloves, crushed
- 1 pound fresh kombu seaweed, boiled and cut into strips
- 2 tablespoons apple cider vinegar
- Salt, to taste
- 2 tablespoons coconut aminos

**Directions:**
Mix together the kombu, garlic, apple cider vinegar, and coconut aminos in a large bowl.     Season with salt and combine well.     Dish out in a glass bowl and serve immediately.
**Nutrition Info:**Calories: 257;Carbs: 16.9g;Fats: 19.;Proteins: 6.5g;Sodium: 294mg;Sugar: 2.7g

## Turkey Meatball And Ditalini Soup

Servings: 4     Cooking Time: 40 Minutes
**Ingredients:**
- meatballs:
- 1 pound 93% lean ground turkey
- 1/3 cup seasoned breadcrumbs
- 3 tablespoons grated Pecorino Romano cheese
- 1 large egg, beaten
- 1 clove crushed garlic
- 1 tablespoon fresh minced parsley
- 1/2 teaspoon kosher salt
- Soup:
- cooking spray
- 1 teaspoon olive oil
- 1/2 cup chopped onion
- 1/2 cup chopped celery
- 1/2 cup chopped carrot
- 3 cloves minced garlic
- 1 can (28 ounces diced San Marzano tomatoes
- 4 cups reduced sodium chicken broth
- 4 torn basil leaves
- 2 bay leaves
- 1 cup ditalini pasta
- 1 cup zucchini, diced small
- Parmesan rind, optional
- Grated parmesan cheese, optional for serving

**Directions:**
Thoroughly combine turkey with egg, garlic, parsley, salt, pecorino and breadcrumbs in a bowl.     Make 30 equal sized meatballs out of this mixture.     Preheat olive oil in the insert of the Instant Pot on Sauté mode. Sear the meatballs in the heated oil in batches, until brown.     Set the meatballs aside in a plate.     Add more oil to the insert of the Instant Pot.     Stir in carrots, garlic, celery, and onion. Sauté for 4 minutes. Add basil, bay leaves, tomatoes, and Parmesan rind. Return the seared meatballs to the pot along with the broth.     Secure and sear the Instant Pot lid and select Manual mode for 15 minutes at high pressure.     Once done, release the pressure completely then remove the lid.     Add zucchini and pasta, cook it for 4 minutes on Sauté mode.     Garnish with cheese and basil.     Serve.
**Nutrition Info:**Calories: 261;Carbohydrate: 11.2g;Protein: 36.6g;Fat: 7g;Sugar: 3g;Sodium: 198g

## Mint Avocado Chilled Soup

Servings: 2     Cooking Time: 5 Minutes
**Ingredients:**
- 1 cup coconut milk, chilled
- 1 medium ripe avocado
- 1 tablespoon lime juice
- Salt, to taste
- 20 fresh mint leaves

**Directions:**
Put all the ingredients into an immersion blender and blend until a thick mixture is formed.     Allow to cool in the fridge for about 10 minutes and serve chilled.
**Nutrition Info:**Calories: 286;Carbs: 12.6g;Fats: 26.9g;Proteins: 4.2g;Sodium: 70mg;Sugar: 4.6g

## Split Pea Soup

Servings: 6    Cooking Time: 30 Minutes
**Ingredients:**
- 3 tablespoons butter
- 1 onion diced
- 2 ribs celery diced
- 2 carrots diced
- 6 oz. diced ham
- 1 lb. dry split peas sorted and rinsed
- 6 cups chicken stock
- 2 bay leaves
- kosher salt and black pepper

**Directions:**
Set your Instant Pot on Sauté mode and melt butter in it.    Stir in celery, onion, carrots, salt, and pepper. Sauté them for 5 minutes then stir in split peas, ham bone, chicken stock, and bay leaves.    Seal and lock the Instant Pot lid then select Manual mode for 15 minutes at high pressure.    Once done, release the pressure completely then remove the lid.    Remove the ham bone and separate meat from the bone.    Shred or dice the meat and return it to the soup.    Adjust seasoning as needed then serve warm.    Enjoy.

**Nutrition Info:**Calories: 190;Carbohydrate: 30.5g;Protein: 8g;Fat: 3.5g;Sugar: 4.2g;Sodium: 461mg

## Butternut Squash Soup

Servings: 4    Cooking Time: 40 Minutes
**Ingredients:**
- 1 tablespoon olive oil
- 1 medium yellow onion chopped
- 1 large carrot chopped
- 1 celery rib chopped
- 3 cloves of garlic minced
- 2 lbs. butternut squash, peeled chopped
- 2 cups vegetable broth
- 1 green apple peeled, cored, and chopped
- 1/4 teaspoon ground cinnamon
- 1 sprig fresh thyme
- 1 sprig fresh rosemary
- 1 teaspoon kosher salt
- 1/2 teaspoon black pepper
- Pinch of nutmeg optional

**Directions:**
Preheat olive oil in the insert of the Instant Pot on Sauté mode.    Add celery, carrots, and garlic, sauté for 5 minutes.    Stir in squash, broth, cinnamon, apple nutmeg, rosemary, thyme, salt, and pepper.    Mix well gently then seal and secure the lid.    Select Manual mode to cook for 10 minutes at high pressure.    Once done, release the pressure completely then remove the lid.    Puree the soup using an immersion blender. Serve warm.

**Nutrition Info:**Calories: 282;Carbohydrate: 50g;Protein: 13g;Fat: 4.7g;Sugar: 12.8g;Sodium: 213mg

## Creamy Cilantro Lime Coleslaw

Servings: 2    Cooking Time: 10 Minutes
**Ingredients:**
- ¾ avocado
- 1 lime, juiced
- 1/8 cup water
- Cilantro, to garnish
- 6 oz coleslaw, bagged
- 1/8 cup cilantro leaves
- 1 garlic clove
- ¼ teaspoon salt

**Directions:**
Put garlic and cilantro in a food processor and process until chopped.    Add lime juice, avocado and water and pulse until creamy.    Put coleslaw in a large bowl and stir in the avocado mixture.    Refrigerate for a few hours before serving.

**Nutrition Info:**Calories: 240;Carbs: 17.4g;Fats: 19.6g;Proteins: 2.8g;Sodium: 0mg;Sugar: 0.5g

## Snap Pea Salad

Servings: 2    Cooking Time: 15 Minutes
**Ingredients:**
- 1/8 cup lemon juice
- ½ clove garlic, crushed
- 4 ounces cauliflower riced
- 1/8 cup olive oil
- ¼ teaspoon coarse grain Dijon mustard
- ½ teaspoon granulated stevia
- ¼ cup sugar snap peas, ends removed and each pod cut into three pieces
- 1/8 cup chives
- 1/8 cup red onions, minced
- Sea salt and black pepper, to taste
- ¼ cup almonds, sliced

**Directions:**
Pour water in a pot fitted with a steamer basket and bring water to a boil.    Place riced cauliflower in the steamer basket and season with sea salt.    Cover the pot and steam for about 10 minutes until tender. Drain the cauliflower and dish out in a bowl to refrigerate for about 1 hour.    Meanwhile, make a dressing by mixing olive oil, lemon juice, garlic, mustard, stevia, salt and black pepper in a bowl.    Mix together chilled cauliflower, peas, chives, almonds and red onions in another bowl.    Pour the dressing over this mixture and serve.

**Nutrition Info:**Calories: 203;Carbs: 7.6g;Fats: 18g;Proteins: 4.2g;Sodium: 28mg;Sugar: 2.9g

## Spinach And Bacon Salad

Servings: 4     Cooking Time: 15 Minutes
**Ingredients:**
- 2 eggs, boiled, halved, and sliced
- 10 oz. organic baby spinach, rinsed, and dried
- 8 pieces thick bacon, cooked and sliced
- ½ cup plain mayonnaise
- ½ medium red onion, thinly sliced

**Directions:**
Mix together the mayonnaise and spinach in a large bowl.     Stir in the rest of the ingredients and combine well.     Dish out in a glass bowl and serve well.
**Nutrition Info:**Calories: 373;Carbs: ;Fats: 34.5g;Proteins: 11g;Sodium: 707mg;Sugar: 1.1g

## Beef Stroganoff Soup

Servings: 6     Cooking Time: 35 Minutes
**Ingredients:**
- 1.5 pounds stew meat
- 6 cups beef broth
- 4 tablespoons Worcestershire sauce
- 1/2 teaspoon Italian seasoning blend
- 1 1/2 teaspoons onion powder
- 2 teaspoons garlic powder
- salt and pepper to taste
- 1/2 cup sour cream
- 8 ounces mushrooms, sliced
- 8 ounces short noodles, cooked
- 1/3 cup cold water
- 1/4 cup corn starch

**Directions:**
Add meat, 5 cups broth, Italian seasoning, Worcestershire sauce, garlic powder, salt, pepper, and onion powder to the insert of the Instant Pot.     Secure and seal the Instant Pot lid then select Manual mode for 1 hour at high pressure.     Once done, release the pressure completely then remove the lid.     Set the Instant pot on Soup mode and add sour cream along with 1 cup broth.     Mix well then add mushrooms and mix well.     Whisk corn-starch with water and pour this mixture into the pot.     Cook this mixture until it thickens then add noodles, salt, and pepper.     Garnish with cheese parsley, black pepper.     Enjoy.

**Nutrition Info:**Calories: 320;Carbohydrate: 21.6g;Protein: 26.9g;Fat: 13.7g;Sugar: 7.1g;Sodium: 285mg

## Egg, Avocado And Tomato Salad

Servings: 4     Cooking Time: 40 Minutes
**Ingredients:**
- 2 boiled eggs, chopped into chunks
- 1 ripe avocado, chopped into chunks
- 1 medium-sized tomato, chopped into chunks
- Salt and black pepper, to taste
- 1 lemon wedge, juiced

**Directions:**
Mix together all the ingredients in a large bowl until well combined.     Dish out in a glass bowl and serve immediately.
**Nutrition Info:**Calories: 140;Carbs: 5.9g;Fats: 12.1g;Proteins: 4g;Sodium: mg;Sugar: 1.3g

## Creamy Low Carb Butternut Squash Soup

Servings: 8     Cooking Time: 1 Hour 10 Minutes
**Ingredients:**
- 2 tablespoons avocado oil, divided
- 2 pounds butternut squash, cut in half length-wise and seeds removed
- Sea salt and black pepper, to taste
- 1 (13.5-oz can coconut milk
- 4 cups chicken bone broth

**Directions:**
Preheat the oven to 400 degrees F and grease a baking sheet.     Arrange the butternut squash halves with open side up on the baking sheet.     Drizzle with half of the avocado oil and season with sea salt and black pepper.     Flip over and transfer into the oven.     Roast the butternut squash for about  minutes.     Heat the remaining avocado oil over medium heat in a large pot and add the broth and coconut milk.     Let it simmer for about 20 minutes and scoop the squash out of the shells to transfer into the soup.     Puree this mixture in an immersion blender until smooth and serve immediately.
**Nutrition Info:**Calories: 185;Carbs: 12.6g;Fats: 12.6g;Proteins: 4.7g;Sodium: 3mg;Sugar: 4.5g

# Desserts Recipes

## Cherry Brownies With Walnuts

Servings: 9     Cooking Time: 25 To 30 Minutes
**Ingredients:**
- 9 fresh cherries that are stemmed and pitted or 9 frozen cherries
- ½ cup sugar or sweetener substitute
- ¼ cup extra virgin olive oil
- 1 teaspoon vanilla extract
- ¼ teaspoon sea salt
- ½ cup whole-wheat pastry flour
- ¼ teaspoon baking powder
- ⅓ cup walnuts, chopped
- 2 eggs
- ½ cup plain Greek yogurt
- ⅓ cup cocoa powder, unsweetened

**Directions:**
Make sure one of the metal racks in your oven is set in the middle.     Turn the temperature on your oven to 375 degrees Fahrenheit.     Using cooking spray, grease a 9-inch square pan.     Take a large bowl and add the oil and sugar or sweetener substitute. Whisk the ingredients well.     Add the eggs and use a mixer to beat the ingredients together.     Pour in the yogurt and continue to beat the mixture until it is smooth.     Take a medium bowl and combine the cocoa powder, flour, sea salt, and baking powder by whisking them together. Combine the powdered ingredients into the wet ingredients and use your electronic mixer to incorporate the ingredients together thoroughly.     Add in the walnuts and stir.     Pour the mixture into the pan. Sprinkle the cherries on top and push them into the batter. You can use any design, but it is best to make three rows and three columns with the cherries. This ensures that each piece of the brownie will have one cherry.     Put the batter into the oven and turn your timer to 20 minutes.     Check that the brownies are done using the toothpick test before removing them from the oven. Push the toothpick into the middle of the brownies and once it comes out clean, remove the brownies.     Let the brownies cool for 5 to 10 minutes before cutting and serving.
**Nutrition Info:**calories: 225, fats: 10 grams, carbohydrates: 30 grams, protein: 5 grams.

## Fruit Dip

Servings: 10     Cooking Time: 10 To 15 Minutes
**Ingredients:**
- ¼ cup coconut milk, full-fat is best
- ¼ cup vanilla yogurt
- ⅓ cup marshmallow creme
- 1 cup cream cheese, set at room temperature
- 2 tablespoons maraschino cherry juice

**Directions:**
In a large bowl, add the coconut milk, vanilla yogurt, marshmallow creme, cream cheese, and cherry juice. Using an electric mixer, set to low speed and blend the ingredients together until the fruit dip is smooth. Serve the dip with some of your favorite fruits and enjoy!
**Nutrition Info:**calories: 110, fats: 11 grams, carbohydrates: 3 grams, protein: 3 grams.

## A Lemony Treat

Servings: 4     Cooking Time: 30 Minutes
**Ingredients:**
- 1 lemon, medium in size
- 1 ½ teaspoons cornstarch
- 1 cup Greek yogurt, plain is best
- Fresh fruit
- ¼ cup cold water
- ⅔ cup heavy whipped cream
- 3 tablespoons honey
- Optional: mint leaves

**Directions:**
Take a large glass bowl and your metal, electric mixer and set them in the refrigerator so they can chill.     In a separate bowl, add the yogurt and set that in the fridge. Zest the lemon into a medium bowl that is microwavable.     Cut the lemon in half and then squeeze 1 tablespoon of lemon juice into the bowl. Combine the cornstarch and water. Mix the ingredients thoroughly.     Pour in the honey and whisk the ingredients together.     Put the mixture into the microwave for 1 minute on high.     Once the microwave stops, remove the mixture and stir.     Set it back into the microwave for 15 to 30 seconds or until the mixture starts to bubble and thicken.     Take the bowl of yogurt from the fridge and pour in the warm mixture while whisking.     Put the yogurt mixture back into the fridge.     Take the large bowl and beaters out of the fridge.     Put your electronic mixer together and pour the whipped cream into the chilled bowl.     Beat the cream until soft peaks start to form. This can take up to 3 minutes, depending on how fresh your cream is. Remove the yogurt from the fridge.     Fold the yogurt into the cream using a rubber spatula. Remember to lift and turn the mixture so it doesn't deflate.     Place back into the fridge until you are serving the dessert or for 15 minutes. The dessert should not be in the fridge for longer than 1 hour.     When you serve the lemony goodness, you will spoon it into four dessert dishes and drizzle with extra honey or even melt some chocolate to drizzle on top.     Add a little fresh mint and enjoy!
**Nutrition Info:**calories: 241, fats: 16 grams, carbohydrates: 21 grams, protein: 7 grams.

## Melon With Ginger

Servings: 4     Cooking Time: 10 To 15 Minutes
**Ingredients:**
- ½ cantaloupe, cut into 1-inch chunks
- 2 cups of watermelon, cut into 1-inch chunks
- 2 cups honeydew melon, cut into 1-inch chunks
- 2 tablespoons of raw honey
- Ginger, 2 inches in size, peeled, grated, and preserve the juice

**Directions:**
In a large bowl, combine your cantaloupe, honeydew melon, and watermelon. Gently mix the ingredients. Combine the ginger juice and stir.     Drizzle on the honey, serve, and enjoy! You can also chill the mixture for up to an hour before serving.
**Nutrition Info:**calories: 91, fats: 0 grams, carbohydrates: 23 grams, protein: 1 gram.

## Almond Shortbread Cookies

Servings: 16     Cooking Time: 25 Minutes
**Ingredients:**
- ½ cup coconut oil
- 1 teaspoon vanilla extract
- 2 egg yolks
- 1 tablespoon brandy
- 1 cup powdered sugar
- 1 cup finely ground almonds
- 3 ½ cups cake flour
- ½ cup almond butter
- 1 tablespoon water or rose flower water

**Directions:**
In a large bowl, combine the coconut oil, powdered sugar, and butter. If the butter is not soft, you want to wait until it softens up. Use an electric mixer to beat the ingredients together at high speed.     In a small bowl, add the egg yolks, brandy, water, and vanilla extract. Whisk well.     Fold the egg yolk mixture into the large bowl.     Add the flour and almonds. Fold and mix with a wooden spoon.     Place the mixture into the fridge for at least 1 hour and 30 minutes.     Preheat your oven to 325 degrees Fahrenheit.     Take the mixture, which now looks like dough, and divide it into 1-inch balls. With a piece of parchment paper on a baking sheet, arrange the cookies and flatten them with a fork or your fingers.     Place the cookies in the oven for 13 minutes, but watch them so they don't burn.     Transfer the cookies onto a rack to cool for a couple of minutes before enjoying!
**Nutrition Info:**calories: 250, fats: 14 grams, carbohydrates: 30 grams, protein: 3 grams.

## Chocolate Fruit Kebabs

Servings: 6     Cooking Time: 30 Minutes
**Ingredients:**
- 24 blueberries
- 12 strawberries with the green leafy top part removed
- 12 green or red grapes, seedless
- 12 pitted cherries
- 8 ounces chocolate

**Directions:**
Line a baking sheet with a piece of parchment paper and place 6, -inch long wooden skewers on top of the paper.     Start by threading a piece of fruit onto the skewers. You can create and follow any pattern that you like with the ingredients. An example pattern is 1 strawberry, 1 cherry, blueberries, 2 grapes. Repeat the pattern until all of the fruit is on the skewers.     In a saucepan on medium heat, melt the chocolate. Stir continuously until the chocolate has melted completely. Carefully scoop the chocolate into a plastic sandwich bag and twist the bag closed starting right above the chocolate.     Snip the corner of the bag with scissors. Drizzle the chocolate onto the kebabs by squeezing it out of the bag.     Put the baking pan into the freezer for 20 minutes.     Serve and enjoy!
**Nutrition Info:**calories: 254, fats: 15 grams, carbohydrates: 28 grams, protein: 4 grams.

## Peaches With Blue Cheese Cream

Servings: 4     Cooking Time: 20 Hours 10 Minutes
**Ingredients:**
- 4 peaches
- 1 cinnamon stick
- 4 ounces sliced blue cheese
- ⅓ cup orange juice, freshly squeezed is best
- 3 whole cloves
- 1 teaspoon of orange zest, taken from the orange peel
- ¼ teaspoon cardamom pods
- ⅔ cup red wine
- 2 tablespoons honey, raw or your preferred variety
- 1 vanilla bean
- 1 teaspoon allspice berries
- 4 tablespoons dried cherries

**Directions:**
Set a saucepan on top of your stove range and add the cinnamon stick, cloves, orange juice, cardamom, vanilla, allspice, red wine, and orange zest. Whisk the ingredients well.     Add your peaches to the mixture and poach them for hours or until they become soft. Take a spoon to remove the peaches and boil the rest of the liquid to make the syrup. You want the liquid to reduce itself by at least half.     While the liquid is boiling, combine the dried cherries, blue cheese, and honey into a bowl.     Once your peaches are cooled, slice them into halves.     Top each peach with the blue cheese mixture and then drizzle the liquid onto the top. Serve and enjoy!
**Nutrition Info:**calories: 211, fats: 24 grams, carbohydrates: 15 grams, protein: 6 grams.

## Mediterranean Blackberry Ice Cream

Servings: 6     Cooking Time: 15 Minutes
**Ingredients:**
- 3 egg yolks
- 1 container of Greek yogurt
- 1 pound mashed blackberries
- ½ teaspoon vanilla essence
- 1 teaspoon arrowroot powder
- ¼ teaspoon ground cloves
- 5 ounces sugar or sweetener substitute
- 1 pound heavy cream

**Directions:**
In a small bowl, add the arrowroot powder and egg yolks. Whisk or beat them with an electronic mixture until they are well combined.     Set a saucepan on top of your stove and turn your heat to medium.     Add the heavy cream and bring it to a boil.     Turn off the heat and add the egg mixture into the cream through folding. Turn the heat back on to medium and pour in the sugar. Cook the mixture for 10 minutes or until it starts to thicken.     Remove the mixture from heat and place it in the fridge so it can completely cool. This should take about one hour.     Once the mixture is cooled, add in the Greek yogurt, ground cloves, blackberries, and vanilla by folding in the ingredients.     Transfer the ice cream into a container and place it in the freezer for at least two hours.     Serve and enjoy!

**Nutrition Info:** calories: 402, fats: 20 grams, carbohydrates: 52 grams, protein: 8 grams.

## Stuffed Figs

Servings: 6     Cooking Time: 20 Minutes
**Ingredients:**
- 10 halved fresh figs
- 20 chopped almonds
- 4 ounces goat cheese, divided
- 2 tablespoons of raw honey

**Directions:**
Turn your oven to broiler mode and set it to a high temperature.     Place your figs, cut side up, on a baking sheet. If you like to place a piece of parchment paper on top you can do this, but it is not necessary.     Sprinkle each fig with half of the goat cheese.     Add a tablespoon of chopped almonds to each fig.     Broil the figs for 3 to 4 minutes.     Take them out of the oven and let them cool for 5 to 7 minutes.     Sprinkle with the remaining goat cheese and honey.

**Nutrition Info:** calories: 209, fats: 9 grams, carbohydrates: 26 grams, protein: grams.

## Chia Pudding With Strawberries

Servings: 4     Cooking Time: 4 Hours 5 Minutes
**Ingredients:**
- 2 cups unsweetened almond milk
- 1 tablespoon vanilla extract
- 2 tablespoons raw honey
- ¼ cup chia seeds
- 2 cups fresh and sliced strawberries

**Directions:**
In a medium bowl, combine the honey, chia seeds, vanilla, and unsweetened almond milk. Mix well.     Set the mixture in the refrigerator for at least 4 hours. When you serve the pudding, top it with strawberries. You can even create a design in a glass serving bowl or dessert dish by adding a little pudding on the bottom, a few strawberries, top the strawberries with some more pudding, and then top the dish with a few strawberries.

**Nutrition Info:** calories: 108, fats: grams, carbohydrates: 17 grams, protein: 3 grams.

# Snacks Recipes

## Chunky Monkey Trail Mix

Servings: 6    Cooking Time: 1 Hour 30 Minutes
**Ingredients:**
- 1 cup cashews, halved
- 2 cups raw walnuts, chopped or halved
- ⅓ cup coconut sugar
- 1 cup coconut flakes, unsweetened and make sure you have big flakes and not shredded
- 6 ounces dried banana slices
- 1 ½ teaspoons coconut oil at room temperature
- 1 teaspoon vanilla extract
- ½ cup of chocolate chips

**Directions:**
Turn your crockpot to high and add the cashews, walnuts, vanilla, coconut oil, and sugar. Combine until the ingredients are well mixed and then cook for 45 minutes.    Reduce the temperature on your crockpot to low.    Continue to cook the mixture for another 20 minutes.    Place a piece of parchment paper on your counter.    Once the mix is done cooking, remove it from the crockpot and set on top of the parchment paper.    Let the mixture sit and cool for 20 minutes. Pour the contents into a bowl and add the dried bananas and chocolate chips. Gently mix the ingredients together. You can store the mixture in Ziplock bags for a quick and easy snack.
**Nutrition Info:**calories: 250, fats: 6 grams, carbohydrates: 1grams, protein: 4 grams

## Fig-pecan Energy Bites

Servings: 6    Cooking Time: 20 Minutes
**Ingredients:**
- ½ cup chopped pecans
- 2 tablespoons honey
- ¾ cup dried figs, about 6 to 8, diced
- 2 tablespoons wheat flaxseed
- ¼ cup quick oats
- 2 tablespoons regular or powdered peanut butter

**Directions:**
Combine the figs, quick oats, pecans, peanut butter, and flaxseed into a bowl. Stir the ingredients well.    Drizzle honey onto the ingredients and mix everything with a wooden spoon. Do your best to press all the ingredients into the honey as you are stirring. If you start to struggle because the mixture is too sticky, set it in the freezer for 3 to 5 minutes.    Divide the mixture into four sections. Take a wet rag and get your hands damp. You don't want them too wet or they won't work well with the mixture.    Divide each of the four sections into 3 separate sections.    Take one of the three sections and roll them up. Repeat with each section so you have a dozen energy bites once you are done.    If you want to firm them up, you can place them into the freezer for a few minutes. Otherwise, you can enjoy them as soon as they are little energy balls.    To store them, you'll want to keep them in a sealed container and set them in the fridge. They can be stored for about a week.

**Nutrition Info:**calories: 157, fats: 6 grams, carbohydrates: 26 grams, protein: 3 grams.

## Baked Apples Mediterranean Style

Servings: 4    Cooking Time: 25 Minutes
**Ingredients:**
- ½ lemon, squeezed for juice
- 1 ½ pounds of peeled and sliced apples
- ¼ teaspoon cinnamon

**Directions:**
Set the temperature of your oven to 350 degrees Fahrenheit so it can preheat.    Take a piece of parchment paper and lay on top of a baking pan. Combine your lemon juice, cinnamon, and apples into a medium bowl and mix well.    Pour the apples onto the baking pan and arrange them so they are not doubled up.    Place the pan in the oven and set your timer to 2minutes. The apples should be tender but not mushy. Remove from the oven, plate and enjoy!
**Nutrition Info:**calories: 90, fats: 0.3 grams, carbohydrates: 24 grams, protein: 0.5 grams.

## Strawberry Popsicle

Servings: 5    Cooking Time: 10 Minutes
**Ingredients:**
- ½ cup almond milk
- 1 ½ cups fresh strawberries

**Directions:**
Using a blender or hand mixer, combine the almond milk and strawberries thoroughly in a bowl.    Using popsicle molds, pour the mixture into the molds and place the sticks into the mixture.    Set in the freezer for at least 4 hours.    Serve and enjoy—especially on a hot day!

## Frozen Blueberry Yogurt

Servings: 6    Cooking Time: 30 Minutes
**Ingredients:**
⅔ cup honey        2 cups chilled yogurt
- 1 pint fresh blueberries
- 1 juiced and zested lime or lemon. You can even substitute an orange if your tastes prefer.

**Directions:**
With a saucepan on your burner set to medium heat, add the honey, juiced fruit, zest, and blueberries.    Stir the mixture continuously as it begins to simmer for 15 minutes.    When the liquid is nearly gone, pour the contents into a bowl and place in the fridge for several minutes. You will want to stir the ingredients and check to see if they are chilled.    Once the fruit is chilled, combine with the yogurt.    Mix until the ingredients are well incorporated and enjoy.
**Nutrition Info:**calories: 233, fats: 3 grams, carbohydrates: 52 grams, protein: 3.5 grams.

# Meat Recipes

## Authentic Aioli Baked Chicken Wings

Servings: 4    Cooking Time: 35 Minutes
**Ingredients:**
- 4 chicken wings
- 1 cup Halloumi cheese, cubed
- 1 tablespoon garlic, finely minced
- 1 tablespoon fresh lime juice
- 1 tablespoon fresh coriander, chopped
- 6 black olives, pitted and halved
- 1 ½ tablespoons butter
- 1 hard-boiled egg yolk
- 1 tablespoon balsamic vinegar
- 1/2 cup extra-virgin olive oil
- 1/4 teaspoon flaky sea salt
- Sea salt and pepper, to season

**Directions:**
In a saucepan, melt the butter until sizzling. Sear the chicken wings for 5 minutes per side. Season with salt and pepper to taste.    Place the chicken wings on a parchment-lined baking pan    Mix the egg yolk, garlic, lime juice, balsamic vinegar, olive oil, and salt in your blender until creamy, uniform and smooth.    Spread the Aioli over the fried chicken. Now, scatter the coriander and black olives on top of the chicken wings. Bake in the preheated oven at 380 degrees F for 20 to 2minutes. Top with the cheese and bake an additional 5 minutes until hot and bubbly.    Storing    Place the chicken wings in airtight containers or Ziploc bags; keep in your refrigerator for up to 3 to 4 days.    For freezing, place the chicken wings in airtight containers or heavy-duty freezer bags. Freeze up to 3 months. Once thawed in the refrigerator, heat in the preheated oven at 375 degrees F for 20 to 25 minutes or until heated through. Enjoy!
**Nutrition Info:**562 Calories; 43.8g Fat; 2.1g Carbs; 40.8g Protein; 0.4g Fiber

## Smoked Pork Sausage Keto Bombs

Servings: 6    Cooking Time: 15 Minutes
**Ingredients:**
- 3/4 pound smoked pork sausage, ground
- 1 teaspoon ginger-garlic paste
- 2 tablespoons scallions, minced
- 1 tablespoon butter, room temperature
- 1 tomato, pureed
- 4 ounces mozzarella cheese, crumbled
- 2 tablespoons flaxseed meal
- 8 ounces cream cheese, room temperature
- Sea salt and ground black pepper, to taste

**Directions:**
Melt the butter in a frying pan over medium-high heat. Cook the sausage for about 4 minutes, crumbling with a spatula.    Add in the ginger-garlic paste, scallions, and tomato; continue to cook over medium-low heat for a further 6 minutes. Stir in the remaining ingredients.

Place the mixture in your refrigerator for 1 to 2 hours until firm. Roll the mixture into bite-sized balls.
Storing    Transfer the balls to the airtight containers and place in your refrigerator for up to 3 days.    For freezing, place in a freezer safe containers and freeze up to 1 month. Enjoy!
**Nutrition Info:**383 Calories; 32. Fat; 5.1g Carbs; 16.7g Protein; 1.7g Fiber

## Turkey Meatballs With Tangy Basil Chutney

Servings: 6    Cooking Time: 30 Minutes
**Ingredients:**
- 2 tablespoons sesame oil
- For the Meatballs:
- 1/2 cup Romano cheese, grated
- 1 teaspoon garlic, minced
- 1/2 teaspoon shallot powder
- 1/4 teaspoon dried thyme
- 1/2 teaspoon mustard seeds
- 2 small-sized eggs, lightly beaten
- 1 ½ pounds ground turkey
- 1/2 teaspoon sea salt
- 1/4 teaspoon ground black pepper, or more to taste
- 3 tablespoons almond meal
- For the Basil Chutney:
- 2 tablespoons fresh lime juice
- 1/4 cup fresh basil leaves
- 1/4 cup fresh parsley
- 1/2 cup cilantro leaves
- 1 teaspoon fresh ginger root, grated
- 2 tablespoons olive oil
- 2 tablespoons water
- 1 tablespoon habanero chili pepper, deveined and minced

**Directions:**
In a mixing bowl, combine all ingredients for the meatballs. Roll the mixture into meatballs and reserve. Heat the sesame oil in a frying pan over a moderate flame. Sear the meatballs for about 8 minutes until browned on all sides.    Make the chutney by mixing all the ingredients in your blender or food processor.
Storing    Place the meatballs in airtight containers or Ziploc bags; keep in your refrigerator for up to 3 to 4 days.    Freeze the meatballs in airtight containers or heavy-duty freezer bags. Freeze up to 3 to 4 months. To defrost, slowly reheat in a frying pan.    Store the basil chutney in the refrigerator for up to a week. Bon appétit!
**Nutrition Info:**390 Calories; 27.2g Fat; 1. Carbs; 37.4g Protein; 0.3g Fiber

## Roasted Chicken With Cashew Pesto

Servings: 4     Cooking Time: 35 Minutes
**Ingredients:**
- 1 cup leeks, chopped
- 1 pound chicken legs, skinless
- Salt and ground black pepper, to taste
- 1/2 teaspoon red pepper flakes
- For the Cashew-Basil Pesto:
- 1/2 cup cashews
- 2 garlic cloves, minced
- 1/2 cup fresh basil leaves
- 1/2 cup Parmigiano-Reggiano cheese, preferably freshly grated
- 1/2 cup olive oil

**Directions:**
Place the chicken legs in a parchment-lined baking pan. Season with salt and pepper, Then, scatter the leeks around the chicken legs.     Roast in the preheated oven at 390 degrees F for 30 to 35 minutes, rotating the pan occasionally.     Pulse the cashews, basil, garlic, and cheese in your blender until pieces are small. Continue blending while adding olive oil to the mixture. Mix until the desired consistency is reached.     Storing     Place the chicken in airtight containers or Ziploc bags; keep in your refrigerator for up 3 to 4 days.     To freeze the chicken legs, place them in airtight containers or heavy-duty freezer bags. Freeze up to 3 months. Once thawed in the refrigerator, heat in the preheated oven at 375 degrees F for 20 to 25 minutes.     Store your pesto in the refrigerator for up to a week. Bon appétit!
**Nutrition Info:**5 Calories; 44.8g Fat; 5g Carbs; 38.7g Protein; 1g Fiber

## Duck Breasts In Boozy Sauce

Servings: 4     Cooking Time: 20 Minutes
**Ingredients:**
- 1 ½ pounds duck breasts, butterflied
- 1 tablespoon tallow, room temperature
- 1 ½ cups chicken consommé
- 3 tablespoons soy sauce
- 2 ounces vodka
- 1/2 cup sour cream
- 4 scallion stalks, chopped
- Salt and pepper, to taste

**Directions:**
Melt the tallow in a frying pan over medium-high flame. Sear the duck breasts for about 5 minutes, flipping them over occasionally to ensure even cooking.     Add in the scallions, salt, pepper, chicken consommé, and soy sauce. Partially cover and continue to cook for a further 8 minutes.     Add in the vodka and sour cream; remove from the heat and stir to combine well.     Storing     Place the duck breasts in airtight containers or Ziploc bags; keep in your refrigerator for up to 3 to 4 days. For freezing, place duck breasts in airtight containers or heavy-duty freezer bags. Freeze up to 2 to 3 months. Once thawed in the refrigerator, reheat in a saucepan. Bon appétit!
**Nutrition Info:**351 Calories; 24. Fat; 6.6g Carbs; 22.1g Protein; 0.6g Fiber

## White Cauliflower And Chicken Chowder

Servings: 6     Cooking Time: 30 Minutes

**Ingredients:**
- 1 cup leftover roast chicken breasts
- 1 head cauliflower, broken into small-sized florets
- Sea salt and ground white pepper, to taste
- 2 ½ cups water
- 3 cups chicken consommé
- 1 ¼ cups sour cream
- 1/2 stick butter
- 1/2 cup white onion, finely chopped
- 1 teaspoon fresh garlic, finely minced
- 1 celery, chopped

**Directions:**
In a heavy bottomed pot, melt the butter over a moderate heat. Cook the onion, garlic and celery for about 5 minutes or until they've softened.     Add in the salt, white pepper, water, chicken consommé, chicken, and cauliflower florets; bring to a boil. Reduce the temperature to simmer and continue to cook for 30 minutes.     Puree the soup with an immersion blender. Fold in sour cream and stir to combine well.     Storing     Spoon your chowder into airtight containers or Ziploc bags; keep in your refrigerator for up to 3 to 4 days. For freezing, place your chowder in airtight containers. It will maintain the best quality for about 4 to months. Defrost in the refrigerator. Bon appétit!
**Nutrition Info:**231 Calories; 18.2g Fat; 5.9g Carbs; 11.9g Protein; 1.4g Fiber

## Taro Leaf And Chicken Soup

Servings: 4     Cooking Time: 45 Minutes
**Ingredients:**
- 1 pound whole chicken, boneless and chopped into small chunks
- 1/2 cup onions, chopped
- 1/2 cup rutabaga, cubed
- 2 carrots, peeled
- 2 celery stalks
- Salt and black pepper, to taste
- 1 cup chicken bone broth
- 1/2 teaspoon ginger-garlic paste
- 1/2 cup taro leaves, roughly chopped
- 1 tablespoon fresh coriander, chopped
- 3 cups water
- 1 teaspoon paprika

**Directions:**
Place all ingredients in a heavy-bottomed pot. Bring to a boil over the highest heat.     Turn the heat to simmer. Continue to cook, partially covered, an additional 40 minutes.     Storing     Spoon the soup into four airtight containers or Ziploc bags; keep in your refrigerator for up to 3 to days.     For freezing, place the soup in airtight containers. It will maintain the best quality for about to 6 months. Defrost in the refrigerator. Bon appétit!
**Nutrition Info:**25Calories; 12.9g Fat; 3.2g Carbs; 35.1g Protein; 2.2g Fiber

## Creamed Greek-style Soup

Servings: 4     Cooking Time: 30 Minutes
**Ingredients:**
- 1/2 stick butter
- 1/2 cup zucchini, diced
- 2 garlic cloves, minced
- 4 ½ cups roasted vegetable broth
- Sea salt and ground black pepper, to season
- 1 ½ cups leftover turkey, shredded
- 1/3 cup double cream
- 1/2 cup Greek-style yogurt

**Directions:**
In a heavy-bottomed pot, melt the butter over medium-high heat. Once hot, cook the zucchini and garlic for 2 minutes until they are fragrant.     Add in the broth, salt, black pepper, and leftover turkey. Cover and cook for   minutes, stirring periodically.     Then, fold in the cream and yogurt. Continue to cook for 5 minutes more or until thoroughly warmed.     Storing     Spoon the soup into four airtight containers or Ziploc bags; keep in your refrigerator for up to 3 to 4 days.     For freezing, place the soup in airtight containers. It will maintain the best quality for about 4 to months. Defrost in the refrigerator. Enjoy!
**Nutrition Info:**256 Calories; 18.8g Fat; 5.4g Carbs; 15.8g Protein; 0.2g Fiber

## Keto Pork Wraps

Servings: 4     Cooking Time: 15 Minutes
**Ingredients:**
- 1 pound ground pork
- 2 garlic cloves, finely minced
- 1 chili pepper, deveined and finely minced
- 1 teaspoon mustard powder
- 1 tablespoon sunflower seeds
- 2 tablespoons champagne vinegar
- 1 tablespoon coconut aminos
- Celery salt and ground black pepper, to taste
- 2 scallion stalks, sliced
- 1 head lettuce

**Directions:**
Sear the ground pork in the preheated pan for about 8 minutes. Stir in the garlic, chili pepper, mustard seeds, and sunflower seeds; continue to sauté for minute longer or until aromatic.     Add in the vinegar, coconut aminos, salt, black pepper, and scallions. Stir to combine well.     Storing     Place the ground pork mixture in airtight containers or Ziploc bags; keep in your refrigerator for up to 3 to days.     For freezing, place the ground pork mixture it in airtight containers or heavy-duty freezer bags. Freeze up to 2 to 3 months. Defrost in the refrigerator and reheat in the skillet. Add spoonfuls of the pork mixture to the lettuce leaves, wrap them and serve.
**Nutrition Info:**281 Calories; 19.4g Fat; 5.1g Carbs; 22.1g Protein; 1.3g Fiber

## Ground Pork Skillet

Servings: 4     Cooking Time: 25 Minutes
**Ingredients:**
- 1 ½ pounds ground pork

- 2 tablespoons olive oil
- 1 bunch kale, trimmed and roughly chopped
- 1 cup onions, sliced
- 1/4 teaspoon black pepper, or more to taste
- 1/4 cup tomato puree
- 1 bell pepper, chopped
- 1 teaspoon sea salt
- 1 cup chicken bone broth
- 1/4 cup port wine
- 2 cloves garlic, pressed
- 1 chili pepper, sliced

**Directions:**
Heat tablespoon of the olive oil in a cast-iron skillet over a moderately high heat. Now, sauté the onion, garlic, and peppers until they are tender and fragrant; reserve. Heat the remaining tablespoon of olive oil; once hot, cook the ground pork and approximately 5 minutes until no longer pink.     Add in the other ingredients and continue to cook for 15 to 17 minutes or until cooked through.     Storing     Place the ground pork mixture in airtight containers or Ziploc bags; keep in your refrigerator for up to 3 to 4 days.     For freezing, place the ground pork mixture in airtight containers or heavy-duty freezer bags. Freeze up to 2 to 3 months. Defrost in the refrigerator. Bon appétit!
**Nutrition Info:**349 Calories; 13g Fat; 4.4g Carbs; 45.3g Protein; 1.2g Fiber

## Cheesy Chinese-style Pork

Servings: 6     Cooking Time: 20 Minutes
**Ingredients:**
- 1 tablespoon sesame oil
- 1 ½ pounds pork shoulder, cut into strips
- Himalayan salt and freshly ground black pepper, to taste
- 1/2 teaspoon cayenne pepper
- 1/2 cup shallots, roughly chopped
- 2 bell peppers, sliced
- 1/4 cup cream of onion soup
- 1/2 teaspoon Sriracha sauce
- 1 tablespoon tahini (sesame butter
- 1 tablespoon soy sauce
- 4 ounces gouda cheese, cut into small pieces

**Directions:**
Heat he sesame oil in a wok over a moderately high flame.     Stir-fry the pork strips for 3 to 4 minutes or until just browned on all sides. Add in the spices, shallots and bell peppers and continue to cook for a further 4 minutes.     Stir in the cream of onion soup, Sriracha, sesame butter, and soy sauce; continue to cook for to 4 minutes more.     Top with the cheese and continue to cook until the cheese has melted.     Storing Place your stir-fry in six airtight containers or Ziploc bags; keep in your refrigerator for 3 to 4 days.     For freezing, wrap tightly with heavy-duty aluminum foil or freezer wrap. It will maintain the best quality for 2 to 3 months. Defrost in the refrigerator and reheat in your wok.
**Nutrition Info:**424 Calories; 29.4g Fat; 3. Carbs; 34.2g Protein; 0.6g Fiber

## Pork In Blue Cheese Sauce

Servings: 6    Cooking Time: 30 Minutes
**Ingredients:**
- 2 pounds pork center cut loin roast, boneless and cut into 6 pieces
- 1 tablespoon coconut aminos
- 6 ounces blue cheese
- 1/3 cup heavy cream
- 1/3 cup port wine
- 1/3 cup roasted vegetable broth, preferably homemade
- 1 teaspoon dried hot chile flakes
- 1 teaspoon dried rosemary
- 1 tablespoon lard
- 1 shallot, chopped
- 2 garlic cloves, chopped
- Salt and freshly cracked black peppercorns, to taste

**Directions:**
Rub each piece of the pork with salt, black peppercorns, and rosemary.    Melt the lard in a saucepan over a moderately high flame. Sear the pork on all sides about 15 minutes; set aside.    Cook the shallot and garlic until they've softened. Add in port wine to scrape up any brown bits from the bottom.    Reduce the heat to medium-low and add in the remaining ingredients; continue to simmer until the sauce has thickened and reduced.    Storing    Divide the pork and sauce into six portions; place each portion in a separate airtight container or Ziploc bag; keep in your refrigerator for 3 to 4 days.    Freeze the pork and sauce in airtight containers or heavy-duty freezer bags. Freeze up to 4 months. Defrost in the refrigerator. Bon appétit!
**Nutrition Info:**34Calories; 18.9g Fat; 1.9g Carbs; 40.3g Protein; 0.3g Fiber

## Mississippi Pulled Pork

Servings: 4    Cooking Time: 6 Hours
**Ingredients:**
- 1 ½ pounds pork shoulder
- 1 tablespoon liquid smoke sauce
- 1 teaspoon chipotle powder
- Au Jus gravy seasoning packet
- 2 onions, cut into wedges
- Kosher salt and freshly ground black pepper, taste

**Directions:**
Mix the liquid smoke sauce, chipotle powder, Au Jus gravy seasoning packet, salt and pepper. Rub the spice mixture into the pork on all sides.    Wrap in plastic wrap and let it marinate in your refrigerator for 3 hours. Prepare your grill for indirect heat. Place the pork butt roast on the grate over a drip pan and top with onions; cover the grill and cook for about 6 hours.    Transfer the pork to a cutting board. Now, shred the meat into bite-sized pieces using two forks.    Storing    Divide the pork between four airtight containers or Ziploc bags; keep in your refrigerator for up to 3 to 5 days. For freezing, place the pork in airtight containers or heavy-duty freezer bags. Freeze up to 4 months. Defrost in the refrigerator. Bon appétit!
**Nutrition Info:**350 Calories; 11g Fat; 5g Carbs; 53.6g Protein; 2.2g Fiber

## Spicy And Cheesy Turkey Dip

Servings: 4    Cooking Time: 25 Minutes
**Ingredients:**
- 1 Fresno chili pepper, deveined and minced
- 1 ½ cups Ricotta cheese, creamed, 4% fat, softened
- 1/4 cup sour cream
- 1 tablespoon butter, room temperature
- 1 shallot, chopped
- 1 teaspoon garlic, pressed
- 1 pound ground turkey
- 1/2 cup goat cheese, shredded
- Salt and black pepper, to taste
- 1 ½ cups Gruyère, shredded

**Directions:**
Melt the butter in a frying pan over a moderately high flame. Now, sauté the onion and garlic until they have softened.    Stir in the ground turkey and continue to cook until it is no longer pink.    Transfer the sautéed mixture to a lightly greased baking dish. Add in Ricotta, sour cream, goat cheese, salt, pepper, and chili pepper. Top with the shredded Gruyère cheese. Bake in the preheated oven at 350 degrees F for about 20 minutes or until hot and bubbly in top.    Storing    Place your dip in an airtight container; keep in your refrigerator for up 3 to 4 days. Enjoy!
**Nutrition Info:**284 Calories; 19g Fat; 3.2g Carbs; 26. Protein; 1.6g Fiber

## Turkey Chorizo With Bok Choy

Servings: 4    Cooking Time: 50 Minutes
**Ingredients:**
- 4 mild turkey Chorizo, sliced
- 1/2 cup full-fat milk
- 6 ounces Gruyère cheese, preferably freshly grated
- 1 yellow onion, chopped
- Coarse salt and ground black pepper, to taste
- 1 pound Bok choy, tough stem ends trimmed
- 1 cup cream of mushroom soup
- 1 tablespoon lard, room temperature

**Directions:**
Melt the lard in a nonstick skillet over a moderate flame; cook the Chorizo sausage for about 5 minutes, stirring occasionally to ensure even cooking; reserve. Add in the onion, salt, pepper, Bok choy, and cream of mushroom soup. Continue to cook for 4 minutes longer or until the vegetables have softened.    Spoon the mixture into a lightly oiled casserole dish. Top with the reserved Chorizo.    In a mixing bowl, thoroughly combine the milk and cheese. Pour the cheese mixture over the sausage.    Cover with foil and bake at 36degrees F for about 35 minutes.    Storing    Cut your casserole into four portions. Place each portion in an airtight container; keep in your refrigerator for 3 to 4 days.    For freezing, wrap your portions tightly with heavy-duty aluminum foil or freezer wrap. Freeze up to 1 to 2 months. Defrost in the refrigerator. Enjoy!
**Nutrition Info:**18Calories; 12g Fat; 2.6g Carbs; 9.4g Protein; 1g Fiber

## Spicy Chicken Breasts

Servings: 6     Cooking Time: 30 Minutes
**Ingredients:**
- 1 ½ pounds chicken breasts
- 1 bell pepper, deveined and chopped
- 1 leek, chopped
- 1 tomato, pureed
- 2 tablespoons coriander
- 2 garlic cloves, minced
- 1 teaspoon cayenne pepper
- 1 teaspoon dry thyme
- 1/4 cup coconut aminos
- Sea salt and ground black pepper, to taste

**Directions:**
Rub each chicken breasts with the garlic, cayenne pepper, thyme, salt and black pepper. Cook the chicken in a saucepan over medium-high heat.     Sear for about 5 minutes until golden brown on all sides.     Fold in the tomato puree and coconut aminos and bring it to a boil. Add in the pepper, leek, and coriander.     Reduce the heat to simmer. Continue to cook, partially covered, for about 20 minutes.     Storing     Place the chicken breasts in airtight containers or Ziploc bags; keep in your refrigerator for 3 to 4 days.     For freezing, place the chicken breasts in airtight containers or heavy-duty freezer bags. It will maintain the best quality for about 4 months. Defrost in the refrigerator. Bon appétit!
**Nutrition Info:**239 Calories; 6g Fat; 5.5g Carbs; 34.3g Protein; 1g Fiber

## Saucy Boston Butt

Servings: 8     Cooking Time: 1 Hour 20 Minutes
**Ingredients:**
- 1 tablespoon lard, room temperature
- 2 pounds Boston butt, cubed
- Salt and freshly ground pepper
- 1/2 teaspoon mustard powder
- A bunch of spring onions, chopped
- 2 garlic cloves, minced
- 1/2 tablespoon ground cardamom
- 2 tomatoes, pureed
- 1 bell pepper, deveined and chopped
- 1 jalapeno pepper, deveined and finely chopped
- 1/2 cup unsweetened coconut milk
- 2 cups chicken bone broth

**Directions:**
In a wok, melt the lard over moderate heat. Season the pork belly with salt, pepper and mustard powder. Sear the pork for 8 to 10 minutes, stirring periodically to ensure even cooking; set aside, keeping it warm.     In the same wok, sauté the spring onions, garlic, and cardamom. Spoon the sautéed vegetables along with the reserved pork into the slow cooker.     Add in the remaining ingredients, cover with the lid and cook for 1 hour 10 minutes over low heat.     Storing     Divide the pork and vegetables between airtight containers or Ziploc bags; keep in your refrigerator for up to 3 to 5 days.     For freezing, place the pork and vegetables in

airtight containers or heavy-duty freezer bags. Freeze up to 4 months. Defrost in the refrigerator. Bon appétit!
**Nutrition Info:**369 Calories; 20.2g Fat; 2.9g Carbs; 41.3g Protein; 0.7g Fiber

## Old-fashioned Goulash

Servings: 4     Cooking Time: 9 Hours 10 Minutes
**Ingredients:**
- 1 ½ pounds pork butt, chopped
- 1 teaspoon sweet Hungarian paprika
- 2 Hungarian hot peppers, deveined and minced
- 1 cup leeks, chopped
- 1 ½ tablespoons lard
- 1 teaspoon caraway seeds, ground
- 4 cups vegetable broth
- 2 garlic cloves, crushed
- 1 teaspoons cayenne pepper
- 2 cups tomato sauce with herbs
- 1 ½ pounds pork butt, chopped
- 1 teaspoon sweet Hungarian paprika
- 2 Hungarian hot peppers, deveined and minced
- 1 cup leeks, chopped
- 1 ½ tablespoons lard
- 1 teaspoon caraway seeds, ground
- 4 cups vegetable broth
- 2 garlic cloves, crushed
- 1 teaspoons cayenne pepper
- 2 cups tomato sauce with herbs

**Directions:**
Melt the lard in a heavy-bottomed pot over medium-high heat. Sear the pork for 5 to 6 minutes until just browned on all sides; set aside.     Add in the leeks and garlic; continue to cook until they have softened. Place the reserved pork along with the sautéed mixture in your crock pot. Add in the other ingredients and stir to combine.     Cover with the lid and slow cook for 9 hours on the lowest setting.     Storing     Spoon your goulash into four airtight containers or Ziploc bags; keep in your refrigerator for up to 3 to 4 days.     For freezing, place the goulash in airtight containers. Freeze up to 4 to 6 months. Defrost in the refrigerator. Enjoy!
**Nutrition Info:**456 Calories; 27g Fat; 6.7g Carbs; 32g Protein; 3.4g Fiber

## Flatbread With Chicken Liver Pâté

Servings: 4    Cooking Time: 2 Hours 15 Minutes
**Ingredients:**
- 1 yellow onion, finely chopped
- 10 ounces chicken livers
- 1/2 teaspoon Mediterranean seasoning blend
- 4 tablespoons olive oil
- 1 garlic clove, minced
- For Flatbread:
- 1 cup lukewarm water
- 1/2 stick butter
- 1/2 cup flax meal
- 1 ½ tablespoons psyllium husks
- 1 ¼ cups almond flour

**Directions:**
Pulse the chicken livers along with the seasoning blend, olive oil, onion and garlic in your food processor; reserve.    Mix the dry ingredients for the flatbread. Mix in all the wet ingredients. Whisk to combine well. Let it stand at room temperature for 2 hours. Divide the dough into 8 balls and roll them out on a flat surface. In a lightly greased pan, cook your flatbread for 1 minute on each side or until golden.    Storing    Wrap the chicken liver pate in foil before packing it into airtight containers; keep in your refrigerator for up to 7 days.    For freezing, place the chicken liver pate in airtight containers or heavy-duty freezer bags. Freeze up to 2 months. Defrost overnight in the refrigerator. As for the keto flatbread, wrap them in foil before packing them into airtight containers; keep in your refrigerator for up to 4 days.    Bon appétit!
**Nutrition Info:**395 Calories; 30.2g Fat; 3.6g Carbs; 17.9g Protein; 0.5g Fiber

## Sunday Chicken With Cauliflower Salad

Servings: 2    Cooking Time: 20 Minutes
**Ingredients:**
- 1 teaspoon hot paprika
- 2 tablespoons fresh basil, snipped
- 1/2 cup mayonnaise
- 1 teaspoon mustard
- 2 teaspoons butter
- 2 chicken wings
- 1/2 cup cheddar cheese, shredded
- Sea salt and ground black pepper, to taste
- 2 tablespoons dry sherry
- 1 shallot, finely minced
- 1/2 head of cauliflower

**Directions:**
Boil the cauliflower in a pot of salted water until it has softened; cut into small florets and place in a salad bowl. Melt the butter in a saucepan over medium-high heat. Cook the chicken for about 8 minutes or until the skin is crisp and browned. Season with hot paprika salt, and black pepper.    Whisk the mayonnaise, mustard, dry sherry, and shallot and dress your salad. Top with cheddar cheese and fresh basil.    Storing    Place the chicken wings in airtight containers or Ziploc bags; keep in your refrigerator for up 3 to 4 days.    Keep the cauliflower salad in your refrigerator for up 3 days. For freezing, place the chicken wings in airtight containers or heavy-duty freezer bags. Freeze up to 3 months. Once thawed in the refrigerator, reheat in a saucepan until thoroughly warmed.
**Nutrition Info:**444 Calories; 36g Fat; 5.7g Carbs; 20.6g Protein; 4.3g Fiber

## Kansas-style Meatloaf

Servings: 8    Cooking Time: 1 Hour 10 Minutes
**Ingredients:**
- 2 pounds ground pork
- 2 eggs, beaten
- 1/2 cup onions, chopped
- 1/2 cup marinara sauce, bottled
- 8 ounces Colby cheese, shredded
- 1 teaspoon granulated garlic
- Sea salt and freshly ground black pepper, to taste
- 1 teaspoon lime zest
- 1 teaspoon mustard seeds
- 1/2 cup tomato puree
- 1 tablespoon Erythritol

**Directions:**
Mix the ground pork with the eggs, onions, marinara salsa, cheese, granulated garlic, salt, pepper, lime zest, and mustard seeds; mix to combine.    Press the mixture into a lightly-greased loaf pan. Mix the tomato paste with the Erythritol and spread the mixture over the top of your meatloaf.    Bake in the preheated oven at 5 degrees F for about 1 hour 10 minutes, rotating the pan halfway through the cook time.    Storing    Wrap your meatloaf tightly with heavy-duty aluminum foil or plastic wrap. Then, keep in your refrigerator for up to 3 to 4 days.    For freezing, wrap your meatloaf tightly to prevent freezer burn. Freeze up to 3 to 4 months. Defrost in the refrigerator. Bon appétit!
**Nutrition Info:**318 Calories; 14. Fat; 6.2g Carbs; 39.3g Protein; 0.3g Fiber

## Authentic Turkey Kebabs

Servings: 6     Cooking Time: 30 Minutes
**Ingredients:**
- 1 ½ pounds turkey breast, cubed
- 3 Spanish peppers, sliced
- 2 zucchinis, cut into thick slices
- 1 onion, cut into wedges
- 2 tablespoons olive oil, room temperature
- 1 tablespoon dry ranch seasoning

**Directions:**
Thread the turkey pieces and vegetables onto bamboo skewers. Sprinkle the skewers with dry ranch seasoning and olive oil.     Grill your kebabs for about 10 minutes, turning them periodically to ensure even cooking. Storing     Wrap your kebabs in foil before packing them into airtight containers; keep in your refrigerator for up to 3 to days.     For freezing, place your kebabs in airtight containers or heavy-duty freezer bags. Freeze up to 2-3 months. Defrost in the refrigerator. Bon appétit!
**Nutrition Info:**2 Calories; 13.8g Fat; 6.7g Carbs; 25.8g Protein; 1.2g Fiber

## Mexican-style Turkey Bacon Bites

Servings: 4     Cooking Time: 5 Minutes
**Ingredients:**
- 4 ounces turkey bacon, chopped
- 4 ounces Neufchatel cheese
- 1 tablespoon butter, cold
- 1 jalapeno pepper, deveined and minced
- 1 teaspoon Mexican oregano
- 2 tablespoons scallions, finely chopped

**Directions:**
Thoroughly combine all ingredients in a mixing bowl. Roll the mixture into 8 balls.     Storing     Divide the turkey bacon bites between two airtight containers or Ziploc bags; keep in your refrigerator for up 3 to days.
**Nutrition Info:**19Calories; 16.7g Fat; 2.2g Carbs; 8.8g Protein; 0.3g Fiber

## Breakfast Muffins With Ground Pork

Servings: 6     Cooking Time: 25 Minutes
**Ingredients:**
- 1 stick butter
- 3 large eggs, lightly beaten
- 2 tablespoons full-fat milk
- 1/2 teaspoon ground cardamom
- 3 ½ cups almond flour
- 2 tablespoons flaxseed meal
- 1 teaspoon baking powder
- 2 cups ground pork
- Salt and pepper, to your liking
- 1/2 teaspoon dried basil

**Directions:**
In the preheated frying pan, cook the ground pork until the juices run clear, approximately 5 minutes.     Add in the remaining ingredients and stir until well combined. Spoon the mixture into lightly greased muffin cups. Bake in the preheated oven at 5 degrees F for about 17 minutes.     Allow your muffins to cool down before unmolding and storing.     Storing     Place your muffins in the airtight containers or Ziploc bags; keep in the refrigerator for a week.     For freezing, divide your muffins among Ziploc bags and freeze up to 3 months. Defrost in your microwave for a couple of minutes. Bon appétit!
**Nutrition Info:**330 Calories; 30.3g Fat; 2.3g Carbs; 19g Protein; 1.2g Fiber

## Mediterranean-style Cheesy Pork Loin

Servings: 4     Cooking Time: 25 Minutes
**Ingredients:**
- 1 pound pork loin, cut into 1-inch-thick pieces
- 1 teaspoon Mediterranean seasoning mix
- Salt and pepper, to taste     1 onion, sliced
- 1 teaspoon fresh garlic, smashed
- 2 tablespoons black olives, pitted and sliced
- 2 tablespoons balsamic vinegar
- 1/2 cup Romano cheese, grated
- 2 tablespoons butter, room temperature
- 1 tablespoon curry paste
- 1 cup roasted vegetable broth
- 1 tablespoon oyster sauce

**Directions:**
In a frying pan, melt the butter over a moderately high heat. Once hot, cook the pork until browned on all sides; season with salt and black pepper and set aside. In the pan drippings, cook the onion and garlic for 4 to 5 minutes or until they've softened.     Add in the Mediterranean seasoning mix, curry paste, and vegetable broth. Continue to cook until the sauce has thickened and reduced slightly or about 10 minutes. Add in the remaining ingredients along with the reserved pork.     Top with cheese and cook for 10 minutes longer or until cooked through.     Storing Divide the pork loin between four airtight containers; keep in your refrigerator for 3 to 5 days.     For freezing, place the pork loin in airtight containers or heavy-duty freezer bags. Freeze up to 4 to 6 months. Defrost in the refrigerator. Enjoy!
**Nutrition Info:**476 Calories; 35.3g Fat; 6.2g Carbs; 31.1g Protein; 1.4g Fiber

## Oven-roasted Spare Ribs

Servings: 6     Cooking Time: 3 Hour 40 Minutes
**Ingredients:**
- 2 pounds spare ribs
- 1 garlic clove, minced
- 1 teaspoon dried marjoram
- 1 lime, halved
- Salt and ground black pepper, to taste

**Directions:**
Toss all ingredients in a ceramic dish.     Cover and let it refrigerate for 5 to 6 hours.     Roast the foil-wrapped ribs in the preheated oven at 275 degrees F degrees for about hours 30 minutes.     Storing     Divide the ribs into six portions. Place each portion of ribs in an airtight container; keep in your refrigerator for 3 to days.     For freezing, place the ribs in airtight containers or heavy-duty freezer bags. Freeze up to 4 to months. Defrost in the refrigerator and reheat in the preheated oven. Bon appétit!
**Nutrition Info:**385 Calories; 29g Fat; 1.8g Carbs; 28.3g Protein; 0.1g Fiber

## Parmesan Chicken Salad

Servings: 6     Cooking Time: 20 Minutes
**Ingredients:**
- 2 romaine hearts, leaves separated
- Flaky sea salt and ground black pepper, to taste
- 1/4 teaspoon chili pepper flakes
- 1 teaspoon dried basil
- 1/4 cup Parmesan, finely grated
- 2 chicken breasts
- 2 Lebanese cucumbers, sliced
- For the dressing:
- 2 large egg yolks
- 1 teaspoon Dijon mustard
- 1 tablespoon fresh lemon juice
- 1/4 cup olive oil
- 2 garlic cloves, minced

**Directions:**
In a grilling pan, cook the chicken breast until no longer pink or until a meat thermometer registers 5 degrees F. Slice the chicken into strips.     Storing     Place the chicken breasts in airtight containers or Ziploc bags; keep in your refrigerator for to 4 days.     For freezing, place the chicken breasts in airtight containers or heavy-duty freezer bags. It will maintain the best quality for about months. Defrost in the refrigerator.     Toss the chicken with the other ingredients. Prepare the dressing by whisking all the ingredients.     Dress the salad and enjoy! Keep the salad in your refrigerator for 3 to 5 days.
**Nutrition Info:**183 Calories; 12.5g Fat; 1. Carbs; 16.3g Protein; 0.9g Fiber

## Turkey Wings With Gravy

Servings: 6     Cooking Time: 6 Hours
**Ingredients:**
- 2 pounds turkey wings
- 1/2 teaspoon cayenne pepper
- 4 garlic cloves, sliced
- 1 large onion, chopped
- Salt and pepper, to taste
- 1 teaspoon dried marjoram
- 1 tablespoon butter, room temperature
- 1 tablespoon Dijon mustard
- For the Gravy:
- 1 cup double cream
- Salt and black pepper, to taste
- 1/2 stick butter
- 3/4 teaspoon guar gum

**Directions:**
Rub the turkey wings with the Dijon mustard and tablespoon of butter. Preheat a grill pan over medium-high heat.     Sear the turkey wings for 10 minutes on all sides.     Transfer the turkey to your Crock pot; add in the garlic, onion, salt, pepper, marjoram, and cayenne pepper. Cover and cook on low setting for 6 hours. Melt 1/2 stick of the butter in a frying pan. Add in the cream and whisk until cooked through.     Next, stir in the guar gum, salt, and black pepper along with cooking juices. Let it cook until the sauce has reduced by half.     Storing     Wrap the turkey wings in foil before packing them into airtight containers; keep in your refrigerator for up to 3 to 4 days.     For freezing, place the turkey wings in airtight containers or heavy-duty freezer bags. Freeze up to 2 to 3 months. Defrost in the refrigerator. Keep your gravy in refrigerator for up to 2 days.
**Nutrition Info:**280 Calories; 22.2g Fat; 4.3g Carbs; 15.8g Protein; 0.8g Fiber

## Pork Chops With Herbs

Servings: 4     Cooking Time: 20 Minutes
**Ingredients:**
- 1 tablespoon butter
- 1 pound pork chops
- 2 rosemary sprigs, minced
- 1 teaspoon dried marjoram
- 1 teaspoon dried parsley
- A bunch of spring onions, roughly chopped
- 1 thyme sprig, minced
- 1/2 teaspoon granulated garlic
- 1/2 teaspoon paprika, crushed
- Coarse salt and ground black pepper, to taste

**Directions:**
Season the pork chops with the granulated garlic, paprika, salt, and black pepper.     Melt the butter in a frying pan over a moderate flame. Cook the pork chops for 6 to 8 minutes, turning them occasionally to ensure even cooking.     Add in the remaining ingredients and cook an additional 4 minutes.     Storing     Divide the pork chops into four portions; place each portion in a separate airtight container or Ziploc bag; keep in your refrigerator for 3 to 4 days.     Freeze the pork chops in airtight containers or heavy-duty freezer bags. Freeze up to 4 months. Defrost in the refrigerator. Bon appétit!
**Nutrition Info:**192 Calories; 6.9g Fat; 0.9g Carbs; 29.8g Protein; 0.4g Fiber

## Ground Pork Stuffed Peppers

Servings: 4     Cooking Time: 40 Minutes
**Ingredients:**
- 6 bell peppers, deveined
- 1 tablespoon vegetable oil
- 1 shallot, chopped
- 1 garlic clove, minced
- 1/2 pound ground pork
- 1/3 pound ground veal
- 1 ripe tomato, chopped
- 1/2 teaspoon mustard seeds
- Sea salt and ground black pepper, to taste

**Directions:**
Parboil the peppers for 5 minutes.     Heat the vegetable oil in a frying pan that is preheated over a moderate heat. Cook the shallot and garlic for 3 to 4 minutes until they've softened.     Stir in the ground meat and cook, breaking apart with a fork, for about 6 minutes. Add the chopped tomatoes, mustard seeds, salt, and pepper. Continue to cook for 5 minutes or until heated through. Divide the filling between the peppers and transfer them to a baking pan.     Bake in the preheated oven at 36degrees F approximately 25 minutes.     Storing Place the peppers in airtight containers or Ziploc bags; keep in your refrigerator for up to 3 to 4 days.     For freezing, place the peppers in airtight containers or heavy-duty freezer bags. Freeze up to 2 to 3 months. Defrost in the refrigerator. Bon appétit!
**Nutrition Info:**2 Calories; 20.5g Fat; 8.2g Carbs; 18.2g Protein; 1.5g Fiber

## Grilled Chicken Salad With Avocado

Servings: 4     Cooking Time: 20 Minutes
**Ingredients:**
- 1/3 cup olive oil
- 2 chicken breasts
- Sea salt and crushed red pepper flakes
- 2 egg yolks
- 1 tablespoon fresh lemon juice
- 1/2 teaspoon celery seeds
- 1 tablespoon coconut aminos
- 1 large-sized avocado, pitted and sliced

**Directions:**
Grill the chicken breasts for about 4 minutes per side. Season with salt and pepper, to taste.     Slice the grilled chicken into bite-sized strips.     To make the dressing, whisk the egg yolks, lemon juice, celery seeds, olive oil and coconut aminos in a measuring cup.     Storing Place the chicken breasts in airtight containers or Ziploc bags; keep in your refrigerator for 3 to 4 days.     For freezing, place the chicken breasts in airtight containers or heavy-duty freezer bags. It will maintain the best quality for about 4 months. Defrost in the refrigerator. Store dressing in your refrigerator for 3 to 4 days. Dress the salad and garnish with fresh avocado. Bon appétit!
**Nutrition Info:**40Calories; 34.2g Fat; 4.8g Carbs; 22.7g Protein; 3.1g Fiber

## Easy Fall-off-the-bone Ribs

Servings: 4     Cooking Time: 8 Hours
**Ingredients:**
- 1 pound baby back ribs
- 4 tablespoons coconut aminos
- 1/4 cup dry red wine
- 1/2 teaspoon cayenne pepper
- 1 garlic clove, crushed
- 1 teaspoon Italian herb mix
- 1 tablespoon butter
- 1 teaspoon Serrano pepper, minced
- 1 Italian pepper, thinly sliced
- 1 teaspoon grated lemon zest

**Directions:**
Butter the sides and bottom of your Crock pot. Place the pork and peppers on the bottom.     Add in the remaining ingredients.     Slow cook for 9 hours on Low heat setting.     Storing     Divide the baby back ribs into four portions. Place each portion of the ribs along with the peppers in an airtight container; keep in your refrigerator for 3 to days.     For freezing, place the ribs in airtight containers or heavy-duty freezer bags. Freeze up to 4 to months. Defrost in the refrigerator. Reheat in your oven at 250 degrees F until heated through.
**Nutrition Info:**192 Calories; 6.9g Fat; 0.9g Carbs; 29.8g Protein; 0.5g Fiber

## Brie-stuffed Meatballs

Servings: 5     Cooking Time: 25 Minutes
**Ingredients:**
- 2 eggs, beaten
- 1 pound ground pork
- 1/3 cup double cream
- 1 tablespoon fresh parsley
- Kosher salt and ground black pepper
- 1 teaspoon dried rosemary
- 10 (1-inch cubes of brie cheese
- 2 tablespoons scallions, minced
- 2 cloves garlic, minced

**Directions:**
Mix all ingredients, except for the brie cheese, until everything is well incorporated.     Roll the mixture into 10 patties; place a piece of cheese in the center of each patty and roll into a ball.     Roast in the preheated oven at 0 degrees F for about 20 minutes.     Storing     Place the meatballs in airtight containers or Ziploc bags; keep in your refrigerator for up to 3 to 4 days.     Freeze the meatballs in airtight containers or heavy-duty freezer bags. Freeze up to 3 to 4 months. To defrost, slowly reheat in a saucepan. Bon appétit!
**Nutrition Info:**302 Calories; 13g Fat; 1.9g Carbs; 33.4g Protein; 0.3g Fiber

## Spicy And Tangy Chicken Drumsticks

Servings: 6    Cooking Time: 55 Minutes
**Ingredients:**
- 3 chicken drumsticks, cut into chunks
- 1/2 stick butter
- 2 eggs
- 1/4 cup hemp seeds, ground
- Salt and cayenne pepper, to taste
- 2 tablespoons coconut aminos
- 3 teaspoons red wine vinegar
- 2 tablespoons salsa
- 2 cloves garlic, minced

**Directions:**
Rub the chicken with the butter, salt, and cayenne pepper.    Drizzle the chicken with the coconut aminos, vinegar, salsa, and garlic. Allow it to stand for 30 minutes in your refrigerator.    Whisk the eggs with the hemp seeds. Dip each chicken strip in the egg mixture. Place the chicken chunks in a parchment-lined baking pan.    Roast in the preheated oven at 390 degrees F for 25 minutes.    Storing    Divide the roasted chicken between airtight containers; keep in your refrigerator for up 3 to 4 days.    For freezing, place the roasted chicken in airtight containers or heavy-duty freezer bags. Freeze up to 3 months. Defrost in the refrigerator and reheat in a pan. Enjoy!
**Nutrition Info:**420 Calories; 22g Fat; 5g Carbs; 35.3g Protein; 0.8g Fiber

## Italian-style Chicken Meatballs With Parmesan

Servings: 6    Cooking Time: 20 Minutes

**Ingredients:**
- For the Meatballs:
- 1 ¼ pounds chicken, ground
- 1 tablespoon sage leaves, chopped
- 1 teaspoon shallot powder
- 1 teaspoon porcini powder
- 2 garlic cloves, finely minced
- 1/3 teaspoon dried basil
- 3/4 cup Parmesan cheese, grated
- 2 eggs, lightly beaten
- Salt and ground black pepper, to your liking
- 1/2 teaspoon cayenne pepper
- For the sauce:
- 2 tomatoes, pureed
- 1 cup chicken consommé
- 2 ½ tablespoons lard, room temperature
- 1 onion, peeled and finely chopped

**Directions:**
In a mixing bowl, combine all ingredients for the meatballs. Roll the mixture into bite-sized balls.    Melt 1 tablespoon of lard in a skillet over a moderately high heat. Sear the meatballs for about 3 minutes or until they are thoroughly cooked; reserve.    Melt the remaining lard and cook the onions until tender and translucent. Add in pureed tomatoes and chicken consommé and continue to cook for 4 minutes longer. Add in the reserved meatballs, turn the heat to simmer and continue to cook for 6 to 7 minutes.    Storing Place the meatballs in airtight containers or Ziploc bags; keep in your refrigerator for up to 3 to 4 days.    Freeze the meatballs in airtight containers or heavy-duty freezer bags. Freeze up to 3 to 4 months. To defrost, slowly reheat in a saucepan. Bon appétit!
**Nutrition Info:**252 Calories; 9.7g Fat; 5.3g Carbs; 34.2g Protein; 1.4g Fiber

# Sides & Appetizers Recipes

## Chicken Bacon Pasta

Servings: 4     Cooking Time: 35 Minutes

**Ingredients:**
- 8 ounces linguine pasta
- 3 slices of bacon
- 1 pound boneless chicken breast, cooked and diced
- salt
- 2 ounce can diced tomatoes, undrained
- 1/4 teaspoon dried rosemary
- 1/3 cup crumbled feta cheese, plus extra for topping
- 2/3 cup pitted black olives
- 1 6-ounce can artichoke hearts

**Directions:**
Fill a large pot with salted water and bring to a boil. Add linguine and cook for 8-10 minutes until al dente. Cook bacon until brown, and then crumble.     Season chicken with salt.     Place chicken and bacon into a large skillet.     Add tomatoes and rosemary and simmer the mixture for about 20 minutes.     Stir in feta cheese, artichoke hearts, and olives, and cook until thoroughly heated.     Toss the freshly cooked pasta with chicken mixture and cool.     Spread over the containers.     Before eating, garnish with extra feta if your heart desires!

**Nutrition Info:Per Serving:**Calories: 755, Total Fat: 22.5 g, Saturated Fat: 6.5 g, Cholesterol: 128 mg, Sodium: 852 mg, Total Carbohydrate: 75.4 g, Dietary Fiber: 7.3 g, Total Sugars: 3.4 g, Protein: 55.6 g, Vitamin D: 0 mcg, Calcium: 162 mg, Iron: 7 mg, Potassium: 524 mg

## Creamy Garlic Shrimp Pasta

Servings: 4     Cooking Time: 15 Minutes

**Ingredients:**
- 6 ounces whole-wheat spaghetti, your favorite
- 12 ounces raw shrimp, peeled, deveined, and cut into 1-inch pieces
- 1 bunch asparagus, trimmed and thinly sliced
- 1 large bell pepper, thinly sliced
- 3 cloves garlic, chopped
- 1¼ teaspoon kosher salt
- 1½ cups non-fat plain yogurt
- 1/4 cup flat-leaf parsley, chopped
- 3 tablespoons lemon juice
- 1 tablespoon extra virgin olive oil
- ½ teaspoon fresh ground black pepper
- 1/4 cup toasted pine nuts

**Directions:**
Bring water to a boil in a large pot.     Add spaghetti and cook for about minutes less than called for by the package instructions.     Add shrimp, bell pepper, asparagus and cook for about 2-4 minutes until the

shrimp are tender.     Drain the pasta.     In a large bowl, mash the garlic until paste forms.     Whisk yogurt, parsley, oil, pepper, and lemon juice into the garlic paste.     Add pasta mixture and toss well.     Cool and spread over the containers.     Sprinkle with pine nuts.     Enjoy!

**Nutrition Info:Per Serving:**Calories: 504, Total Fat: 15.4 g, Saturated Fat: 4.9 g, Cholesterol: 199 mg, Sodium: 2052 mg, Total Carbohydrate: 42.2 g, Dietary Fiber: 3.5 g, Total Sugars: 26.6 g, Protein: 43.2 g, Vitamin D: 0 mcg, Calcium: 723 mg, Iron: 3 mg, Potassium: 3 mg

## Mushroom Fettuccine

Servings: 5     Cooking Time: 15 Minutes

**Ingredients:**
- 12 ounces whole-wheat fettuccine (or any other)
- 1 tablespoon extra virgin olive oil
- 4 cups mixed mushrooms, such as oyster, cremini, etc., sliced
- 4 cups broccoli, divided
- 1 tablespoon minced garlic
- ½ cup dry sherry
- 2 cups low-fat milk
- 2 tablespoons all-purpose flour
- ½ teaspoon salt
- ½ teaspoon freshly ground pepper
- 1 cup finely shredded Asiago cheese, plus some for topping

**Directions:**
Cook pasta in a large pot of boiling water for about 8-minutes.     Drain pasta and set it to the side.     Add oil to large skillet and heat over medium heat.     Add mushrooms and broccoli, and cook for about 8-10 minutes until the mushrooms have released the liquid. Add garlic and cook for about 1 minute until fragrant. Add sherry, making sure to scrape up any brown bits. Bring the mix to a boil and cook for about 1 minute until evaporated.     In a separate bowl, whisk flour and milk. Add the mix to your skillet, and season with salt and pepper.     Cook well for about 2 minutes until the sauce begins to bubble and is thickened.     Stir in Asiago cheese until it has fully melted.     Add the sauce to your pasta and give it a gentle toss.     Spread over the containers. Serve with extra cheese.

**Nutrition Info:Per Serving:**Calories: 503, Total Fat: 19.6 g, Saturated Fat: 6.3 g, Cholesterol: 25 mg, Sodium: 1136 mg, Total Carbohydrate: 57.5 g, Dietary Fiber: 12.4 g, Total Sugars: 6.4 g, Protein: 24.5 g, Vitamin D: 51 mcg, Calcium: 419 mg, Iron: 5 mg, Potassium: 390 mg

## Lemon Garlic Sardine Fettuccine

Servings: 4     Cooking Time: 15 Minutes
**Ingredients:**
- 8 ounces whole-wheat fettuccine
- 4 tablespoons extra-virgin olive oil, divided
- 4 cloves garlic, minced
- 1 cup fresh breadcrumbs
- ¼ cup lemon juice
- 1 teaspoon freshly ground pepper
- ½ teaspoon of salt
- 2 4-ounce cans boneless and skinless sardines, dipped in tomato sauce
- ½ cup fresh parsley, chopped
- ¼ cup finely shredded parmesan cheese

**Directions:**
Fill a large pot with water and bring to a boil.     Cook pasta according to package instructions until tender (about 10 minutes).     In a small skillet, heat 2 tablespoons of oil over medium heat.     Add garlic and cook for about 20 seconds, until sizzling and fragrant. Transfer the garlic to a large bowl.     Add the remaining 2 tablespoons of oil to skillet and heat over medium heat.     Add breadcrumbs and cook for 5-6 minutes until golden and crispy.     Whisk lemon juice, salt, and pepper into the garlic bowl.     Add pasta to the garlic bowl, along with garlic, sardines, parmesan, and parsley; give it a gentle stir.     Cool and spread over the containers.     Before eating, sprinkle with breadcrumbs.     Enjoy!
**Nutrition Info:Per Serving:**Calories: 633, Total Fat: 27.7 g, Saturated Fat: 6.4 g, Cholesterol: 40 mg, Sodium: 771 mg, Total Carbohydrate: 55.9 g, Dietary Fiber: 7.7 g, Total Sugars: 2.1 g, Protein: 38.6 g, Vitamin D: 0 mcg, Calcium: 274 mg, Iron: 7 mg, Potassium: mg

## Spinach Almond Stir-fry

Servings: 2     Cooking Time: 10 Minutes
**Ingredients:**
- 2 ounces spinach
- 1 tablespoon coconut oil
- 3 tablespoons almond, slices
- sea salt or plain salt
- freshly ground black pepper

**Directions:**
Start by heating a skillet with coconut oil; add spinach and let it cook.     Then, add salt and pepper as the spinach is cooking.     Finally, add in the almond slices. Serve warm.
**Nutrition Info:Per Serving:**Calories: 117, Total Fat: 11.4 g, Saturated Fat: 6.2 g, Cholesterol: 0 mg, Sodium: 23 mg, Total Carbohydrate: 2.9 g, Dietary Fiber: 1.7 g, Total Sugars: 0.g, Protein: 2.7 g, Vitamin D: 0 mcg, Calcium: 52 mg, Iron: 1 mg, Potassium: 224 mg

## Bbq Carrots

Servings: 8     Cooking Time: 30 Minutes
**Ingredients:**
- 2 pounds baby carrots (organic)
- 1 tablespoon olive oil
- 1 tablespoon garlic powder
- 1 tablespoon onion powder
- sea salt or plain salt
- freshly ground black pepper

**Directions:**
Mix all the Ingredients: in a plastic bag so that the carrots are well coated with the mixture.     Then, on the BBQ grill place a piece of aluminum foil and spread the carrots in a single layer.     Finally, grill for 30 minutes or until tender.     Serve warm.
**Nutrition Info:Per Serving:**Calories: 388, Total Fat: 1.9 g, Saturated Fat: 0.3 g, Cholesterol: 0 mg, Sodium: 89 mg, Total Carbohydrate: 10.8 g, Dietary Fiber: 3.4 g, Total Sugars: 6 g, Protein: 1 g, Vitamin D: 0 mcg, Calcium: 40 mg, Iron: 1 mg, Potassium: 288 mg

## Mediterranean Baked Zucchini Sticks

Servings: 8     Cooking Time: 20 Minutes
**Ingredients:**
- ¼ cup feta cheese, crumbled
- 4 zucchini
- ¼ cup parsley, chopped
- ½ cup tomatoes, minced
- ½ cup kalamata olives, pitted and minced
- 1 cup red bell pepper, minced
- 1 tablespoon oregano
- ¼ cup garlic, minced
- 1 tablespoon basil
- sea salt or plain salt
- freshly ground black pepper

**Directions:**
Start by cutting zucchini in half (lengthwise) and scoop out the middle.     Then, combine garlic, black pepper, bell pepper, oregano, basil, tomatoes, and olives in a bowl.     Now, fill in the middle of each zucchini with this mixture. Place these on a prepared baking dish and bake the dish at 0 degrees F for about 15 minutes. Finally, top with feta cheese and broil on high for 3 minutes or until done. Garnish with parsley.     Serve warm.
**Nutrition Info:Per Serving:**Calories: 53, Total Fat: 2.2 g, Saturated Fat: 0.9 g, Cholesterol: 4 mg, Sodium: 138 mg, Total Carbohydrate: 7.5 g, Dietary Fiber: 2.1 g, Total Sugars: 3 g, Protein: 2.g, Vitamin D: 0 mcg, Calcium: 67 mg, Iron: 1 mg, Potassium: 353 mg

## Artichoke Olive Pasta

Servings: 4     Cooking Time: 25 Minutes
**Ingredients:**
- salt
- pepper
- 2 tablespoons olive oil, divided
- 2 garlic cloves, thinly sliced
- 1 can artichoke hearts, drained, rinsed, and quartered lengthwise
- 1-pint grape tomatoes, halved lengthwise, divided
- ½ cup fresh basil leaves, torn apart
- 12 ounces whole-wheat spaghetti
- ½ medium onion, thinly sliced
- ½ cup dry white wine
- 1/3 cup pitted Kalamata olives, quartered lengthwise
- ¼ cup grated Parmesan cheese, plus extra for serving

**Directions:**
Fill a large pot with salted water.     Pour the water to a boil and cook your pasta according to package instructions until al dente.     Drain the pasta and reserve 1 cup of the cooking water.     Return the pasta to the pot and set aside.     Heat 1 tablespoon of olive oil in a large skillet over medium-high heat.     Add onion and garlic, season with pepper and salt, and cook well for about 3-4 minutes until nicely browned.     Add wine and cook for 2 minutes until evaporated.     Stir in artichokes and keep cooking 2-3 minutes until brown. Add olives and half of your tomatoes.     Cook well for 1-2 minutes until the tomatoes start to break down. Add pasta to the skillet.     Stir in the rest of the tomatoes, cheese, basil, and remaining oil.     Thin the mixture with the reserved pasta water if needed. Place in containers and sprinkle with extra cheese. Enjoy!

**Nutrition Info:Per Serving:**Calories: 340, Total Fat: 11.9 g, Saturated Fat: 3.3 g, Cholesterol: 10 mg, Sodium: 278 mg, Total Carbohydrate: 35.8 g, Dietary Fiber: 7.8 g, Total Sugars: 4.8 g, Protein: 11.6 g, Vitamin D: 0 mcg, Calcium: 193 mg, Iron: 3 mg, Potassium: 524 mg

## Olive Tuna Pasta

Servings: 4     Cooking Time: 20 Minutes
**Ingredients:**
- 8 ounces of tuna steak, cut into 3 pieces
- ¼ cup green olives, chopped
- 3 cloves garlic, minced
- 2 cups grape tomatoes, halved
- ½ cup white wine
- 2 tablespoons lemon juice
- 6 ounces pasta - whole wheat gobetti, rotini, or penne
- 1 10-ounce package frozen artichoke hearts, thawed and squeezed dry
- 4 tablespoons extra-virgin olive oil, divided
- 2 teaspoons fresh grated lemon zest
- 2 teaspoons fresh rosemary, chopped, divided
- ½ teaspoon salt, divided
- ¼ teaspoon fresh ground pepper
- ¼ cup fresh basil, chopped

**Directions:**
Preheat grill to medium-high heat.     Take a large pot of water and put it on to boil.     Place the tuna pieces in a bowl and add 1 tablespoon of oil, 1 teaspoon of rosemary, lemon zest, a ¼ teaspoon of salt, and pepper. Grill the tuna for about 3 minutes per side.     Transfer tuna to a plate and allow it to cool.     Place the pasta in boiling water and cook according to package instructions.     Drain the pasta.     Flake the tuna into bite-sized pieces.     In a large skillet, heat remaining oil over medium heat.     Add artichoke hearts, garlic, olives, and remaining rosemary.     Cook for about 3-4 minutes until slightly browned.     Add tomatoes, wine, and bring the mixture to a boil.     Cook for about 3 minutes until the tomatoes are broken down.     Stir in pasta, lemon juice, tuna, and remaining salt.     Cook for 1-2 minutes until nicely heated.     Spread over the containers.     Before eating, garnish with some basil and enjoy!

**Nutrition Info:Per Serving:**Calories: 455, Total Fat: 21.2 g, Saturated Fat: 3.5 g, Cholesterol: 59 mg, Sodium: 685 mg, Total Carbohydrate: 38.4 g, Dietary Fiber: 6.1 g, Total Sugars: 3.5 g, Protein: 25.5 g, Vitamin D: 0 mcg, Calcium: 100 mg, Iron: 5 mg, Potassium: 800 mg

## Braised Artichokes

Servings: 6     Cooking Time: 30 Minutes
**Ingredients:**
- 6 tablespoons olive oil
- 2 pounds baby artichokes, trimmed
- ½ cup lemon juice
- 4 garlic cloves, thinly sliced
- ½ teaspoon salt
- 1½ pounds tomatoes, seeded and diced
- ½ cup almonds, toasted and sliced

**Directions:**
Heat oil in a skillet over medium heat.     Add artichokes, garlic, and lemon juice, and allow the garlic to sizzle.     Season with salt.     Reduce heat to medium-low, cover, and simmer for about 15 minutes. Uncover, add tomatoes, and simmer for another 10 minutes until the tomato liquid has mostly evaporated. Season with more salt and pepper.     Sprinkle with toasted almonds.     Enjoy!

**Nutrition Info:Per Serving:**Calories: 265, Total Fat: 1g, Saturated Fat: 2.6 g, Cholesterol: 0 mg, Sodium: 265 mg, Total Carbohydrate: 23 g, Dietary Fiber: 8.1 g, Total Sugars: 12.4 g, Protein: 7 g, Vitamin D: 0 mcg, Calcium: 81 mg, Iron: 2 mg, Potassium: 1077 mg

## Fried Green Beans

Servings: 2    Cooking Time: 15 Minutes
**Ingredients:**
- ½ pound green beans, trimmed
- 1 egg
- 2 tablespoons olive oil
- 1¼ tablespoons almond flour
- 2 tablespoons parmesan cheese
- ½ teaspoon garlic powder
- sea salt or plain salt
- freshly ground black pepper

**Directions:**
Start by beating the egg and olive oil in a bowl.    Then, mix the remaining Ingredients: in a separate bowl and set aside.    Now, dip the green beans in the egg mixture and then coat with the dry mix.    Finally, grease a baking pan, then transfer the beans to the pan and bake at 5 degrees F for about 12-15 minutes or until crisp.    Serve warm.

**Nutrition Info:Per Serving:**Calories: 334, Total Fat: 23 g, Saturated Fat: 8.3 g, Cholesterol: 109 mg, Sodium: 397 mg, Total Carbohydrate: 10.9 g, Dietary Fiber: 4.3 g, Total Sugars: 1.9 g, Protein: 18.1 g, Vitamin D: 8 mcg, Calcium: 398 mg, Iron: 2 mg, Potassium: 274 mg

## Veggie Mediterranean Pasta

Servings: 4    Cooking Time: 2 Hours
**Ingredients:**
- 1 tablespoon olive oil
- 1 small onion, finely chopped
- 2 small garlic cloves, finely chopped
- 2 14-ounce cans diced tomatoes
- 1 tablespoon sun-dried tomato paste
- 1 bay leaf
- 1 teaspoon dried thyme
- 1 teaspoon dried basil
- 1 teaspoon oregano
- 1 teaspoon dried parsley
- ½ teaspoon salt
- ½ teaspoon brown sugar
- freshly ground black pepper
- 1 piece aubergine
- 2 pieces courgettes
- 2 pieces red peppers, de-seeded
- 2 garlic cloves, peeled
- 2-3 tablespoons olive oil
- 12 small vine-ripened tomatoes
- 16 ounces of pasta of your preferred shape, such as Gigli, conchiglie, etc.
- 3½ ounces parmesan cheese
- bread of your choice

**Directions:**
Heat oil in a pan over medium heat.    Add onions and fry them until tender.    Add garlic and stir-fry for 1 minute.    Add the remaining Ingredients: listed under the sauce and bring to a boil.    Reduce the heat, cover, and simmer for 60 minutes.    Season with black pepper and salt as needed. Set aside.    Preheat oven to 350 degrees F.    Chop up courgettes, aubergine and red peppers into 1-inch pieces.    Place them on a roasting pan along with whole garlic cloves.    Drizzle with olive oil and season with salt and black pepper. Mix the veggies well and roast in the oven for 45 minutes until they are tender.    Add tomatoes just before 20 minutes to end time.    Cook your pasta according to package instructions.    Drain well and stir into the sauce.    Divide the pasta sauce between 4 containers and top with vegetables.    Grate some parmesan cheese on top and serve with bread.    Enjoy!

**Nutrition Info:Per Serving:**Calories: 211, Total Fat: 14.9 g, Saturated Fat: 2.1 g, Cholesterol: 0 mg, Sodium: 317 mg, Total Carbohydrate: 20.1 g, Dietary Fiber: 5.7 g, Total Sugars: 11.7 g, Protein: 4.2 g, Vitamin D: 0 mcg, Calcium: 66 mg, Iron: 2 mg, Potassium: 955 mg

## Basil Pasta

Servings: 4    Cooking Time: 40 Minutes
**Ingredients:**
- 2 red peppers, de-seeded and cut into chunks
- 2 red onions cut into wedges
- 2 mild red chilies, de-seeded and diced
- 3 garlic cloves, coarsely chopped
- 1 teaspoon golden caster sugar
- 2 tablespoons olive oil, plus extra for serving
- 2 pounds small ripe tomatoes, quartered
- 12 ounces pasta
- a handful of basil leaves, torn
- 2 tablespoons grated parmesan
- salt
- pepper

**Directions:**
Preheat oven to 390 degrees F.    On a large roasting pan, spread peppers, red onion, garlic, and chilies. Sprinkle sugar on top.    Drizzle olive oil and season with salt and pepper.    Roast the veggies for 1minutes. Add tomatoes and roast for another 15 minutes.    In a large pot, cook your pasta in salted boiling water according to instructions.    Once ready, drain pasta. Remove the veggies from the oven and carefully add pasta.    Toss everything well and let it cool.    Spread over the containers.    Before eating, place torn basil leaves on top, and sprinkle with parmesan.    Enjoy!

**Nutrition Info:Per Serving:**Calories: 384, Total Fat: 10.8 g, Saturated Fat: 2.3 g, Cholesterol: 67 mg, Sodium: 133 mg, Total Carbohydrate: 59.4 g, Dietary Fiber: 2.3 g, Total Sugars: 5.7 g, Protein: 1 g, Vitamin D: 0 mcg, Calcium: 105 mg, Iron: 4 mg, Potassium: 422 mg

## Red Onion Kale Pasta

Servings: 4     Cooking Time: 25 Minutes
**Ingredients:**
- 2½ cups vegetable broth
- ¾ cup dry lentils
- ½ teaspoon of salt
- 1 bay leaf
- ¼ cup olive oil
- 1 large red onion, chopped
- 1 teaspoon fresh thyme, chopped
- ½ teaspoon fresh oregano, chopped
- 1 teaspoon salt, divided
- ½ teaspoon black pepper
- 8 ounces vegan sausage, sliced into ¼-inch slices
- 1 bunch kale, stems removed and coarsely chopped
- 1 pack rotini

**Directions:**
Add vegetable broth, ½ teaspoons of salt, bay leaf, and lentils to a saucepan over high heat and bring to a boil. Reduce the heat to medium-low and allow to cook for about   minutes until tender.     Discard the bay leaf. Take another skillet and heat olive oil over medium-high heat.     Stir in thyme, onions, oregano, ½ a teaspoon of salt, and pepper; cook for 1 minute.     Add sausage and reduce heat to medium-low.     Cook for 10 minutes until the onions are tender.     Bring water to a boil in a large pot, and then add rotini pasta and kale. Cook for about 8 minutes until al dente.     Remove a bit of the cooking water and put it to the side.     Drain the pasta and kale and return to the pot.     Stir in both the lentils mixture and the onions mixture.     Add the reserved cooking liquid to add just a bit of moistness. Spread over containers.
**Nutrition Info:Per Serving:**Calories: 508, Total Fat: 17 g, Saturated Fat: 3 g, Cholesterol: 0 mg, Sodium: 2431 mg, Total Carbohydrate: 59.3 g, Dietary Fiber: 6 g, Total Sugars: 4.8 g, Protein: 30.9 g, Vitamin D: 0 mcg, Calcium: 256 mg, Iron: 8 mg, Potassium: 1686 mg

## Scallops Pea Fettuccine

Servings: 5     Cooking Time: 15 Minutes
**Ingredients:**
- 8 ounces whole-wheat fettuccine (pasta, macaroni)
- 1 pound large sea scallops
- ¼ teaspoon salt, divided
- 1 tablespoon extra virgin olive oil
- 1 8-ounce bottle of clam juice
- 1 cup low-fat milk
- ¼ teaspoon ground white pepper
- 3 cups frozen peas, thawed
- ¾ cup finely shredded Romano cheese, divided
- 1/3 cup fresh chives, chopped
- ½ teaspoon freshly grated lemon zest
- 1 teaspoon lemon juice

**Directions:**

Boil water in a large pot and cook fettuccine according to package instructions.     Drain well and put it to the side.     Heat oil in a large, non-stick skillet over medium-high heat.     Pat the scallops dry and sprinkle them with 1/8 teaspoon of salt.     Add the scallops to the skillet and cook for about 2-3 minutes per side until golden brown. Remove scallops from pan.     Add clam juice to the pan you removed the scallops from.     In another bowl, whisk in milk, white pepper, flour, and remaining 1/8 teaspoon of salt.     Once the mixture is smooth, whisk into the pan with the clam juice.     Bring the entire mix to a simmer and keep stirring for about 1-2 minutes until the sauce is thick.     Return the scallops to the pan and add peas. Bring it to a simmer.     Stir in fettuccine, chives, ½ a cup of Romano cheese, lemon zest, and lemon juice.     Mix well until thoroughly combined.     Cool and spread over containers. Before eating, serve with remaining cheese sprinkled on top.     Enjoy!
**Nutrition Info:Per Serving:**Calories: 388, Total Fat: 9.2 g, Saturated Fat: 3.7 g, Cholesterol: 33 mg, Sodium: 645 mg, Total Carbohydrate: 50.1 g, Dietary Fiber: 10.4 g, Total Sugars: 8.7 g, Protein: 24.9 g, Vitamin D: 25 mcg, Calcium: 293 mg, Iron: 4 mg, Potassium: 247 mg

## Baked Mushrooms

Servings: 2     Cooking Time: 20 Minutes
**Ingredients:**
- ½ pound mushrooms (sliced)
- 2 tablespoons olive oil (onion and garlic flavored)
- 1 can tomatoes
- 1 cup Parmesan cheese
- ½ teaspoon oregano
- 1 tablespoon basil
- sea salt or plain salt
- freshly ground black pepper

**Directions:**
Heat the olive oil in the pan and add the mushrooms, salt, and pepper. Cook for about 2 minutes.     Then, transfer the mushrooms into a baking dish.     Now, in a separate bowl mix the tomatoes, basil, oregano, salt, and pepper, and layer it on the mushrooms. Top it with Parmesan cheese.     Finally, bake the dish at 0 degrees F for about 18-22 minutes or until done.     Serve warm.
**Nutrition Info:Per Serving:**Calories: 358, Total Fat: 27 g, Saturated Fat: 10.2 g, Cholesterol: 40 mg, Sodium: 535 mg, Total Carbohydrate: 13 g, Dietary Fiber: 3.5 g, Total Sugars: 6.7 g, Protein: 23.2 g, Vitamin D: 408 mcg, Calcium: 526 mg, Iron: 4 mg, Potassium: 797 mg

## Mint Tabbouleh

Servings: 6     Cooking Time: 15 Minutes

**Ingredients:**
- ¼ cup fine bulgur
- 1/3 cup water, boiling
- 3 tablespoons lemon juice
- ¼ teaspoon honey
- 1 1/3 cups pistachios, finely chopped
- 1 cup curly parsley, finely chopped
- 1 small cucumber, finely chopped
- 1 medium tomato, finely chopped
- 4 green onions, finely chopped
- 1/3 cup fresh mint, finely chopped
- 3 tablespoons olive oil

**Directions:**

Take a large bowl and add bulgur and 3 cup of boiling water.    Allow it to stand for about 5 minutes.    Stir in honey and lemon juice and allow it to stand for 5 minutes more.    Fluff up the bulgur with a fork and stir in the rest of the Ingredients:.    Season with salt and pepper.    Enjoy!

**Nutrition Info:Per Serving:**Calories: 15 Total Fat: 13.5 g, Saturated Fat: 1.8 g, Cholesterol: 0 mg, Sodium: 78 mg, Total Carbohydrate: 9.2 g, Dietary Fiber: 2.8 g, Total Sugars: 2.9 g, Protein: 3.8 g, Vitamin D: 0 mcg, Calcium: 46 mg, Iron: 2 mg, Potassium: 359 mg

# Great Mediterranean Diet Recipes

## Italian Herb Bread

Servings: 25     Cooking Time: 40 Minutes
**Ingredients:**
- 1 2/3 teaspoons active dry yeast
- 3½ cups all-purpose flour
- 2 1/4 cup rye flour
- 1 tablespoon salt
- 2 tablespoons olive oil
- 1 tablespoon flat-leaf parsley, finely chopped
- 10 sprigs fresh thyme leaves, stems removed
- 1 garlic clove, peeled and finely chopped
- ¼ cup black olives, pitted and chopped
- 3 green chilies, deseeded and chopped
- ¾ cup sun-dried tomatoes, drained and chopped

**Directions:**
Take a bowl of lukewarm water (temperature of 0 degrees F) and dissolve 1 and 2/3 cups of yeast.     Add flour, yeast water, and salt to another bowl.     Mix well to prepare the dough using a mixer or your hands.     Put the dough in a large, clean bowl and allow it to rest covered for 2 hours.     Transfer dough to a lightly floured surface and knead, adding the parsley, garlic, olives, thyme, tomatoes, and chilies.     Place the kneaded dough in an 8½-inch bread-proofing basket. Cover and allow to rest for about 60 minutes. Preheat oven to 400 degrees F.     Line a baking sheet with parchment paper.     Bake for about 30-40 minutes.     Once done, enjoy it!
**Nutrition Info:Per Serving:**Calories: 338, Total Fat: 2.5 g, Saturated Fat: 0.4 g, Cholesterol: 0 mg, Sodium: 294 mg, Total Carbohydrate: 68.6 g, Dietary Fiber: 5.5 g, Total Sugars: 0.5 g, Protein: 10 g, Vitamin D: 0 mcg, Calcium: 53 mg, Iron: 7 mg, Potassium: 202 mg

## Kidney Bean, Veggie, And Grape Salad With Feta

Servings:4     Cooking Time: 25 Minutes
**Ingredients:**
- 1½ cups red grapes, halved
- 1 (15-ounce) can red kidney beans, drained and rinsed
- 10 ounces cherry tomatoes, halved (quartered if tomatoes are large)
- 4 (6-inch) Persian cucumbers, quartered vertically and chopped
- ½ cup green pumpkin seeds (pepitas)
- ½ cup feta cheese
- 2½ ounces baby spinach leaves (about 4 cups)
- ½ cup Dijon Red Wine Vinaigrette

**Directions:**
Place the grapes, kidney beans, cherry tomatoes, cucumbers, pumpkin seeds, and feta in a large mixing bowl and mix to combine.     Place cups of the salad mixture in each of 4 containers. Then place 1 cup of spinach leaves on top of each salad. Pour 2 tablespoons of vinaigrette into each of 4 sauce containers. Refrigerate all the containers.     STORAGE: Store covered containers in the refrigerator for up to 5 days.

**Nutrition Info:Per Serving:** Total calories: 5; Total fat: 25g; Saturated fat: 6g; Sodium: 435mg; Carbohydrates: 37g; Fiber: 10g; Protein: 16g

## Sumac Chickpea Bowl

Servings: 4     Cooking Time: 25 Minutes
**Ingredients:**
- ⅔ cup uncooked bulgur
- 1⅓ cups water
- ⅛ teaspoon kosher salt
- 1 teaspoon olive oil
- 2 tablespoons olive oil
- 2 (15.5-ounce) cans low-sodium chickpeas, drained and rinsed
- 3 tablespoons sumac
- ¼ teaspoon kosher salt
- 4 Persian cucumbers, quartered lengthwise and chopped (about 2 cups)
- 10 ounces cherry tomatoes, quartered (halved if you have small tomatoes)
- ¼ cup chopped fresh mint
- 1 cup chopped fresh parsley
- 4 teaspoons olive oil
- 2 tablespoons plus 2 teaspoons freshly squeezed lemon juice
- ¼ teaspoon kosher salt
- 2 tablespoons unsalted tahini
- ¼ teaspoon garlic powder
- 5 tablespoons water

**Directions:**
TO MAKE THE BULGUR     Place the bulgur, water, and salt in a saucepan, and bring to a boil. Once it boils, cover the pot with a lid and turn off the heat. Let the covered pot stand for     minutes. Stir the oil into the cooked bulgur. Cool.     Place ½ cup of bulgur in each of 4 microwaveable containers.     TO MAKE THE CHICKPEAS     Heat the oil in a 12-inch skillet over medium-high heat. Once the oil is shimmering, add the chickpeas, sumac, and salt, and stir to coat. Cook for 2 minutes without stirring. Give the chickpeas a stir and cook for another 2 minutes without stirring. Stir and cook for 2 more minutes.     Place ¾ cup of cooled chickpeas in each of the 4 bulgur containers.     TO MAKE THE SALAD     Combine all the ingredients for the salad in a medium mixing bowl. Taste for salt and lemon, and add more if you need it.     Place 1¼ cup of salad in each of 4 containers. These containers will not be reheated.     TO MAKE THE TAHINI SAUCE Combine the tahini and garlic powder in a small bowl. Whisk in 1 tablespoon of water at a time until all 5 tablespoons have been incorporated and a thin sauce has formed. It will thicken as it sits.     Place 1 tablespoon of tahini sauce in each of 4 small sauce containers.     STORAGE: Store covered containers in the refrigerator for up to 5 days. When serving, reheat the bulgur and chickpeas, add them to the salad, and drizzle the tahini sauce over the top.
**Nutrition Info:Per Serving:** Total calories: 485; Total fat: 19g; Saturated fat: 2g; Sodium: 361mg; Carbohydrates: 67g; Fiber: 19g; Protein: 16g

## Smoked Salmon And Lemon-dill Ricotta Bento Box

Servings: 4     Cooking Time: 10 Minutes
**Ingredients:**
- FOR THE LEMON-DILL RICOTTA
- 1 (16-ounce) container whole-milk ricotta cheese
- 1 teaspoon finely grated lemon zest
- 3 tablespoons chopped fresh dill
- FOR THE BENTO BOX
- 8 ounces smoked salmon
- 4 (6-inch) Persian cucumbers or 2 small European cucumbers, sliced
- 2 cups sugar snap peas
- 4 whole-wheat pitas, each cut into 4 pieces

**Directions:**
Mix all the ingredients for the lemon-dill ricotta in a medium bowl.     Divide the salmon, cucumbers, and snap peas among 4 containers.     Place 1 pita in each of 4 resealable bags.     Place ½ cup of ricotta spread in each of separate small containers, since it may release some liquid after a couple of days.     STORAGE: Store covered containers in the refrigerator for up to 4 days. Store the pita at room temperature or in the refrigerator.

**Nutrition Info:Per Serving:** Total calories: 4; Total fat: 20g; Saturated fat: 11g; Sodium: 1,388mg; Carbohydrates: 40g; Fiber: 8g; Protein: 32g

## Mediterranean Baked Tilapia With Roasted Baby Red Potatoes

Servings: 2     Cooking Time: 35 Minutes
**Ingredients:**
- 3 teaspoons olive oil, divided
- 1 small yellow onion, very thinly sliced (about 2½ cups)
- 1 large red bell pepper, thinly sliced (about 2 cups)
- 10 ounces baby red potatoes, quartered (about 1-inch pieces)
- ⅜ teaspoon kosher salt, divided
- 1 teaspoon chopped garlic
- 1 tablespoon capers, drained, rinsed, and roughly chopped
- ¼ cup golden raisins
- 1 (½-ounce) pack fresh basil, roughly chopped
- 2½ ounces baby spinach, large leaves torn in half (about 4 cups)
- 2 teaspoons freshly squeezed lemon juice
- 8 ounces tilapia or other thin white fish (see tip)

**Directions:**
Preheat the oven to 450°F. Line a sheet pan with a silicone baking mat or parchment paper.     Heat teaspoons of oil in a 12-inch skillet over medium heat. When the oil is shimmering, add the onions and peppers. Cook for 12 minutes, stirring occasionally. The onions should be very soft.     While the onions and peppers are cooking, place the potatoes on the sheet pan and toss with ⅛ teaspoon of salt and the remaining

1 teaspoon of oil. Spread the potatoes out evenly across half of the pan. Roast in the oven for 10 minutes. Once the onions are soft, add the garlic, capers, raisins, basil, ⅛ teaspoon of salt, and the spinach. Stir to combine and cook for 3 more minutes to wilt the spinach.     Carefully remove the sheet pan from the oven after 10 minutes. Add half of the onion mixture to the empty side of the pan to form a nest for the fish. Place the fish on top and season with the remaining ⅛ teaspoon of salt and the lemon juice. Spread the rest of the onion mixture evenly across the top of the fish. Place the pan back in the oven and cook for 10 minutes. The fish should be flaky.     When the fish and potatoes have cooled, place 1 piece of fish plus half of the potatoes and half of the onion mixture in each of 2 containers. Refrigerate.     STORAGE: Store covered containers in the refrigerator for up to 4 days.

**Nutrition Info:Per Serving:** Total calories: 427; Total fat: ; Saturated fat: 2g; Sodium: 952mg; Carbohydrates: 59g; Fiber: 10g; Protein: 31g

## Mediterranean Focaccia

Servings: 4     Cooking Time: 30 Minutes
**Ingredients:**
- 3 3/5 cups flour
- 1 1/7 cups warm water
- 2 tablespoons olive oil
- 2 teaspoons dry yeast
- 1½ teaspoons salt
- 1 cup black olives, pitted and coarsely chopped
- sea salt
- olive oil

**Directions:**
Place flour and yeast in a large bowl.     Make a well and pour in water, salt, and oil.     Gradually keep mixing until everything is incorporated well.     Knead for about 20 minutes.     Add black olives and mix well. Form a ball and allow it to rise for about 45 minutes (in a bowl covered with a towel).     Once the dough is ready, push air out of it by crushing it using your palm. Roll out the dough onto a floured surface to a thickness of about ½ an inch.     Place it on a baking sheet covered with parchment paper, and allow the dough to rise for another 45 minutes.     Preheat oven to 425 degrees Fahrenheit.     Press fingers into the dough at regular intervals to pierce the dough.     When ready to bake, pour a bit of olive oil into the holes and sprinkle with salt.     Bake for 20-30 minutes.     Enjoy!

**Nutrition Info:Per Serving:**Calories: 523, Total Fat: 11.7 g, Saturated Fat: 1.7 g, Cholesterol: 0 mg, Sodium: 3495 mg, Total Carbohydrate: 89.4 g, Dietary Fiber: 4.6 g, Total Sugars: 0.3 g, Protein: 13.8 g, Vitamin D: 0 mcg, Calcium: 50 mg, Iron: 7 mg, Potassium: 124 mg

## Cheesy Olive Bread

Servings: 8      Cooking Time: 15 Minutes
**Ingredients:**
- ½ cup softened butter
- ¼ cup mayo
- 1 teaspoon garlic powder
- 1 teaspoon onion powder
- 2 cups shredded mozzarella cheese
- ½ cup chopped black olives
- 1 loaf of French Bread, halved longways

**Directions:**
Preheat oven to a temperature of 350 degrees Fahrenheit.     Stir butter and mayo together in a bowl until it is smooth and creamy.     Add onion powder, garlic powder, olives, and cheese and stir.     Spread the mixture over French bread.     Place bread on a baking sheet and bake for 10-12 minutes.     Increase the heat to broil and cook until the cheese has melted and the bread is golden brown.     Cool and chill.     Pre-heat before eating.
**Nutrition Info:Per Serving:**Calories: 307, Total Fat: 17.7 g, Saturated Fat: 2 g, Cholesterol: 38 mg, Sodium: 482 mg, Total Carbohydrate: 30.1 g, Dietary Fiber: 1.5 g, Total Sugars: 1.9 g, Protein: 8 g, Vitamin D: 0 mcg, Calcium: 40 mg, Iron: 2 mg, Potassium: 73 mg

## Red Wine–marinated Flank Steak With Brussels Sprout Slaw

Servings: 2      Cooking Time: 10 Minutes
**Ingredients:**
- FOR THE STEAK
- 8 ounces flank steak, trimmed of visible fat
- ½ cup red wine
- 2 tablespoons low-sodium soy sauce
- 1 tablespoon olive oil
- ½ teaspoon garlic powder
- FOR THE BRUSSELS SPROUT SLAW
- 8 ounces Brussels sprouts, stemmed, halved, and very thinly sliced
- 3 tablespoons unsalted sunflower seeds
- 3 tablespoons freshly squeezed lemon juice
- 1 tablespoon plus 1 teaspoon olive oil
- 2 tablespoons dried cranberries
- ⅛ teaspoon kosher salt
- ⅔ cup Artichoke-Olive Compote

**Directions:**
TO MAKE THE STEAK     Place all the ingredients for the steak in a gallon-size resealable bag. Allow the steak to marinate overnight or up to    hours.     Place the oven rack about 6 inches from the heating element. Preheat the oven to the broil setting (use the high setting if you have multiple settings).     Cover a sheet pan with foil. Lift the steak out of the marinade and place on top of the foil-lined sheet pan. Place the pan in the oven and cook for to 6 minutes on one side. Flip the steak over to the other side and broil for 4 to 6 minutes more.     Remove from the oven and allow to rest for to 10 minutes. Medium-rare will be about 135°F when an instant-read meat thermometer is inserted.     On a cutting board, slice the steak thinly against the grain and divide the steak between 2 containers.     TO MAKE THE BRUSSELS SPROUT SLAW     Combine the Brussels sprouts, sunflower seeds, lemon juice, olive

oil, cranberries, and salt in a medium bowl.     Place 1 cup of Brussels sprout slaw and ⅓ cup of artichoke-olive compote in each of 2 containers. The slaw and compote are meant to be eaten at room temperature, while the steak can be eaten warm. However, if you want to eat the steak at room temperature as well, all the items can be put in the same container.     STORAGE: Store covered containers in the refrigerator for up to 5 days.
**Nutrition Info:Per Serving:** Total calories: 601; Total fat: 31g; Saturated fat: 3g; Sodium: 1,098mg; Carbohydrates: 26g; Fiber: 5g; Protein: 29g

## One-pot Spanish Chicken Sausage And Shrimp With Rice

Servings: 4      Cooking Time: 30 Minutes
**Ingredients:**
- 4 teaspoons olive oil, divided
- 1 (12-ounce) package cooked chicken sausage, sliced
- 6 ounces uncooked peeled, deveined medium shrimp
- 1 large green bell pepper, chopped (about 1½ cups)
- 1 small yellow onion, chopped (about 2 cups)
- 2 teaspoons chopped garlic
- 2 teaspoons smoked paprika
- 1 teaspoon dried thyme leaves
- 1 teaspoon dried oregano
- ½ teaspoon kosher salt
- ½ cup quick-cooking or instant brown rice
- 1 (14.5-ounce) can no-salt-added diced tomatoes in juice
- 1 cup low-sodium chicken broth
- 1 medium zucchini, halved vertically and sliced into half-moons

**Directions:**
Heat 2 teaspoons of oil in a soup pot over medium-high heat. When the oil is shimmering, add the sausage and brown for 5 minutes. Add the shrimp and cook for more minute. Remove the sausage and shrimp, and place them on a plate.     Add the remaining teaspoons of oil to the pot, and when the oil is shimmering, add the bell pepper, onion, and garlic. Sauté until soft, about 5 minutes.     Add the sausage, shrimp, paprika, thyme, oregano, salt, rice, tomatoes, and broth to the pot, and stir to combine. Bring to a boil, then cover the pot and turn the heat down to low. Simmer for 15 minutes. After 15 minutes, add the zucchini, return the cover to the pot, and continue to simmer for 5 to 10 more minutes, until the zucchini is crisp-tender and the rice has absorbed most of the liquid.     Place about 2 cups of the rice mixture in each of 4 containers.
STORAGE: Store covered containers in the refrigerator for up to 5 days.
**Nutrition Info:Per Serving:** Total calories: 333; Total fat: 14g; Saturated fat: 3g; Sodium: 954mg; Carbohydrates: 29g; Fiber: 6g; Protein: 26g

## Broccoli, Roasted Red Pepper, Cheddar, And Olive Frittata

Servings: 5     Cooking Time: 25 Minutes
**Ingredients:**
- Oil or cooking spray for greasing the pan
- 8 large eggs
- ½ cup low-fat (2%) milk
- 1 teaspoon smoked paprika
- 6 ounces broccoli florets, finely chopped (about 2 cups)
- ½ cup chopped jarred roasted red peppers, drained of liquid
- ⅓ cup pitted black olives, chopped (or other olive of your choice)
- ¼ cup shredded sharp Cheddar cheese, plus 2 tablespoons

**Directions:**
Preheat the oven to 375°F and rub an 8-inch round cake or pie pan with oil, or spray with cooking spray. Break the eggs into a large mixing bowl. Add the milk and smoked paprika, and whisk until well combined. Add the chopped broccoli, red peppers, olives, and ¼ cup of cheese, and mix.     Pour the mixture into the oiled pan and top with the remaining 2 tablespoons of cheese. Bake for 20 to 25 minutes.     Once the frittata is cool, run a spatula around the sides and slice into pieces.     Place 1 slice in each of 5 containers and refrigerate.     STORAGE: Store covered containers in the refrigerator for up to 5 days.
**Nutrition Info:Per Serving:** Total calories: 193; Total fat: 12g; Saturated fat: 5g; Sodium: 295mg; Carbohydrates: 7g; Fiber: 1g; Protein: 13g

## Chutney-dijon Pork Tenderloin With Mushroom And Kale Farro Pilaf

Servings: 2     Cooking Time: 40 Minutes
**Ingredients:**
- 8 ounces pork tenderloin (freeze half if you can only find a 1-pound package)
- ⅓ cup prepared mango or apricot chutney, plus 1 tablespoon
- 2 tablespoons Dijon mustard
- 1 teaspoon chopped garlic
- 2 teaspoons olive oil
- 2 teaspoons olive oil
- 4 ounces mushrooms, sliced
- 1 small bunch (about 7 ounces) lacinato or curly kale, ribs removed, leaves roughly chopped
- ½ teaspoon chopped garlic
- ⅔ cup farro
- ¼ cup dry red wine, such as red zinfandel, merlot, or cabernet
- 1¼ cups low-sodium vegetable broth (or chicken broth)
- ¼ teaspoon kosher salt

**Directions:**
TO MAKE THE PORK     Remove the tough silver skin from the tenderloin with a sharp knife.     In a small bowl, combine ⅓ cup of chutney and the mustard, garlic, and oil.     Place the pork in a gallon-size resealable bag or shallow dish and rub the chutney mixture over the pork. Marinate for at least 8 hours.

When you're ready to cook, preheat the oven to 0°F and line a sheet pan with a silicone baking mat or foil. Remove the pork from the marinade and place it on the sheet pan. Discard the marinade. Place the pork in the oven for 10 minutes. Turn it over, rub the remaining 1 tablespoon of chutney over the top and sides, and roast for another 8 minutes. (Don't worry if extra marinade burns on the baking mat. The pork will be okay.)     Let the pork cool for at least 10 minutes and slice.     Divide the slices between 2 containers.     TO MAKE THE MUSHROOM AND KALE FARRO PILAF     Heat the oil in a soup pot or Dutch oven over medium-high heat. When the oil is shimmering, add the mushrooms and cook for 4 minutes.     Add the kale and garlic, stir, and cook for another 5 minutes.     Add the farro, stir, and cook for 1 minute. Add the red wine and allow to cook for 1 more minute.     Add the broth and salt, increase the heat to high, and bring to a boil. Once it is boiling, turn the heat down to low, cover, and simmer for 30 minutes, until the farro is tender but still has some bite to it.     After it has cooled, place 1 heaping cup of pilaf in each of the 2 pork containers. Refrigerate.
STORAGE: Store covered containers in the refrigerator for up to 5 days. Freeze farro pilaf for up to 6 months.
**Nutrition Info:Per Serving:** Total calories: 677; Total fat: 18g; Saturated fat: 3g; Sodium: 1,041mg; Carbohydrates: 76g; Fiber: 10g; Protein: 48g

## Tuna, Kale Slaw, Edamame, And Strawberry Salad

Servings: 3     Cooking Time: 15 Minutes
**Ingredients:**
- 2 (5-ounce) cans light tuna packed in water
- 8 tablespoons Honey-Lemon Vinaigrette, divided
- 3 cups prepackaged kale-and-cabbage slaw
- 1 cup shelled frozen edamame, thawed
- 2 Persian cucumbers, quartered vertically and chopped
- 1¼ cups sliced strawberries
- 3 tablespoons chopped fresh dill

**Directions:**
Place the tuna in a small bowl and mix with 2 tablespoons of vinaigrette.     In a large mixing bowl, place the slaw, edamame, cucumbers, strawberries, and dill. Toss to combine.     Place ⅓ cup of tuna in each of containers. Place one third of the salad on top of the tuna in each container to lessen the chance of the salad getting soggy. Spoon 2 tablespoons of the remaining vinaigrette into each of 3 separate sauce containers. STORAGE: Store covered containers in the refrigerator for up to days.
**Nutrition Info:Per Serving:** Total calories: 317; Total fat: 18g; Saturated fat: 2g; Sodium: 414mg; Carbohydrates: 22g; Fiber: 9g; Protein: 22g

## Avocado Green Goddess Dip With Veggie Dippers

Servings: 4     Cooking Time: 10 Minutes
**Ingredients:**
- ½ teaspoon chopped garlic
- 1 cup packed fresh parsley leaves
- ½ cup fresh mint leaves
- ¼ cup fresh tarragon leaves
- ¼ teaspoon plus ⅛ teaspoon kosher salt
- ¼ cup freshly squeezed lemon juice
- ¼ cup extra-virgin olive oil
- ½ cup water
- 1 medium avocado
- 1 (1-pound) bag baby carrots
- 2 heads endive, leaves separated

**Directions:**
Place the garlic, parsley, mint, tarragon, salt, lemon juice, oil, water, and avocado in a blender and blend until smooth.     Place 4 ounces of carrots and half a head of endive leaves in each of 4 containers. Spoon ¼ cup of dip into each of 4 sauce containers.
STORAGE: Store covered containers in the refrigerator for up to 5 days.
**Nutrition Info:Per Serving:** Total calories: 301; Total fat: 21g; Saturated fat: 2g; Sodium: 373mg; Carbohydrates: 2; Fiber: 13g; Protein: 23g

## Black Olive Bread

Servings: 6     Cooking Time: 45 Minutes
**Ingredients:**
- 3 cups bread flour
- 2 teaspoons active dry yeast
- 2 tablespoons white sugar
- 1 teaspoon salt
- ½ cup black olives, chopped
- 3 tablespoons olive oil
- 1¼ cups warm water (about 110 degrees Fahrenheit)
- 1 tablespoon cornmeal

**Directions:**
In a large bowl, combine flour, sugar, yeast, salt, black olives, water, and olive oil.     Mix well to prepare the dough.     Turn the dough onto a floured surface and knead well for 5-10 minutes until elastic.     Set dough aside and allow it to rise for about minutes until it has doubled in size.     Punch the dough down and knead again for 10 minutes.     Allow it to rise for 30 minutes more.     Round up the dough on a kneading board, place upside down in a bowl, and line it with a lint-free, well-floured towel.     Allow it to rise until it has doubled in size again.     While the bread is rising up for the third and final time, take a pan, fill it up with water, and place it at the bottom of your oven.     Preheat oven to a temperature of 500 degrees Fahrenheit.     Turn the loaf out onto a sheet pan, lightly oil it, and dust with cornmeal.     Bake for about 15 minutes.     Reduce heat to 375 degrees Fahrenheit and bake for another 30 minutes.     Cool and chill.     Enjoy!
**Nutrition Info:Per Serving:**Calories: 324, Total Fat: 8.9 g, Saturated Fat: 1.3 g, Cholesterol: 0 mg, Sodium: 488 mg, Total Carbohydrate: 53.9 g, Dietary Fiber: 2.4 g, Total Sugars: 4.2 g, Protein: 7.2 g, Vitamin D: 0 mcg, Calcium: 20 mg, Iron: 4 mg, Potassium: 98 mg

## Cocoa-almond Bliss Bites

Servings: 10     Cooking Time: 1 Hour
**Ingredients:**
- 1 medium ripe banana, mashed
- 3 tablespoons ground flaxseed
- ½ cup rolled oats
- ½ cup plain, unsalted almond butter
- 2 tablespoons unsweetened cocoa powder
- ¼ cup almond meal
- ¼ teaspoon ground cinnamon
- 2 teaspoons pure maple syrup

**Directions:**
Combine all the ingredients in a medium mixing bowl. Roll the mixture into 10 balls, slightly smaller than a golf ball, and place on a plate.     Freeze the bites for 1 hour to harden.     Place 2 bites in each of 5 small containers or resealable bags and store in the refrigerator.     STORAGE: Store covered containers or resealable bags in the refrigerator for up to days. If you want to make a big batch, the bites can be frozen for up to 3 months.
**Nutrition Info:**Per Serving (2 bites): Total calories: 130; Total fat: 9g; Saturated fat: 1g; Sodium: 1mg; Carbohydrates: 11g; Fiber: 3g; Protein: 5g

## Crispbread With Mascarpone And Berry-chia Jam

Servings: 3     Cooking Time: 5 Minutes
**Ingredients:**
- 1 (1-pound) bag frozen mixed berries
- 2 teaspoons freshly squeezed lemon juice
- 2 teaspoons pure maple syrup
- 2 tablespoons plus 2 teaspoons chia seeds
- 6 slices crispbread
- 3 tablespoons mascarpone cheese

**Directions:**
Place the frozen berries in a saucepan over medium heat. When the berries are defrosted, about 5 minutes, mash with a potato masher. You can leave them chunky.     Turn the heat off and add the lemon juice, maple syrup, and chia seeds.     Allow the jam to cool, then place in the refrigerator to thicken for about an hour.     Place 2 slices of crispbread in each of 3 resealable sandwich bags. Place 1 tablespoon of mascarpone and 2 tablespoons of jam in each of 3 containers with dividers. Alternatively, put the mascarpone and jam in separate small sauce containers.     STORAGE: Store crispbread at room temperature and jam and mascarpone in the refrigerator. Mascarpone will last for 7 days in the refrigerator, while jam will last for 2 weeks. Jam can be frozen for up to 3 months.
**Nutrition Info:Per Serving:** Total calories: 2; Total fat: 9g; Saturated fat: 3g; Sodium: 105mg; Carbohydrates: 40g; Fiber: 14g; Protein: 6g

## Spiced Chicken-stuffed Zucchini With Brown Rice And Lentils

Servings: 3    Cooking Time: 35 Minutes
**Ingredients:**
- ⅓ cup long-grain brown rice
- 1⅔ cups water
- ⅛ teaspoon kosher salt
- ⅓ cup brown lentils
- 2 teaspoons olive oil
- 3 tablespoons chopped fresh dill
- 3 medium zucchini, halved lengthwise and flesh scooped out with a teaspoon (zucchini flesh reserved)
- 3 teaspoons olive oil, divided
- 1 small yellow onion, chopped
- 1 teaspoon chopped garlic
- ½ pound ground lean chicken
- ¾ teaspoon ground cumin
- ¾ teaspoon ground coriander
- ¾ teaspoon caraway seeds
- ⅛ teaspoon red chili flakes
- 3 tablespoons tomato paste
- ¼ teaspoon kosher salt
- ¼ cup feta cheese

**Directions:**
TO MAKE THE BROWN RICE AND LENTILS    Place the rice, water, and salt in a saucepan over high heat. Once the water is boiling, cover the pan and reduce the heat to low. Simmer for 15 minutes.    After 15 minutes, add the lentils and stir. Cover the pan and cook for another 15 minutes.    If there is a little bit of water still in the pan after the rice and lentils are tender, cook uncovered for a couple of minutes.    Stir in the oil and chopped dill.    Once the mixture has cooled, place ⅔ cup in each of 3 containers.    TO MAKE THE STUFFED ZUCCHINI    Preheat the oven to 400°F and line a sheet pan with a silicone baking mat or parchment paper. Place the zucchini boats on a lined sheet pan and coat with 1 teaspoon of oil.    In a 12-inch skillet, heat the remaining 2 teaspoons of oil over medium-high heat. When the oil is shimmering, add the onion and garlic and cook for 5 minutes. Add the zucchini flesh and cook for 2 more minutes.    Add the ground chicken, breaking it up with a spatula. Cook for 5 more minutes.    Add the cumin, coriander, caraway seeds, chili flakes, tomato paste, and salt, and cook for another 2 minutes.    Mound the chicken mixture into the zucchini boats. Top each zucchini boat with 2 teaspoons of feta cheese. Bake for 20 minutes.    Once cooled, place 2 zucchini halves in each of the 3 rice-and-lentil containers.    STORAGE: Store covered containers in the refrigerator for up to 5 days. Brown rice and lentils can be frozen for up to 3 months.
**Nutrition Info:Per Serving:** Total calories: 414; Total fat: 19g; Saturated fat: 5g; Sodium: 645mg; Carbohydrates: 39g; Fiber: 10g; Protein: 26g

## Apple, Cinnamon, And Walnut Baked Oatmeal

Servings: 8    Cooking Time: 40 Minutes
**Ingredients:**
- Cooking spray or oil for greasing the pan
- 3 small Granny Smith apples (about 1 pound), skin-on, chopped into ½-inch dice
- 3 cups rolled oats
- 1 teaspoon baking powder
- 3 tablespoons ground flaxseed
- 1 teaspoon ground cinnamon
- 2 eggs
- ¼ cup olive oil
- 1½ cups low-fat (2%) milk
- ⅓ cup pure maple syrup
- ½ cup walnut pieces (if you buy walnut halves, roughly chop the nuts)

**Directions:**
Preheat the oven to 350°F and spray an 8-by--inch baking dish with cooking spray or rub with oil. Combine the apples, oats, baking powder, flaxseed, cinnamon, eggs, oil, milk, and maple syrup in a large mixing bowl and pour into the prepared baking dish. Sprinkle the walnut pieces evenly across the oatmeal and bake for 40 minutes.    Allow the oatmeal to cool and cut it into 8 pieces. Place 1 piece in each of 5 containers. Take the other 3 pieces and either eat as a snack during the week or freeze for a later time. STORAGE: Store covered containers in the refrigerator for up to 6 days. If frozen, oatmeal will last 6 months.
**Nutrition Info:Per Serving:** Total calories: 349; Total fat: 18g; Saturated fat: 3g; Sodium: 108mg; Carbohydrates: 43g; Fiber: ; Protein: 9g

## Chocolate–peanut Butter Yogurt With Berries

Servings: 4    Cooking Time: 15 Minutes
**Ingredients:**
- 2 cups low-fat (2%) plain Greek yogurt
- 4 tablespoons unsweetened cocoa powder
- 4 tablespoons natural-style peanut butter
- 1 tablespoon pure maple syrup
- 1 cup fresh or frozen berries of your choice

**Directions:**
In a medium bowl, mix the yogurt, cocoa powder, peanut butter, and maple syrup until well combined. Spoon ½ cup of the yogurt mixture and ¼ cup of berries into each of 4 containers.    STORAGE: Store covered containers in the refrigerator for up to 5 days.
**Nutrition Info:Per Serving:** Total calories: 225; Total fat: 12g; Saturated fat: ; Sodium: 130mg; Carbohydrates: 19g; Fiber: 4g; Protein: 16g

## Olive Fougasse

Servings: 4    Cooking Time: 20 Minutes
**Ingredients:**
- 3 2/3 cups bread flour
- 3 1/2 tablespoons olive oil
- 1 2/3 tablespoons bread yeast
- 1 1/4 cups black olives, chopped
- 1 teaspoon oregano
- 1 teaspoon salt
- 1 cup water

**Directions:**
Add flour to a bowl.    Make a well in the center and add the water and remaining Ingredients:.    Knead the dough well until it becomes slightly elastic.    Mold it into a ball and let stand for about 1 hour.    Divide the pastry into four pieces of equal portions.    Flatten the balls using a rolling pin and place it on a floured baking tray.    Make incisions on the bread.    Allow them to rest for about 30 minutes    Preheat oven to 425 degrees Fahrenheit.    Brush the Fougasse with olive oil and allow it to bake for 20 minutes.    Turn the oven off and allow it to rest for 5 minutes.    Remove and allow it to cool.    Enjoy!

**Nutrition Info:Per Serving:**Calories: 586, Total Fat: 18.1 g, Saturated Fat: 2.6 g, Cholesterol: 0 mg, Sodium: 371 mg, Total Carbohydrate: 92.2 g, Dietary Fiber: 5.6 g, Total Sugars: 0.3 g, Protein: 2 g, Vitamin D: 0 mcg, Calcium: 63 mg, Iron: 8 mg, Potassium: 232 mg

## Tofu And Vegetable Provençal

Servings: 4    Cooking Time: 30 Minutes
**Ingredients:**
- 1 pound super-firm tofu, cut into ¾-inch cubes
- 2 tablespoons freshly squeezed lemon juice
- 2 tablespoons olive oil
- 1 teaspoon garlic powder
- 1 teaspoon herbes de Provence
- ¼ teaspoon kosher salt
- 4 teaspoons olive oil, divided
- 1 (14-ounce) eggplant, cubed into 1-inch pieces (5 to 6 cups)
- 1 small yellow onion, chopped (about 2 cups)
- 2 teaspoons chopped garlic
- 10 ounces cherry tomatoes, halved if tomatoes are fairly large
- 1 (14-ounce) can artichoke hearts, drained
- 1 teaspoon herbes de Provence
- ¼ teaspoon kosher salt
- ½ cup dry white wine, such as sauvignon blanc
- ⅓ cup pitted kalamata olives, roughly chopped
- 1 (½-ounce) package fresh basil, chopped

**Directions:**
TO MAKE THE TOFU    Place the tofu in a container with the lemon juice, oil, garlic powder, herbes de Provence, and salt. Allow to marinate for 1 hour. When you're ready to cook the tofu, preheat the oven to 400°F and line a sheet pan with a silicone baking mat or parchment paper. Lift the tofu out of the marinade and place it on the sheet pan. Bake for    minutes, flipping the tofu over after 15 minutes. Cool, then place about ½ cup of tofu cubes in each of 4 containers.    TO MAKE THE VEGETABLE RAGOUT    While the tofu is marinating, heat 2 teaspoons of oil in a 12-inch skillet over medium-high heat. When the oil is shimmering,

add the eggplant and cook for 4 minutes, stirring occasionally. Remove the eggplant and place on a plate. Add the remaining 2 teaspoons of oil to the pan, and add the onion and garlic. Cook for 2 minutes. Add the tomatoes and cook for 5 more minutes. Add the eggplant, artichokes, herbes de Provence, salt, and wine. Cover the pan, lower the heat, and simmer for 20 minutes.    Turn the heat off and stir in the olives and basil.    Spoon about 1½ cups of vegetables into each of the 4 tofu containers.    STORAGE: Store covered containers in the refrigerator for up to 5 days.
**Nutrition Info:Per Serving:** Total calories: 362; Total fat: 17g; Saturated fat: 3g; Sodium: 728mg; Carbohydrates: 32g; Fiber: 9g; Protein: 23g

## Banana, Orange, And Pistachio Smoothie

Servings: 3    Cooking Time: 25 Minutes
**Ingredients:**
- 1 (17.6-ounce) container plain low-fat (2%) Greek yogurt
- 3 very ripe medium bananas
- 1½ cups orange juice
- ¾ cup unsalted shelled pistachios

**Directions:**
Place all the ingredients in a blender and blend until smooth.    Pour 1¾ cups of the smoothie into each of 3 smoothie containers.    STORAGE: Store covered containers in the refrigerator for up to 4 days.
**Nutrition Info:Per Serving:** Total calories: 9; Total fat: 19g; Saturated fat: 4g; Sodium: 71mg; Carbohydrates: 55g; Fiber: 3g; Protein: 26g

## Breakfast Bento Box

Servings: 2    Cooking Time: 12 Minutes
**Ingredients:**
- 2 eggs
- 2 ounces sliced prosciutto
- 20 small whole-grain crackers
- 20 whole, unsalted almonds (about ¼ cup)
- 2 (6-inch) Persian cucumbers, sliced
- 1 large pear, sliced

**Directions:**
Place the eggs in a saucepan and cover with water. Bring the water to a boil. As soon as the water starts to boil, place a lid on the pan and turn the heat off. Set a timer for    minutes.    When the timer goes off, drain the hot water and run cold water over the eggs to cool. Peel the eggs when cool and cut in half.    Place 2 egg halves and half of the prosciutto, crackers, almonds, cucumber slices, and pear slices in each of 2 containers. STORAGE: Store covered containers in the refrigerator for up to 5 days.
**Nutrition Info:Per Serving:** Total calories: 370; Total fat: 20g; Saturated fat: ; Sodium: 941mg; Carbohydrates: 35g; Fiber: 7g; Protein: 16g

## Maple-cardamom Chia Pudding With Blueberries

Servings: 5     Cooking Time: 5 Minutes
**Ingredients:**
- 2½ cups low-fat (2%) milk
- ½ cup chia seeds
- 1 tablespoon plus 1 teaspoon pure maple syrup
- ¼ teaspoon ground cardamom
- 2½ cups frozen blueberries

**Directions:**
Place the milk, chia seeds, maple syrup, and cardamom in a large bowl and stir to combine.    Spoon ½ cup of the mixture into each of 5 containers.    Place ½ cup of frozen blueberries in each container and stir to combine. Let the pudding sit for at least an hour in the refrigerator before eating.    STORAGE: Store covered containers in the refrigerator for up to 5 days.
**Nutrition Info:Per Serving:** Total calories: 218; Total fat: 8g; Saturated fat: 2g; Sodium: 74mg; Carbohydrates: 28g; Fiber: 10g; Protein: 10g

## Cheesy Bread

Servings: 12     Cooking Time: 15 Minutes
**Ingredients:**
- 3 cups shredded cheddar cheese
- 1 cup mayonnaise
- 1 1-ounce pack dry ranch dressing mix
- 1 2-ounce can chopped black olives, drained
- 4 green onions, sliced
- 2 French baguettes, cut into ½ inch slices

**Directions:**
Preheat oven to 350 degrees Fahrenheit.    In a medium-sized bowl, combine cheese, ranch dressing mix, mayonnaise, onions, and olives.    Increase mayo if you want a juicier mixture.    Spread cheese mixture on top of your French baguette slices.    Arrange the slices in a single layer on a large baking sheet.    Bake for about 15 minutes until the cheese is bubbly and browning.    Cool and chill.    Serve warm!
**Nutrition Info:Per Serving:** Calories: 2, Total Fat: 17 g, Saturated Fat: 7.2 g, Cholesterol: 35 mg, Sodium: 578 mg, Total Carbohydrate: 23.9 g, Dietary Fiber: 1.1 g, Total Sugars: 2.4 g, Protein: 11.1 g, Vitamin D: 3 mcg, Calcium: 229 mg, Iron: 2 mg, Potassium: 85 mg

## Carrot-chickpea Fritters

Servings: 3     Cooking Time: 10 Minutes
**Ingredients:**
- 2 teaspoons olive oil, plus 1 tablespoon
- 3 cups shredded carrots
- 1 (4-ounce) bunch scallions, white and green parts chopped
- 1 (15-ounce) can low-sodium chickpeas, drained and rinsed
- ⅓ cup dried apricots (about 10 small apricot halves), chopped
- 1 teaspoon garlic powder
- 1½ teaspoons dried mint
- ⅓ cup chickpea flour
- 1 egg
- ¼ teaspoon kosher salt
- 1 tablespoon freshly squeezed lemon juice
- 1 (5-ounce) package arugula
- ¾ cup Garlic Yogurt Sauce

**Directions:**
Heat 2 teaspoons of oil in a -inch skillet over medium-high heat. Once the oil is hot, add the carrots and scallions, and cook for 5 minutes. Allow to cool. While the carrots are cooking, mash the chickpeas in a large mixing bowl with the bottom of a coffee mug. (I find a coffee mug works better than a potato masher.) Add the apricots, garlic powder, mint, chickpea flour, egg, salt, lemon juice, and cooked carrot mixture to the bowl, and stir until well combined.    Form 6 patties and place them on a plate.    Heat the remaining 1 tablespoon of oil in the same skillet over medium-high heat. Once the oil is hot, add the patties. Cook for 3 minutes on each side, or until each side is browned. Place 2 cooled fritters in each of 3 containers. Place about 2 cups of arugula in each of 3 other containers, and spoon ¼ cup Garlic Yogurt Sauce into each of 3 separate containers, or next to the arugula. The arugula and sauce are served at room temperature, while the fritters will be reheated.    STORAGE:Store covered containers in the refrigerator for up to 5 days. Uncooked patties can be frozen for 3 to 4 months.
**Nutrition Info:Per Serving:** Total calories: 461; Total fat: 17g; Saturated fat: 3g; Sodium: 393mg; Carbohydrates: 61g; Fiber: 15g; Protein: 21g

## Whole-wheat Pasta With Lentil Bolognese

Servings: 4     Cooking Time: 55 Minutes
**Ingredients:**
- 2 tablespoons olive oil, divided
- 1 small yellow onion, chopped (about 2 cups)
- 1 tablespoon chopped garlic
- 2 medium carrots, peeled, halved vertically, and sliced (about 1¼ cup)
- 8 ounces button or cremini mushrooms, roughly chopped (about 4 cups)
- 1 teaspoon dried Italian herbs
- 2 tablespoons tomato paste
- ½ cup dry red wine
- 1 (28-ounce) can no-salt-added crushed tomatoes
- 2 cups water
- 1 cup uncooked brown lentils
- ½ teaspoon kosher salt
- 8 ounces dry whole-wheat penne pasta
- ¼ cup nutritional yeast

**Directions:**
Heat a soup pot on medium-high heat with tablespoon of oil. Once the oil is shimmering, add the onion and garlic, and cook for 2 minutes.    Add the carrots and mushrooms, then stir and cook for another 5 minutes. Add the Italian herbs and tomato paste, stir to evenly incorporate, and cook for 5 more minutes, without stirring.    Add the wine and scrape up any bits from the bottom of the pan. Cook for 2 more minutes.    Add the tomatoes, water, lentils, and salt. Bring to a boil, then turn the heat down to low and simmer for 40 minutes.    While the sauce is cooking, cook the pasta according to the package directions, drain, and cool. When the sauce is done simmering, stir in the remaining 1 tablespoon of oil and the nutritional yeast. Cool the sauce.    Combine 1 cup of cooked pasta and 1⅓ cups of sauce in each of 4 containers. Freeze the remaining sauce for a later meal.    STORAGE: Store covered containers in the refrigerator for up to 5 days.
**Nutrition Info:Per Serving:** Total calories: 570; Total fat: 9g; Saturated fat: 1g; Sodium: 435mg; Carbohydrates: 96g; Fiber: 17g; Protein: 27g

## Strawberries With Cottage Cheese And Pistachios

Servings: 5     Cooking Time: 35 Minutes
**Ingredients:**
- 16 ounces low-fat cottage cheese
- 16 ounces strawberries, hulled and sliced
- ½ cup plus 2 tablespoons unsalted shelled pistachios

**Directions:**
Spoon ⅓ cup of cottage cheese into each of 5 containers. Top each scoop of cottage cheese with ⅔ cup of strawberries and tablespoons of pistachios. Refrigerate.     STORAGE: Store covered containers in the refrigerator for up to 5 days.
**Nutrition Info:Per Serving:** Total calories: 184; Total fat: 9g; Saturated fat: 2g; Sodium: 26g; Carbohydrates: 14g; Fiber: 4g; Protein: 15g

## Turkey Meatballs With Tomato Sauce And Roasted Spaghetti Squash

Servings: 3     Cooking Time: 35 Minutes
**Ingredients:**
- FOR THE SPAGHETTI SQUASH
- 3 pounds spaghetti squash
- 1 teaspoon olive oil
- ¼ teaspoon kosher salt
- FOR THE MEATBALLS
- ½ pound lean ground turkey
- 4 ounces mushrooms, finely chopped (about 1½ cups)
- 2 tablespoons onion powder
- 1 tablespoon garlic powder
- 1 teaspoon dried Italian herbs
- ⅛ teaspoon kosher salt
- 1 large egg
- FOR THE SAUCE
- 1 (28-ounce) can crushed tomatoes
- 1 cup shredded carrots
- 1 teaspoon garlic powder
- 1 teaspoon onion powder
- ¼ teaspoon kosher salt

**Directions:**
TO MAKE THE SPAGHETTI SQUASH     Preheat the oven to 4°F and place a silicone baking mat or parchment paper on a sheet pan.     Using a heavy, sharp knife, cut the ends off the spaghetti squash. Stand the squash upright and cut down the middle. Scrape out the seeds and stringy flesh with a spoon and discard. Rub the oil on the cut sides of the squash and sprinkle with the salt. Lay the squash cut-side down on the baking sheet. Roast for 30 to 35 minutes, until the flesh is tender when poked with a sharp knife.     When the squash is cool enough to handle, scrape the flesh out with a fork and place about 1 cup in each of 3 containers.     TO MAKE THE MEATBALLS AND SAUCE     Place all the ingredients for the meatballs in a large bowl. Mix with your hands until all the ingredients are combined.     Place all the sauce ingredients in an by-11-inch glass or ceramic baking dish, and stir to combine.     Form 12 golf-ball-size meatballs and place each directly in the baking dish of tomato sauce.     Place the baking dish in the oven and bake for 25 minutes. Cool.     Place 4 meatballs and 1 cup of sauce in each of the 3 squash containers. STORAGE:Store covered containers in the refrigerator for up to 5 days.
**Nutrition Info:Per Serving:** Total calories: 406; Total fat: ; Saturated fat: 5g; Sodium: 1,296mg; Carbohydrates: 45g; Fiber: 10g; Protein: 29g

## Salmon Cakes With Steamed Green Bean Gremolata

Servings: 4     Cooking Time: 6 Minutes
**Ingredients:**
- 2 (6-ounce) cans skinless, boneless salmon, drained
- ½ teaspoon garlic powder
- ⅓ cup minced shallot
- 2 tablespoons Dijon mustard
- 2 eggs
- ½ cup panko bread crumbs
- 1 tablespoon capers, chopped
- 1 cup chopped parsley
- ⅓ cup chopped sun-dried tomatoes
- 1 tablespoon freshly squeezed lemon juice
- 1 tablespoon olive oil
- Zest of 2 lemons (about 2 tablespoons when zested with a Microplane)
- ¼ cup minced parsley
- 1 teaspoon minced garlic
- ¼ teaspoon kosher salt
- 1 teaspoon olive oil
- 1 pound green beans, trimmed

**Directions:**
TO MAKE THE SALMON CAKES     In a large bowl, place the salmon, garlic, shallot, mustard, eggs, bread crumbs, capers, parsley, tomatoes, and lemon juice. Stir well to combine.     Form 8 patties and place them on a plate.     Heat the oil in a 12-inch skillet over medium-high heat. Once the oil is hot, add the patties. Cook for 3 minutes on each side, or until each side is browned. Place 2 cooled salmon cakes in each of 4 containers. TO MAKE THE GREEN BEANS     In a small bowl, combine the lemon zest, parsley, garlic, salt, and oil. Bring about ¼ to ½ inch of water to a boil in a soup pot, Dutch oven, or skillet.     Once the water is boiling, add the green beans, cover, and set a timer for 3 minutes. The green beans should be crisp-tender. Drain the green beans and transfer to a large bowl. Add the gremolata (lemon zest mixture) and toss to combine.     Divide the green beans among the 4 salmon cake containers. If using, place ¼ cup of Garlic Yogurt Sauce in each of 4 sauce containers. Refrigerate. STORAGE: Store covered containers in the refrigerator for up to 5 days. Uncooked patties can be frozen for 3 to 4 months.
**Nutrition Info:Per Serving:** Total calories: 268; Total fat: 9g; Saturated fat: 2g; Sodium: 638mg; Carbohydrates: 21g; Fiber: 6g; Protein: 27g

## Popcorn Trail Mix

Servings: 5     Cooking Time: 35 Minutes
**Ingredients:**
- 12 dried apricot halves, quartered
- ⅔ cup whole, unsalted almonds
- ½ cup green pumpkin seeds (pepitas)
- 4 cups air-popped lightly salted popcorn

**Directions:**
Place the apricots, almonds, and pumpkin seeds in a medium bowl and toss with clean hands to evenly mix. Scoop about ⅓ cup of the mixture into each of 5 containers or resealable sandwich bags. Place ¾ cup of popcorn in each of 5 separate containers or resealable bags. You will have one extra serving.     Mix the popcorn and the almond mixture together when it's time to eat. (The apricots make the popcorn stale quickly, which is why they're stored separately.) STORAGE: Store covered containers or resealable bags at room temperature for up to 5 days.
**Nutrition Info:Per Serving:** Total calories: 244; Total fat: 16g; Saturated fat: 2g; Sodium: 48mg; Carbohydrates: 19g; Fiber: ; Protein: 10g

## Creamy Shrimp-stuffed Portobello Mushrooms

Servings: 3     Cooking Time: 40 Minutes
**Ingredients:**
- 1 teaspoon olive oil, plus 2 tablespoons
- 6 portobello mushrooms, caps and stems separated and stems chopped
- 6 ounces broccoli florets, finely chopped (about 2 cups)
- 2 teaspoons chopped garlic
- 10 ounces uncooked peeled, deveined shrimp, thawed if frozen, roughly chopped
- 1 (14.5-ounce) can no-salt-added diced tomatoes
- 4 tablespoons roughly chopped fresh basil
- ½ cup mascarpone cheese
- ¼ cup panko bread crumbs
- 4 tablespoons grated Parmesan, divided
- ¼ teaspoon kosher salt

**Directions:**
Preheat the oven to 350°F. Line a sheet pan with a silicone baking mat or parchment paper.     Rub 1 teaspoon of oil over the bottom (stem side) of the mushroom caps and place on the lined sheet pan, stem-side up.     Heat the remaining 2 tablespoons of oil in a 12-inch skillet on medium-high heat. Once the oil is shimmering, add the chopped mushroom stems and broccoli, and sauté for 2 to minutes. Add the garlic and shrimp, and continue cooking for 2 more minutes. Add the tomatoes, basil, mascarpone, bread crumbs, 3 tablespoons of Parmesan, and the salt. Stir to combine and turn the heat off.     With the mushroom cap openings facing up, mound slightly less than 1 cup of filling into each mushroom. Top each with ½ teaspoon of the remaining Parmesan cheese.     Bake the mushrooms for 35 minutes.     Place 2 mushroom caps

in each of 3 containers.     STORAGE: Store covered containers in the refrigerator for up to 4 days.
**Nutrition Info:Per Serving:** Total calories: 47 Total fat: 31g; Saturated fat: 10g; Sodium: 526mg; Carbohydrates: 26g; Fiber: 7g; Protein: 26g

## Rosemary Edamame, Zucchini, And Sun-dried Tomatoes With Garlic-chive Quinoa

Servings: 4     Cooking Time: 15 Minutes
**Ingredients:**
- FOR THE GARLIC-CHIVE QUINOA
- 1 teaspoon olive oil
- 1 teaspoon chopped garlic
- ⅔ cup quinoa
- 1⅓ cups water
- ¼ teaspoon kosher salt
- 1 (¾-ounce) package fresh chives, chopped
- FOR THE ROSEMARY EDAMAME, ZUCCHINI, AND SUN-DRIED TOMATOES
- 1 teaspoon oil from sun-dried tomato jar
- 2 medium zucchini, cut in half lengthwise and sliced into half-moons (about 3 cups)
- 1 (12-ounce) package frozen shelled edamame, thawed (2 cups)
- ½ cup julienne-sliced sun-dried tomatoes in olive oil, drained
- ¼ teaspoon dried rosemary
- ⅛ teaspoon kosher salt

**Directions:**
TO MAKE THE GARLIC-CHIVE QUINOA     Heat the oil over medium heat in a saucepan. Once the oil is shimmering, add the garlic and cook for 1 minute, stirring often so it doesn't burn.     Add the quinoa and stir a few times. Add the water and salt and turn the heat up to high. Once the water is boiling, cover the pan and turn the heat down to low. Simmer the quinoa for 15 minutes, or until the water is absorbed.     Stir in the chives and fluff the quinoa with a fork.     Place ½ cup quinoa in each of 4 containers.     TO MAKE THE ROSEMARY EDAMAME, ZUCCHINI, AND SUN-DRIED TOMATOES     Heat the oil in a 12-inch skillet over medium-high heat. Once the oil is shimmering, add the zucchini and cook for 2 minutes.     Add the edamame, sun-dried tomatoes, rosemary, and salt, and cook for another 6 minutes, or until the zucchini is crisp-tender.     Spoon 1 cup of the edamame mixture into each of the 4 quinoa containers.     STORAGE: Store covered containers in the refrigerator for up to 5 days.
**Nutrition Info:Per Serving:** Total calories: 312; Total fat: ; Saturated fat: 1g; Sodium: 389mg; Carbohydrates: 39g; Fiber: 9g; Protein: 15g

## Cherry, Vanilla, And Almond Overnight Oats

Servings: 5      Cooking Time: 10 Minutes
**Ingredients:**
- 1⅔ cups rolled oats
- 3⅓ cups unsweetened vanilla almond milk
- 5 tablespoons plain, unsalted almond butter
- 2 teaspoons vanilla extract
- 1 tablespoon plus 2 teaspoons pure maple syrup
- 3 tablespoons chia seeds
- ½ cup plus 2 tablespoons sliced almonds
- 1⅔ cups frozen sweet cherries

**Directions:**
In a large bowl, mix the oats, almond milk, almond butter, vanilla, maple syrup, and chia seeds until well combined.      Spoon ¾ cup of the oat mixture into each of 5 containers.      Top each serving with 2 tablespoons of almonds and ⅓ cup of cherries.      STORAGE: Store covered containers in the refrigerator for up to 5 days. Overnight oats can be eaten cold or warmed up in the microwave.
**Nutrition Info:Per Serving:** Total calories: 373; Total fat: 20g; Saturated fat: 1g; Sodium: 121mg; Carbohydrates: 40g; Fiber: 11g; Protein: 13g

## Rotisserie Chicken, Baby Kale, Fennel, And Green Apple Salad

Servings: 3      Cooking Time: 15 Minutes
**Ingredients:**
- 1 teaspoon olive oil
- 1 teaspoon chopped garlic
- ⅔ cup quinoa
- 1⅓ cups water
- 1 cooked rotisserie chicken, meat removed and shredded (about 9 ounces)
- 1 fennel bulb, core and fronds removed, thinly sliced (about 2 cups)
- 1 small green apple, julienned (about 1½ cups)
- 8 tablespoons Honey-Lemon Vinaigrette, divided
- 1 (5-ounce) package baby kale
- 6 tablespoons walnut pieces

**Directions:**
Heat the oil over medium heat in a saucepan. Once the oil is shimmering, add the garlic and cook for minute, stirring often so that it doesn't burn.      Add the quinoa and stir a few times. Add the water and turn the heat up to high. Once the water is boiling, cover the pan and turn the heat down to low. Simmer the quinoa for 15 minutes, or until the water is absorbed. Cool.      Place the chicken, fennel, apple, and cooled quinoa in a large bowl. Add 2 tablespoons of the vinaigrette to the bowl and mix to combine.      Divide the baby kale, chicken

mixture, and walnuts among 3 containers. Pour 2 tablespoons of the remaining vinaigrette into each of 3 sauce containers.      STORAGE: Store covered containers in the refrigerator for up to days.
**Nutrition Info:Per Serving:** Total calories: 9; Total fat: 39g; Saturated fat: 6g; Sodium: 727mg; Carbohydrates: 49g; Fiber: 8g; Protein: 29g

## Roasted Za'atar Salmon With Peppers And Sweet Potatoes

Servings: 4      Cooking Time: 25 Minutes
**Ingredients:**
- FOR THE VEGGIES
- 2 large red bell peppers, cut into ½-inch strips
- 1 pound sweet potatoes, peeled and cut into 1-inch chunks
- 1 tablespoon olive oil
- ¼ teaspoon kosher salt
- FOR THE SALMON
- 2¾ teaspoons sesame seeds
- 2¾ teaspoons dried thyme leaves
- 2¾ teaspoons sumac
- 1 pound skinless, boneless salmon fillet, divided into 4 pieces
- ⅛ teaspoon kosher salt
- 1 teaspoon olive oil
- 2 teaspoons freshly squeezed lemon juice

**Directions:**
TO MAKE THE VEGGIES      Preheat the oven to 4°F. Place silicone baking mats or parchment paper on two sheet pans.      On the first pan, place the peppers and sweet potatoes. Pour the oil and sprinkle the salt over both and toss to coat. Spread everything out in an even layer. Place the sheet pan in the oven and set a timer for 10 minutes.      TO MAKE THE SALMON      Mix the sesame seeds, thyme, and sumac together in a small bowl to make the za'atar spice mix.      Place the salmon fillets on the second sheet pan. Sprinkle the salt evenly across the fillets. Spread ¼ teaspoon of oil and ½ teaspoon of lemon juice over each piece of salmon. Pat 2 teaspoons of the za'atar spice mix over each piece of salmon.      When the veggie timer goes off, place the salmon in the oven with the veggies and bake for 10 minutes for salmon that is ½ inch thick and for 15 minutes for salmon that is 1 inch thick. The veggies should be done when the salmon is done cooking. Place one quarter of the veggies and 1 piece of salmon in each of 4 separate containers.      STORAGE:Store covered containers in the refrigerator for up to 4 days.
**Nutrition Info:Per Serving:** Total calories: 295; Total fat: 10g; Saturated fat: 2g; Sodium: 249mg; Carbohydrates: 29g; Fiber: 6g; Protein: 25g

# 28-Day Meal Plan

**Day 1**
Breakfast: Cauliflower Fritters With Hummus
Lunch: Marinated Tuna Steak
Dinner: Garlic And Shrimp Pasta

**Day 2**
Breakfast: Italian Breakfast Sausage With Baby Potatoes And Vegetables
Lunch: Paprika Butter Shrimps
Dinner: Mediterranean Avocado Salmon Salad

**Day 3**
Breakfast: Greek Quinoa Breakfast Bowl
Lunch: Moroccan Fish
Dinner: Beet Kale Salad

**Day 4**
Breakfast: Egg, Prosciutto, And Cheese Freezer Sandwiches
Lunch: Grilled Lamb Chops
Dinner: Niçoise-inspired Salad With Sardines

**Day 5**
Breakfast: Healthy Zucchini Kale Tomato Salad
Lunch: Broiled Chili Calamari
Dinner: Mediterranean Chicken Pasta Bake

**Day 6**
Breakfast: Cheese And Cauliflower Frittata With Peppers
Lunch: Seafood Paella
Dinner: Mediterranean Pearl Couscous

**Day 7**
Breakfast: Avocado Kale Omelet
Lunch: Greek-style Braised Pork With Leeks, Greens, And Potatoes
Dinner: Delicious Broccoli Tortellini Salad

**Day 8**
Breakfast: Mediterranean Breakfast Burrito
Lunch: Greek Baked Cod
Dinner: Quinoa Stuffed Eggplant With Tahini Sauce

**Day 9**
Breakfast: Spinach, Feta And Egg Breakfast Quesadillas
Lunch: Zoodles With Turkey Meatballs
Dinner: Lettuce Tomato Salad

**Day 10**
Breakfast: Egg-topped Quinoa Bowl With Kale
Lunch: Lasagna
Dinner: Cheese Onion Soup

**Day 11**
Breakfast: Strawberry Greek Frozen Yogurt
Lunch: Tuna With Vegetable Mix
Dinner: Mixed Spice Burgers

**Day 12**
Breakfast: Almond Peach Oatmeal
Lunch: Pistachio Sole Fish
Dinner: Beef Tomato Soup

**Day 13**

Breakfast: Peanut Butter Banana Pudding
Lunch: Baked Tilapia
Dinner: A Great Mediterranean Snapper

**Day 14**
Breakfast: Raspberry-lemon Olive Oil Muffins
Lunch: Italian Skillet Chicken With Mushrooms And Tomatoes
Dinner: Mediterranean Pizza

**Day 15**
Breakfast: Pearl Couscous Salad
Lunch: Herbal Lamb Cutlets With Roasted Veggies
Dinner: Roasted Vegetable Quinoa Bowl

**Day 16**
Breakfast: Mushroom Tomato Egg Cups
Lunch: Heartthrob Mediterranean Tilapia
Dinner: Tabouli Salad

**Day 17**
Breakfast: Mediterranean Breakfast Salad
Lunch: Beef Sausage Pancakes
Dinner: Greek Lemon Chicken Soup

**Day 18**
Breakfast: Breakfast Carrot Oatmeal
Lunch: Mediterranean-style Pesto Chicken
Dinner: Lobster Salad

**Day 19**
Breakfast: Rum-raisin Arborio Pudding
Lunch: Italian Tuna Sandwiches
Dinner: Chicken Lentil Soup

**Day 20**
Breakfast: Mediterranean Quinoa And Feta Egg Muffins
Lunch: Mediterranean Baked Sole Fillet
Dinner: Luncheon Fancy Salad

**Day 21**
Breakfast: Vegetable Breakfast Bowl
Lunch: North African - inspired Sautéed Shrimp With Leeks And Peppers
Dinner: Salmon Skillet Dinner

**Day 22**
Breakfast: Egg-artichoke Breakfast Casserole
Lunch: Red Wine - braised Pot Roast With Carrots And Mushrooms
Dinner: Italian Platter

**Day 23**
Breakfast: Breakfast Cauliflower Rice Bowl
Lunch: Garlic And Cajun Shrimp Bowl With Noodles
Dinner: Grilled Salmon Tzatziki Bowl

**Day 24**
Breakfast: Savory Cucumber-dill Yogurt
Lunch: Smoky Chickpea, Chard, And Butternut Squash Soup
Dinner: Mediterranean Potato Salad

**Day 25**

Breakfast: Zucchini Pudding
Lunch: Crispy Baked Chicken
Dinner: Italian Baked Beans

**Day 26**
Breakfast: Healthy Dry Fruit Porridge
Lunch: Moroccan Spiced Stir-fried Beef With Butternut Squash And Chickpeas
Dinner: Greek Chicken Wraps

**Day 27**
Breakfast: Peach Blueberry Oatmeal
Lunch: Italian Chicken With Sweet Potato And Broccoli
Dinner: Vegetable Soup

**Day 28**
Breakfast: Tahini Egg Salad With Pita
Lunch: Herb-crusted Halibut
Dinner: Spinach And Beans Mediterranean Style Salad

# Appendix : Recipes Index

Made in the USA
Coppell, TX
28 October 2020